PRAYERS
FOR THE WEEK

Muḥyiddīn Ibn ʿArabī

PRAYERS FOR THE WEEK

The Seven Days of the Heart

Awrād al-usbūʿ

Translation, study, transliteration
and critical edition by

Pablo Beneito and Stephen Hirtenstein

ANQA PUBLISHING • OXFORD

Published by Anqa Publishing
PO Box 1178
Oxford OX2 8YS, UK
www.anqa.co.uk

A CIP catalogue record for this book is available from the British Library

ISBN 978 1 905937 65 3 (HB)
ISBN 978 1 905937 66 0 (PB)

Cover design: meadencreative.com

Back cover: Ibn ʿArabī's signature

Printed and bound in the UK by 4Edge Ltd, Hockley

Contents

And God said, 'Let there be light': and there was light.
And God saw the light, that it was good: and God divided the
light from the darkness.
And God called the light Day and the darkness He called Night:
and the evening and the morning were the first day.

Genesis 1:3–5

Indeed your Lord is God who has created the heavens and the earth in six days, and then He settled Himself upon the Throne. He makes the night cover the day, pursuing it swiftly; and the sun, the moon and the stars, subservient by His Command. Does not the creation and the command belong to Him? Blessed be God, Lord of all beings!

Quran 7:54

The son of Adam wrongs me when he curses the time, for I am Time. In My Hand is the Order. I cause the night and day to turn, one upon the other.

Hadith

Between Adhriʿāt and Buṣrā a maid of fourteen rose to my sight
like a full moon.
She was exalted in majesty above time and transcended it in pride
and glory.

Tarjumān al-ashwāq XL: 1–2

For all who recite these prayers,
past, present and future

Acknowledgements

A new edition of this special set of prayers by Ibn ʿArabī has been long in the making. There are several versions of the *Awrād al-usbūʿ* available in modern printings, including that published by the Muhyiddin Ibn ʿArabi Society as *Wird* (Oxford, 1979), but this is the first time that any serious attempt to collate the many manuscript versions and provide a stable recitation text and translation has been made. We would like to express our heartfelt gratitude to all those who have helped to make this book possible. There have been many, and the following deserve special mention for this new edition:

Nevsat Kaya and Bekir Şahin and all the staff at the Süleymaniye and Yusuf Ağa libraries in Turkey; the Muhyiddin Ibn ʿArabi Society for their unstinting support of the Archive project, which allowed me to investigate many manuscript libraries and collect digital copies; the late Maurice Gloton and Michel Chodkiewicz for their encouragement; Jennifer Heald and Michael Tiernan for their precious technical support over the years and the typesetting of this new version; Daud Sutton and David Apthorp for providing the interior images; Abdellah Cherif Ouazzani for the recording; Barbara for insisting on a translation; and above all, Bulent Rauf for demonstrating the subtle art of translating Ibn ʿArabī.

November 2021

Abbreviations

The following works are all cited in the notes to the prayers. Full details can be found in the Bibliography. The Quranic citations (Q.) are based on Alan Jones' translation, *The Quran*, Gibb Memorial Trust, 2007.

Fuṣ *Fuṣūṣ al-ḥikam* by Ibn ʿArabī, Arabic edition by Mahmud Kılıç

Fusus *Fusus al-Hikam*, with Ottoman commentary, rendered into English by Bulent Rauf

Bezels *The Bezels of Wisdom*, translated by Ralph Austin

Fut. *al-Futūḥāt al-Makkiyya* by Ibn ʿArabī, Beirut edition in 4 vols.

JMIAS *Journal of the Muhyiddin Ibn ʿArabi Society*, 1984 to present

Kashf *Kashf al-maʿnā* by Ibn ʿArabī

Mishkāt *Mishkāt al-anwār* by Ibn ʿArabī

Praise *JMIAS* special volume (21, 1997)

RG *Répertoire Général des oeuvres d'Ibn ʿArabī*, referring to the numbers given in Osman Yahia's classification of the work of Ibn ʿArabī

SDG *The Self-Disclosure of God*, William Chittick

SPK *The Sufi Path of Knowledge*, William Chittick

UM *The Unlimited Mercifier*, Stephen Hirtenstein

Concordance *Concordance et indices de la tradition musulmane*, edited by A. J. Wensinck

On this new edition

This book is an expanded and fully revised version of *The Seven Days of the Heart*, which was first published in 2000. Over the intervening years we have been able to consult a large number of manuscript copies of the *Awrād* in libraries worldwide, and compare different readings. As a result, we have included this new Arabic edition, based on the oldest and best manuscripts available, as well as a full transliteration of the prayers for non-Arabic speakers, and an updated translation and notes, with an accompanying recitation recording. We also decided to reflect the generally accepted title of these prayers by changing the main title to *Prayers for the Week.*

A special recording of all the prayers recited in Arabic by Abdellah Cherif Ouazzani can be downloaded from the Anqa website. For details please go to:
https://anqa.co.uk/publications/prayers-week-audio

Introduction

The Prayers of Ibn ʿArabī

Ibn ʿArabī (1165–1240) has long been known as a great spiritual master. Author of over 350 works, he has exerted an unparalleled influence, not only on his immediate circle of friends and disciples, but on succeeding generations who have taken his teaching as a superlative exposition of Unity (*tawḥīd*). He views the world according to a fundamental harmony, in which all things are intricately interconnected and the human being is given a place of immeasurable dignity. His writings, which were set down in a torrent of inspiration, are living documents, where meanings cascade from the page and no two readings are ever quite the same. Striking to the heart of essential human questions, they illuminate and challenge our view of mankind and the world. His many works of prose and poetry are now becoming more accessible in translation in Western languages, and they possess the remarkable quality of being able to speak to people of all walks of life and belief, across the apparent barrier of many centuries and differing cultures. Despite this growing interest in his works, the prayers which are attributed to him remain little-known. By virtue of their intimate nature, they provide a precious glimpse into the real practice of the spiritual life in the Sufi tradition. This is the first time that any of these prayers have been published in another language, although they have had wide circulation in the Arabic original.

This particular collection of prayers is one of the most celebrated and remarkable. It can be found under many variant titles: 'Daily Prayers' (*al-Awrād al-yawmiyya*), 'Prayers for the Week' (*Awrād al-usbūʿ*), 'Prayers for the Days and Nights' (*Awrād al-ayyām wa-l-layālī*) or simply 'Devotional Prayer' (*Wird*). The term *wird* (pl. *awrād*) is difficult to translate into English: the Arabic root carries connotations of arriving, reaching, appearing or being received. For the nomads of the desert, the root primarily refers to a watering place or well, where travellers come to drink. In the context of spiritual practice, the term *wird* itself is normally applied to private devotional prayers at specific times of day or night. These are supererogatory acts, in addition to the five prayers prescribed for the Muslim community. They often consist of passages from the Quran or prayers upon the Prophet, which are commonly recited at public gatherings. There are several famous devotional prayers of this kind that have come from spiritual teachers. We may mention the following examples by Ibn ʿArabī's Maghribi contemporaries: the Prayer of ʿAbd al-Salām Ibn Mashīsh (d. 625/1228), the Prayer of the Sea (*Ḥizb al-baḥr*) of Abū al-Ḥasan ʿAlī al-Shādhilī (d. 656/1258), or the less well-known Prayer of Blessing (*al-Ṣalāt al-mubāraka*) of ʿAbd al-ʿAzīz al-Mahdawī (d. 621/1224). We also find fine later examples such as the *Burda* of al-Buṣīrī (d. 694/1294) and the *Dalāʾil al-khayrāt* of al-Jazūlī (d. 870/1465), as well as the Blessing-prayer of Effusion (*al-Ṣalāt al-fayḍiyya*) of Abdullah Bosnevi (d. 1054/1644).[1]

Unlike the above, Ibn ʿArabī's 'Prayers for the Week' are neither devotional in any ordinary sense, nor do they appear to be intended as prayers for communal recitation. On the contrary, they seem to be more private and intimate affairs, where the requests imply a high degree of understanding and self-knowledge. In reading them, one is immediately struck by the precision and depth of their formulation, which is consecrated primarily to the clarification and celebration of Union (*tawḥīd*). They are founded upon the detailed exposition of spiritual Union, expressing the most intimate of converse with the Divine Beloved, and situating the one who prays as the true adorer. Here the reciter and the one recited to are understood to be two sides of the same reality. What is recited is that which 'arrives in the heart' (*wārid*) and is 'received' by the adorer, on the one hand, and the request that reaches the Real (*al-ḥaqq*) and is responded to, on

1. See our book *Patterns of Contemplation: Ibn ʿArabī, Abdullah Bosnevi and the Blessing-prayer of Effusion* (Oxford, 2021).

the other. For the one who reads them, these prayers are as much educational as devotional.

The Divine Work: request and response

> Whosoever is in the heavens and the earth is in request of Him; every day He is at work.[2]

For Ibn ʿArabī, this Quranic verse expresses a central issue of existence. At every moment each being, from the greatest galaxy to the smallest particle, is requesting and receiving its nourishment, physically and spiritually. In his comment on the verse, he remarks:

> The [Divine] work is the request of those who ask. There is not a single existent that is not requesting [of] Him, but they are according to different degrees in the asking.[3]

Thus the Divine labour consists in constantly fulfilling the requests of created beings, from the highest to the lowest. God's response is as inherently necessary as the asking of the creature. With the injunction: '*Call upon Me and I shall answer you*',[4] God has promised to respond to the constant request of the creatures, and this in itself is a request:

> He asks the servants to call Him, while the servants ask Him to respond. Thus both are asking and asked for (*ṭālib wa maṭlūb*).[5]

The response is equally mutual:

> Whoever responds when he is called is responded to when he himself calls. His Lord responds when he calls Him, since he has responded to Him when He called him on the tongue of the Envoy of God.[6]

2. Q 55:29.
3. *Ayyām al-sha'n*, 2/54. For a résumé of some parts of this work concerning Time, see Appendix A.
4. Q 40:60.
5. *Fut.* IV:101.
6. *K. al-ʿAbādila* 76: 8 (ʿAbd Allāh b. al-Yasʿa b. ʿAbd al-Mujīb), in *Rasā'il*, 1/255.

> If someone responds to the call of God when He calls him by the language of Revealed Law – and He does not call him except through it – God responds to him [favourably] in whatever he has asked for. So tell His faithful servants to *listen to God and His Envoy when they call you*, since neither He, glory to Him, nor His Envoy call you except *towards that which brings you life.*[7]

Ultimately in reality, according to Ibn ʿArabī, it is always God Himself who is being asked for, since there is no other than He. However, from a limited point of view this quickly becomes obscured by the innumerable forms of manifestation. Hence there are different degrees of knowledge in the asking. Given that there is always a Divine response to our request, it is essential to become conscious of what is actually being asked for. In a highly illuminating passage, Ibn ʿArabī describes this intimate moment-by-moment consciousness in terms of Divine closeness. After commenting on the Quranic verse, '*I am close, I respond to the call of the caller when he calls upon Me*',[8] he writes:

> In respect of His attributing to Himself closeness in listening and responding, this is analogous to His describing Himself as being 'closer' to man 'than his jugular vein'.[9] Here He compares His closeness to His servant with the closeness of man to his own self. When man asks himself to do something and then does it, there is no time-gap between the asking and the response, which is simply listening. The moment of asking actually is the very moment of responding. So the closeness of God in responding to His servant is [identical to] the closeness of the servant in responding to his own self. Then [we can say that] what he asks of his self in any state is akin to what he asks of his Lord as a specific need.[10]

The *Awrād* of Ibn ʿArabī are a most wonderful example of the possibility of theophanic prayer. Underlying the specific requests, there is a primary aim: to see things as they are from the perspective of the Real. In this sense, the prayers are equally a form of invocation or

7. *K. al-ʿAbādila* 76: 5. The verse quoted is Q 8:24.
8. Q 2:186.
9. Q 50:16.
10. *Fut.* IV:255.

remembrance (*dhikr*). In reciting them, the servant is not indulging in mere mechanical repetition, but consciously acknowledging the Presence of God, opening up to the full force of the Divine Revelation and savouring its manifold 'tastes'. This realisation of prayer becomes a mutual remembrance, as God says: '*Remember Me, and I shall remember You*'.[11]

Originally we chose to call these prayers 'The Seven Days of the Heart' to emphasise the intimacy of this relationship. They are a dialogue with the Unseen, a private communion where only one side of the discourse can be visible. We might compare this to what happens in a telephone conversation: on the one side, we can hear and see the speaker talking into the handset, while the other party remains hidden, invisible and inaudible to any but the person making the call. Likewise, the visible text of the prayers is only one part of the conversation, and their recitation is to be drawn into an intimate dialogue with God Himself, invoking Him and being invoked, inviting Him and being invited. This is a returning to Reality, a 'conversion' (*tawba*) that requires constant reiteration. All spiritual traditions emphasise that this is not to be achieved through the normal intellectual processes but only in the deepest centre of the self, referred to as the heart (*qalb*). It is the heart which is capable of acting as a mirror to the divine revelation, 'turning' or 'being turned' (*taqallub*, from the same root as *qalb*) according to the way He makes Himself known. The capacity of the heart to 'see' is precisely what transforms prayer from a repetitive act into meaningful conversation.

> Since [prayer] is a secret intimate converse, it is thus an invocation or remembrance (*dhikr*). And whoever remembers God finds himself sitting with God and God sits with him, according to the Divine tradition: 'I sit with whosoever remembers Me.' Whoever finds himself sitting with the One he remembers, and is capable of inner vision, sees his 'sitting-companion'. This is witnessing (*mushāhada*) and vision (*ru'ya*). If he does not have this inner capacity, he will not see Him. It is from this actuality or absence of vision in the prayer, that the one who prays will know his own spiritual degree.[12]

11. Q 2:152.
12. *Fuṣ*, p. 214; *Wisdom*, p. 128; *Bezels*, p. 280.

The three worlds and the three persons

Throughout the prayers there are references to two fundamental aspects of existence: on the one hand, the visible or witnessed (*shuhūd*) realm, the world of Creation (*khalq*) and of the King's domain (*mulk*); on the other, the invisible or unseen (*ghayb*) realm, the world of Command (*amr*) and of the King's presence (*malakūt*).[13] These correspond to 'day' and 'night', respectively.[14] Between the two realms, in Ibn 'Arabī's teaching, there lies an isthmus (*barzakh*) or threshold which both joins them together and keeps them separate: it is the place where meanings take on form and forms are given meaning. He calls it the world of Compelling Power (*jabarūt*) or Imagination (*khayāl*). It is a realm where the Magnificence of the Divine Presence is witnessed by virtue of inner sight, and where the one who prays is invited for converse. Real prayer takes place in this isthmus between the visible and invisible worlds.

These two realms can equally be viewed as that which is present to us here and now (*shuhūd*), as opposed to that which is absent and hidden from us (*ghayb*). Ibn 'Arabī defines the unseen or absent (*ghayb*) as 'that of you which God has concealed from you, though not from Himself, and thus it indicates Him'. The third person (he) denotes someone who is not here, while the first and second persons (I and you) refer to those present and visible.[15] The contemplation of this distinction opens up a different realm. To enter into converse with God is to step from apparent absence into His Presence. This renders the absent One ('He') into the One present ('You'), so that He may be addressed. At the same time there is always that aspect of 'Him' which remains unseen and eludes 'my' comprehension, for He is too

13. Although the terms express different relationships, they can be taken as generally synonymous. See *Fut.* II:129 for the definition of *malakūt* as 'the world of meanings and the Unseen' and the *mulk* as 'the world of witnessing'.

14. See Chapter 69 of the *Futūḥāt al-Makkiyya*, translated by Chittick, *SDG*, pp. 263–5.

15. The Arabic language, unlike English, reflects this polarity of present–absent. In English 'I' and 'you' do not appear to be semantically related, but in Arabic there is a clear correlation through the shared letters *alif* and *nūn*, which are found in the first two letters of *ana* (I) and of *anta, anti, antum* (you).

Majestic to be encompassed. Nonetheless, within the ultimate mystery of Union, the 'You' who listens is not other than the 'I' who speaks. God is thus simultaneously present and absent, I/You and He. As Ibn 'Arabī says: '... and amongst them [the Divine Names and Attributes] are the personal pronouns of the first, second and third persons.'[16]

We may speak, in fact, of three worlds, Kingdom (*mulk*), Kingship (*malakūt*) and Compelling Power (*jabarūt*), which in a certain sense correspond to the three persons. From our perspective, the 'I' refers to the Kingdom, that which is present to me and as me, while the 'He' refers to the King's immediate Presence, the realm of the invisible. The 'You' is then a bridge between the two, an isthmus, in the same way as the realm of Divine Power (*jabarūt*) separates and unites the two worlds.

'He' (in Arabic *Hū*), the third person singular, denotes 'the Unseen which cannot be contemplated. He is neither manifest nor a place of manifestation, but He is the Sought which the tongue seeks to elucidate.'[17] It refers directly to the Essence Itself, without in any way qualifying It, even as unqualifiable. Although indicated as 'unseen' or 'absent', this He-ness or Ipseity (*huwiyya*) runs through everything: 'Nothing becomes manifest in the adorer and the adored except His Ipseity ... He alone adores and is adored.'[18] Many formulations in the *Awrād* are based upon this recognition. For example: 'O You, who is the Unlimited 'He', while I am the limited 'He'! O 'He', apart from whom there is no other!'[19]

There are various ways in which God is addressed in the *Awrād*: sometimes as 'lord' (*rabb*), sometimes as 'master' (*sayyid*), sometimes by a particular Divine Name whose special quality is thus invoked. By far the most common are *ilāhī* (translated as 'O my God')

16. *Fut.* IV:196. In Arabic the first person is called the 'speaking person' (*mutakallim*), the third is the 'absent person' (*ghā'ib*) and the second is the 'person who is addressed' (*mukhāṭab*).

17. *Fut.* II:128.

18. *Fut.* IV:102. See also *Fut.* II:529.

19. See Sunday Eve prayer, p. 27. In one astonishing short poem in the *Futūḥāt*, Ibn 'Arabī manages to convey the sheer perplexity of the three persons. See *Fut.* I:497, translated by R. Austin in *Prayer & Contemplation*, p. 16. See also M. Chodkiewicz, *An Ocean Without Shore*, p. 36.

and *allāhumma* ('O God'). These are not simply used for stylistic variation, but are a precise mode of address. The first establishes a relationship between the degree of divinity (*ulūhiyya*) and the one who is the place where divinity is exercised (*ma'lūh*). Like the Name Lord (*rabb*), *ilāh* requires an apparent 'other', a creature over whom He can be God (hence the use of 'my God'). The Quran, for example, speaks of the 'God of mankind' (*ilāh al-nās*). The second, *allāhumma*, is an invocational form of the Name *Allāh*. This denotes the absolute transcendent divinity (*ulūha*), by which none other than He can be qualified. Nor is He to be qualified as the *Allāh* of someone, since the Name *Allāh* unites all the Names and rejects such a specific relationship.[20]

Furthermore, we may observe the precise modes of address that are used in each prayer: for example, Sunday Morning only uses *allāhumma* (× 5), Thursday Morning uses *allāhumma* (× 9) and *ilāhī* (× 21), Wednesday and Friday Morning only use *rabbi*; the two Saturday prayers are the only ones to use all the major modes (*allāhumma*, *ilāhī*, *rabbi*, *sayyidī*).

The structure of the Awrād

At first sight it might seem as if the prayers have been arranged somewhat simply: fourteen prayers, one for each night and day of the week. Is there perhaps a deeper structure? While there is no explicit explanation as to why the individual prayers have been set out in this way, we can find many clues in other parts of Ibn 'Arabī's work which enable us to discern a most remarkable underlying pattern.

First of all, Ibn 'Arabī considers the weekly cycle as sacred. It is a Divine Sign, which points to the reality of Being. The seven days and nights express aspects of Being or spiritual realities, which, when taken together, form a complete whole and encompass all of existence. As we shall see, the seven days have a subtle relationship with seven prophets.

20. These two modes of address might be compared with the Biblical Hebrew words, *eloha* and *elohim*, which are often translated as 'God' and 'the Lord God', respectively.

The number 14 itself is charged with significance. In relation to the 28-day lunar cycle, 14 represents the midpoint or full moon, and is thus a symbol of the most complete beauty, wherein the light of the sun is reflected. It stands for the perfect human soul (*nafs kāmila*), who is fully receptive to the action of the Divine Spirit. In the Arabic language, true beauty is symbolised as 'a young maid of fourteen'. In his commentary on the fortieth poem of the *Tarjumān al-ashwāq*, Ibn 'Arabī explains another meaning in attributing 14 to a young woman: 'The attribute of perfection is related to her, so the most perfect of the numbers is given to her, which is the number 4, and that is also 10 (1 + 2 + 3 + 4 = 10). From it comes 14 (4 + 10). The number 4 thus contains 3 and 2 and 1, as well as also containing the number 10.'[21] In mathematical terms, the numbers 4 and 14 are both divisors of 28, which was known to the Greeks as the second perfect number (a number which is the sum of its divisors: 1 + 2 + 4 + 7 + 14). We may also view 14 as a doubling of 7: this recalls the 7 verses of the *Fātiḥa* which are known as the 'seven repeated' (*sabʿ mathānī*), or the seven heavens and seven earths of Islamic cosmology, which include all the worlds of manifestation from the highest to the lowest. The number 7 itself underpins a major part of Ibn 'Arabī's teaching and can be found in texts relating to the spiritual ascension, the spiritual 'climes' or regions and to the human faculties.

The seven days and seven nights

The seven days of the week are an ancient symbol of the complete cycle of creation. In both the Biblical and Quranic accounts there are six days of Divine action followed by one day of repose and rest. The association of the seven days with the seven major planets of our solar system has permeated Western languages. Whilst Hebrew and Arabic

21. *Dhakhāʾir al-aʿlāq*, p. 443. He is alluding also to the Pythagorean doctrine of the tetraktys or tetrahedron: this is the first three-dimensional form which fits perfectly within a sphere, its 4 faces, 6 edges and 4 vertices making a sum of 14. The Pythagoreans specifically associated the number 4 with harmony.

have retained a basic numerical system, European languages have called each day directly after a planet, as shown in Table 1 below:

Table 1

	Planet	English	Latin language (Fr/Sp)	Arabic	Prophet according to Ibn ʿArabī
1	SUN	Sunday	dimanche domingo	*yawm al-aḥad*	IDRIS
2	MOON	Monday	lundi lunes	*yawm al-ithnayn*	ADAM
3	MARS	Tuesday	mardi martes	*yawm al-thulathāʾ*	AARON & JOHN
4	MERCURY	Wednesday	mercredi miércoles	*yawm al-arbiʿāʾ*	JESUS
5	JUPITER	Thursday	jeudi jueves	*yawm al-khamīs*	MOSES
6	VENUS	Friday	vendredi viernes	*yawm al-jumuʿa*	JOSEPH
7	SATURN	Saturday	samedi sábado	*yawm al-sabt*	ABRAHAM

The long-standing association of prophets to planets is here extended to the days of the week. Thus, for Ibn ʿArabī there are two cycles involving the seven prophets (or eight if we include John): the order of the planets in the physical universe, and their order in terms of days of the week. Whether he is considering physical space or temporal space, Ibn ʿArabī views these role- models of mankind as spiritual realities who give meaning to both dimensions.

The spiritual dimension of the physical order is shown in the tradition of Muhammad's night-journey (*isrāʾ*) or heavenly ascension (*miʿrāj*): when he ascended through the seven heavens, he passed through each sphere and there met the prophet appropriate to it. This bodily journey of the Prophet is re-enacted spiritually by the saints. In no less than four separate works, Ibn ʿArabī speaks of the way that he himself experienced the night-journey, in more or less autobiographical detail, and it is clear that it forms one of the cornerstones of his teaching.[22]

The long-standing association of prophets to planets is here extended to the days of the week. Thus, for Ibn ʿArabī there are two cycles involving the seven prophets (or eight if we include John): the order of the planets in the physical universe, and their order in terms of days of the week. Whether he is considering physical space or temporal space, Ibn ʿArabī views these role- models of mankind as spiritual realities who give meaning to both dimensions.

Likewise, there is a spiritual dimension to the days of the week, similarly linked to the same seven prophets. These spiritual days, Ibn ʿArabī says, are 'times' in which we receive spiritual knowledge, contemplations and mysteries, just like the body receives its nourishment during the day. In several works he specifically mentions this inner dimension to the weekly cycle. The following passage from his *Mawāqiʿ al-nujūm*, composed in 595/1199 within a year of his

22. The first experience of heavenly ascension (*miʿrāj*) of which Ibn ʿArabī provides an account took place in 594H in Fez. Detailed accounts appear in *K. al-Isrāʾ*, written soon afterwards, *Tanazzulāt al-Mawṣiliyya* (written in 601H), *R. al-Anwār* (written in 602H) and of course the *Futūḥāt al-Makkiyya*, chapters 167 and 367 (written over a period of many years). Further research on the relationship of the days, prophets, Divine Names and letters would need to take into consideration all these books. See *UM*, pp.115–23.

great ascension in Fez, describes how 'one who has a heart' may be given knowledge of spiritual secrets:

> Know, my son, that for every day [of the week] there is a prophet from among the prophets, from whom descends a secret upon the heart of the verifying witness, a secret in which he takes delight during his day and by which he knows something of that which requires to be known. This only happens to those who possess a heart.
>
> Now on the first day [Sunday] it is Idris [Enoch] who addresses him with a secret revealing to him the causes of things before the existence of their effects. On Monday it is Adam who addresses him with a secret by which he comes to know the reasons why the stations wax or wane with respect to the seekers, and how God reveals Himself. On Tuesday it is either Aaron or John who addresses him with a secret by which he comes to know what is beneficial or harmful about the influences that come upon him from the world of the Unseen. On Wednesday it is Jesus who addresses him with a secret by which he comes to know the completion of the stations, how they are sealed and by whom. On Thursday it is Moses who addresses him with a secret by which he comes to know the religious prescriptions and the mysteries of intimate converse. On Friday it is Joseph who addresses him with a secret by which he comes to know the mysteries of constant ascension through the stations, the [Divine] decree and where it is established. And on Saturday it is Abraham who addresses him with a secret whereby he comes to know how to deal with enemies and when they are to be fought against, and this is the presence of the Substitutes (*abdāl*).[23]

Sunday (the 'first day' or the 'day of the One, *al-Aḥad*') is coupled with Idris, who is associated with the Sun. Just as the Sun is the fourth heaven and the centre of the seven planets in physical space, so the secrets that Idris reveals, namely 'the causes of things before the existence of their effects', shows his privileged position as the heavenly Pole (*quṭb*).[24] At the same time, here we find him as the beginning of the cycle, the 'founder of wisdoms' as he is called in the *Futūḥāt al-Makkiyya*, with a strong association with the principle of *aḥadiyya* (uniqueness). There

23. *Mawāqiʿ al-nujūm*, p.157.

24. In the *R. al-Anwār*, Ibn ʿArabī writes of this degree that in it 'you are given the power of symbols and a view of the whole, and authority over the veil and the unveiling' (see *Journey to the Lord of Power*, p.43).

are several relevant passages in Ibn ʿArabī's work,[25] especially those that discuss the knowledge of unity (*tawḥīd*).[26] However, to avoid any kind of fixity, Ibn ʿArabī also specifies that these are not the only mysteries revealed by each prophet, merely the first.

In his book on the meaning of the Seal of the Saints, the *ʿAnqāʾ mughrib*, composed in the same period as the *Mawāqiʿ al-nujūm*, we find him explicitly reiterating this prophetic correlation:

> If your day is Sunday (the Day of the One), then Idris is your Companion, so follow not behind anyone! And if it is Monday, then Adam is your Companion in the isthmus of the two worlds. If your day is Tuesday, then Aaron is your Companion, so adhere to Right Guidance; and John [the Baptist] will be your Intimate, so cleave to Purity and Contentment. If it is Wednesday, Jesus is your Companion, so hold fast to the holy life and persevere in the desert. If it is Thursday, then it is Moses: for the covering is quite lifted away, and you are addressed in the manner of an Unveiling, not [by] any man or fire; and indeed, the Angel rejoiced [at the mention of God's Name], while the Devil withdrew. And if your day is Friday (ʿArūba), then Joseph, possessor of the qualities of the passionately beloved, is your Companion; while if your day is Saturday, then it is Abraham, so hasten to the honouring of your Guest before [He] vanishes. These are the Days of the Gnostics (*ayyām al-ʿārifīn*) and the radiant stars of the Spheres of the Wayfarers![27]

Ibn ʿArabī attaches particular importance to Wednesday, the fourth of the seven days.[28] He views it as the day of Light (*nūr*) and the centre of the week, just as the Sun occupies the central fourth position amongst the physical planets. As Wednesday is the day of Jesus, it equally alludes to his central position in Time, as the Seal of Universal Sainthood. There are indications of the importance of this prophetic

25. See, for example, *Fut.* I:152–7 and III: 348–9; *Fuṣ*, pp. 54–60 (*Wisdom*, pp. 35–9; *Bezels*, pp. 82–9); or *Tanazzulāt al-Mawṣiliyya*, pp. 112ff. Compare also *Fut.* II:421–56 on the *tawajjuhāt al-asmāʾ*.

26. As Idris explained to Ibn ʿArabī during his spiritual ascension: 'I was a prophet calling them to the word of *tawḥīd*, not to *tawḥīd* itself, for no-one has ever denied *tawḥīd*' (*Fut.* III:348).

27. *ʿAnqāʾ mughrib*, ed. Meftah, p. 236, translated by G. Elmore as *Islamic Sainthood in the Fullness of Time*, pp. 439–41.

28. It is the only day in which all the spiritual realities of the spheres take part. See Appendix B.

principle throughout the day-prayers of the *Awrād*. The most evident is in the marginal note on the prayer for Tuesday Morning, which is found in several manuscripts. Two awesome men appeared to him during a retreat, and one of them gave Ibn ʿArabī this prayer to recite. Although there is no explicit mention of who these men were, we may perhaps identify them as the prophets associated with Tuesday, Aaron and John.[29] In addition, in his *Ayyām al-shaʾn*, Ibn ʿArabī outlines a more complex relationship between these seven prophets and each day (see Appendix B).

In the Judaic and Islamic traditions each day begins not at sunrise but at sunset. The precedence of the night is already attested in the fifth verse of Genesis, when the first 'day' of creation is being described: 'And God called the light Day and the darkness He called Night: and the evening and the morning were the first day.' With the introduction of clock-time and its rigorous division of days beginning at midnight, this natural rhythm is no longer so evident, let alone the basis of our everyday cycle of living.

The night is associated by Ibn ʿArabī with the world of the Unseen (*ghayb*), in which the soul appears in its true condition, a moon reflecting the pure light of the Divine Spirit. While the days belong to the prophets, the nights correspond to the saints (*awliyāʾ*). The contemplative knowledge that underpins all others in Ibn ʿArabī's teaching, and is the prerogative of the saints, is the science of the letters.[30] It is therefore not surprising that the key to understanding the structure of the eve-prayers should lie in the Arabic alphabet.

In a little-known work attributed to Ibn ʿArabī, entitled *Tawajjuhāt al-ḥurūf*, a prayer is ascribed to each of the letters of the alphabet. The text begins with the letter *alif* and ends with the double letter *lām-alif*, making a cycle of twenty-nine rather than the standard twenty-eight. Perhaps this was conceived as a cycle that begins and ends in the same place, the *alif* representing the Essence Itself. The composition of letter-prayers is not without precedent: in the Biblical Psalms we can find one (No. 119) containing twenty-two prayers, each of which is

29. See Notes to Tuesday Morning prayer, p. 105.

30. See *K. al-Mīm wa-l-wāw wa-l-nūn*, *Rasāʾil*, 2/77; Rašić, *The Written World of God*.

dedicated to one of the twenty-two letters of the Hebrew alphabet. Each line and the key terms of the prayer begin with the letter concerned. In the *Tawajjuhāt*, there is also a strong emphasis on the use of the letter in the prayer – for example, we can find over seventy uses of the letter *qāf* in the space of a few lines. It is not only the physical articulation of the letter that is important: Ibn ʿArabī establishes a connection between the twenty-eight Arabic letters and the twenty-eight days of the lunar cycle, where each letter has a particular 'temper' and principial meaning in terms of the whole cosmological cycle.[31]

In the *Awrād*, fourteen of these prayers from the *Tawajjuhāt* have been combined to make seven 'doubled' prayers. Each eve-prayer of the *Awrād* is thus composed of two letter-prayers, with Quranic verses joining them together. Is there an underlying order? Are the letter-combinations based upon sound? Or is there some other factor determining the selection? The key may be found in the correspondence between letters and numerical values, commonly known as the *abjad* system (see Appendix C). Table 2 below explains the combinations by laying out the letters and their values on a seven-by-four grid (according to the Eastern *abjad* system):

Table 2

1 *alif*	2 *bāʾ*	3 *jīm*	4 *dāl*	5 *hāʾ*	6 *wāw*	7 *zāy*
8 *ḥāʾ*	9 *ṭāʾ*	10 *yāʾ*	20 *kāf*	30 *lām*	40 *mīm*	50 *nūn*
60 *sīn*	70 *ʿayn*	80 *fāʾ*	90 *ṣād*	100 *qāf*	200 *rāʾ*	300 *shīn*
400 *tāʾ*	500 *thāʾ*	600 *khāʾ*	700 *dhāl*	800 *ḍād*	900 *ẓāʾ*	1000 *ghayn*

31. See the chart drawn up by Titus Burckhardt in *Mystical Astrology according to Ibn ʿArabi*, pp. 32–3. This is taken from *Fut.* II:421–56 on the *Tawajjuhāt al-asmāʾ*.

By treating each column as relating to one of the seven days, we then find the following letter combinations that have been used for the eve-prayers:

Table 3

Wed	Thurs	Fri	Sat	Sun	Mon	Tues
alif	*bāʾ*	*jīm*	*dāl*	*hāʾ*	*wāw*	*shīn*
sīn	*thāʾ*	*khāʾ*	*ṣād*	*qāf*	*rāʾ*	*ghayn*

As shown in Table 3 above, it might appear odd that only fourteen letters have been used and that the weekly cycle starts here on a Wednesday Eve. Why weren't all four letter-prayers used? Why don't the eve-prayers begin on Sunday Eve, like the day-prayers? We may find a key to this by considering the pattern of the week and the importance of letter symbolism.

If we begin the week in the usual way with Sunday, we find the letter *alif* at the heart of the week on the fourth day, with three days on either side. Ibn ʿArabī considers the *alif* to be the letter that denotes the Divine Essence, as the centre or the 'heart' of all things. This is due to its graphic form (as a straight vertical line, free from curvature and detached from other letters), its numerical value (= 1), and the fact that it is the first letter of the alphabet. In addition, we can see an important numerical pattern: 6 letters are related to the first 3 days (Sunday, Monday, Tuesday), and another 6 to the last 3 (Thursday, Friday, Saturday). As the number 6 is equal to the letter *wāw*, the whole week can thus be read as *w* (*wāw*) + *ā* (*alif*) + *w* (*wāw*), which spells the name of the final sounded letter of the alphabet, *wāw*. In the Eastern *abjad* system, even the extra letter on Wednesday, *sīn*, has a value of 60, or 6 in the tens column. By reducing the number to units, it becomes 6, which again equates to *wāw*. In Ibn ʿArabī's doctrine, the *wāw* alludes to the final degree of existence, the Perfect Man, in whom all the preceding 27 degrees of existence are collected together and summarised (for further explanation of the *alif* and *wāw*, see Appendix D). Other aspects of these letters may also be observed: for example, the range of letters extends from *alif* in Wednesday (1, representing the Essence) to *ghayn* on Tuesday (1,000, representing multiplicity).[32]

We can summarise the internal structure of the prayers in Table 4 below:

Table 4

	Sun	Mon	Tues	Wed	Thurs	Fri	Sat
Eve	*hā'*/ *qāf*	*wāw*/ *rā'*	*shīn*/ *ghayn*	*alif*/ *sīn*	*bā'*/ *thā'*	*jīm*/ *khā'*	*dāl*/ *ṣād*
Day	Idris	Adam	Aaron/ John	Jesus	Moses	Joseph	Abraham

From this table we may also observe the fact that Wednesday is not only associated with the letter *alif*, but is also the day of Jesus. His position at the centre of the temporal cycle of the week parallels the position of Idris at the centre of the physical and spiritual revolution of the spheres.

If the eve-prayers of the *Awrād* have been coded to spell *wāw*, the letter-name of the Perfect Man, we could also consider the seven prophets of the day-prayers as manifestations or modalities of this same Man. This deeper structure, a network of letters and prophetic figures pointing to the Muhammadian perfection, seems entirely deliberate, although some questions still remain. Do the two letters for each eve-prayer have some special affinity or connection with each other within

32. In terms of their numerical values (see Appendix C), these letter-combinations are also significant. For example, using the minor Eastern *abjad* system (which reduces all numbers to units): (Wed) 1 + 6 = 7; (Thur) 2 + 5 = 7; (Fri) 3 + 6 = 9; (Sat) 4 + 9 = 13 = 4; (Sun) 5 + 1 = 6; (Mon) 6 + 2 = 8; (Tue) 3 + 1 = 4. If the totals are added together, the sum is 45, which is the numerical value of the name Adam (1 + 4 + 40). This number Ibn ʿArabī uses to allude to the perfection of the Adamic Divine form and the sciences which He taught Adam in the following passage: 'The matrices of the knowledge of God (*ummuhāt al-ʿilm bi-Llāh*), insofar as He is independent of the worlds, are 45 sciences' (*K. al-Ifāda*, Manisa 1183, fol.114a).

the text of the prayer itself?[33] Could there be a particular correlation between them and the prophet of the day? Perhaps, although all this would be a matter for contemplation rather than speculation.

The days of Muhammad

One fundamental question remains. Given that each day is associated with one of the seven prophets, what role does the Prophet Muhammad play? Is he specifically related here to any of the days of the week? The answer can be found at the beginning of a short work entitled *Ayyām al-sha'n*, which asks for the traditional blessing on the Prophet as follows:

> May the blessing of God be upon the one whose day is [universally] known (*maʿrūf*), whose day is Tuesday in terms of being visibly active, and whose day is Friday in terms of being specific to his self-nature – his subtleties permeate every day, and his realities suffuse every hour – with a complete blessing and constant greeting for as long as he is isolated from all created beings by [having] the best of natures.[34]

In this highly condensed sentence, there are three ways of seeing the 'day' of Muhammad. The first is referred to as the 'known' (*maʿrūf*) or universal day, without any further differentiation, the unit that everyone recognises as constituting 'each day'. In this sense, Muhammad is not related to a specific day because he is considered the all-embracing principle. His day is the very unit of 'day', at whatever level it may be considered, as the minute, the hour or the week itself.[35] On the other hand, the particular days of Tuesday and

33. For example, we may observe that the two letters for Sunday Eve, *hā'* and *qāf*, may be combined to produce the word *qahr* (subjugation or overpowering), which features prominently in the text of this prayer. On Monday Eve, *wāw* and *rā'* may be combined to produce *rūḥ* (spirit) or *rawḥ* (ease, joy).

34. *Ayyām al-sha'n*, 2/53.

35. Ibn ʿArabī is specific about this at the beginning of the *Ayyām al-sha'n* (2/53): 'I have called this book the *Ayyām al-sha'n*, as it is whatever happens in the smallest day of the cosmos in terms of divine effects and enactments, in composition and decomposition, ascent and descent, visible and invisible existence. He, exalted may He be, referred to this "small day" as the day which is universally known, using an all-embracing expression so that those addressed might understand, for He said: "Whosoever is in the heavens and

Friday can be specifically related to the Prophet in a certain manner. Tuesday, the third day, expresses the principle of the number 3, the first of the odd or prime (*fard*) numbers. The connection between the Prophet and primeness or singularity is brought out in the Chapter of Muhammad in the *Fuṣūṣ al-ḥikam*:

> His wisdom is prime singularity (*fardiyya*), because he is the most complete and perfect existent in this humankind. For this reason the order begins with him and is sealed by him. He was 'a prophet while Adam was still between water and clay', and then in his elemental, earthly existence, he was the Seal of the Prophets. The first of the odd prime numbers is three, and none of the other prime numbers [such as 5 or 7] can be greater than this firstness, for he is its eye-entity (*ʿayn*). He was the most complete indicator of his Lord, as he was given the all-inclusive totality of the Words (*jawāmiʿ al-kalim*), which are the contents of the Names [which God taught to] Adam.[36]

Friday (*yawm al-jumuʿa*, literally 'the day of gathering-together'), clearly expresses the principle of gathering and synthesis (*jamʿ*). Muhammad is the Seal who gathers and synthesises all the messages of previous prophets, and the model of human perfection who unites all the modalities of perfection within himself. As the sixth day, Friday contains the qualities of 6 (= *wāw*), the first perfect number (the sum of its divisors), but also those of its factors 2 and 3. When we look at the letters of the eve-prayers, we find that both Tuesday and Friday have a special correspondence with the number 3 (using the minor Eastern *abjad* system): Sunday, Monday, Tuesday (*qāf*/1, *rāʾ*/2, *shīn*/3); and Wednesday, Thursday, Friday (*alif*/1, *bāʾ*/2, *jīm*/3). If the sixth day, Friday, expresses the gathering together openly (like the community gathering in the mosque for Friday prayers), the sealing quality of threefold singularity can be found hidden and encoded within the Tuesday Eve letters. If we look at the way that the night prayers are ordered and count from Wednesday Eve (which begins with *alif*) to Tuesday Eve (see Table 3), the normal *abjad* order is adhered to in the first row of letters (*alif*, *bāʾ*, *jīm*, *dāl*, *hāʾ*, *wāw*),

the earth is in request of Him; every day He is at work" ' (Q 55:29).

36. *Fuṣ*, p. 202; *Wisdom*, p. 116; *Bezels*, p. 272.

in a pattern of 1, 2, 3, 4, 5, 6, but this row ends not with *zāy* (= 7) as one might expect, but with *shīn*, the final letter in the Western *abjad* system (= 1000) and the 21st letter (= 300 = 3) in the Eastern. So the seventh day is not simply a continuation of the previous six, but brings their enumeration to an end and seals them with threeness. On the other hand, the second row interlinks the third and fourth rows of the Eastern *abjad* table (as shown in Table 2): *sīn* / *thāʾ*, *khāʾ* / *ṣād*, *qāf*, *rāʾ*), in a pattern of 1 (letter in third row) / 2 (letters in fourth row) / 3 (letters in third row), and ends with *ghayn* (= 1000), the final letter of the Eastern system and the 27th letter (= 900 = 9) in the Western. Again we find a threefold pattern, expressed in the letter combinations of the first six days, as well as in the 9 of 27 and 900, which is the last of the digits and the cube of 3. In this respect, even though it is not usually regarded as the 'end' of the week, Tuesday, the 'day of 3' (*yawm al-thulāthāʾ*), finalises and seals the week with the threeness of the final letters of the alphabet, alluding to the principle that it is the day of Muhammad as the Seal of the prophets.

The Awrād: manuscripts and translation

There are numerous manuscripts of the prayers, reflecting the fact that they have been revered and well-known throughout the Islamic world for centuries. Osman Yahia in his *Classification* listed almost forty manuscripts (RG 64), although this may in fact represent only a small fraction of the total that survive. Some others are listed under different titles (for example, RG 16a), or are to be found in library collections that Yahia did not consult. Perhaps others are still in private hands. Of the manuscripts we know at present, none have been found to date back further than the early tenth century of the Hegira, some 500 years ago and therefore 300 years after Ibn 'Arabī's death. For our critical edition of the text, we have utilised 18 particularly early or important manuscript copies as well as two printed versions, and consulted at least a further 30 in libraries around the world. A list of these 18 can be found at the end of the Arabic edition. One of the factors that became clear during our research is that different families or traditions of reading these prayers developed over the years and in different countries. We have taken account of these variant readings in our critical edition, and included some in the notes to the Arabic text. Since our first translation of the prayers, which was published as *The Seven Days of the Heart*, did not take account of the numerous changes that have been incorporated into this critical edition, it was evident that a fresh translation and transliteration were needed.

It must be emphasised that the Arabic text is extraordinarily full and poetic: an interweaving of rhyme and rhythm which seems to have been inspired by the prose of the Quran and cannot be conveyed in translation. There is also a richness of allusion to the Quran and Hadith that is staggering, and we have indicated the many references by using italics in the text and providing fuller quotations in the notes. We have used Alan Jones' translation of the Quran as a basis, but have had to adapt it to the context, because of the way that Ibn ʿArabī draws on the implied and subtle meanings of the Arabic language.

As in the case of the Quran, there can be no substitute for the rich sounds and meanings of the original language, no translation that can stand in place of reciting the Arabic. The sheer beauty of the original, its elegance of style, the lexical interconnections that Ibn ʿArabī weaves, the sublimity of the knowledge implied – all these establish the *Awrād* as a unique spiritual masterpiece. Above all else they are prayers, whether they be understood in the sense of acts of devotion that can be performed before or after other actions, or seen as the unceasing prayer of the heart in contemplation. They appear as the natural expression of a heart completely given up to God. They explicitly and implicitly refer to the true reality of Man, created in the Divine Likeness, who recognises his Origin and acts in total conscious conformity to his Lord, thus realising pure servanthood. This constitutes the true imitation of the Prophet:

> As he [Muhammad] was by origin created a pure servant, he never lifted his head to make himself a master, but continued prostrating and standing [before Him], in the condition of [total] receptivity, until God brought forth from him that which He brought forth.[37]

37. *Fuṣ*, p. 210; *Wisdom*, p. 124; *Bezels*, p. 278.

Such imitation of the Prophet in terms of prayers can be seen most explicitly in the way that Ibn ʿArabī cites many well-known prayers and supplications of Muhammad at the very end of his *Futūḥāt*[38]. This final section, specifically entitled 'the conclusion of the chapter' (*khātimat al-bāb*), comes at the end of the direct counsels (*waṣiyya*) that make up the last chapter of the work, ch. 560. Not only is it remarkable that he chose to complete his masterwork with a series of specific prayers for particular circumstances followed by some 50 intimate prophetic prayers (drawn from Quran and Hadith); but it is also very striking how closely the formulation of the prayers parallels the rhymes, rhythms and phrasing found in the *Awrād*. For example, the third prayer of Muhammad which Ibn ʿArabī cites in this general listing[39] reads: *Allāhumma, innī as'aluka l-hudā wa-t-tuqā, wa-l-ʿafāfa wa-l-ghinā, wa-min al-ʿamali mā tarḍā* ('O God, I ask of You guidance and righteous conduct, that I may abstain and be free [from all that is unlawful], and that I may accomplish whatever pleases You'). A very similar phrasing, rhyme and meaning is to be found in the Monday morning prayer: *Allāhumma, innī as'aluka n-nūra wa-l-hudā, wa-l-adaba fi l-iqtidā'* ('O God, I ask of You light and guidance, and good behaviour in conformity [to You]'). The model for the *Awrād*, then, is to be found in the daily supplications and comportment of the Prophet.

For many centuries these prayers have been taken, and are still taken, as recitation by men and women throughout the world in a litany of praise. As a friend has remarked, they teach us to talk to God in the best of ways, for this is not something we automatically know how to do. We can only trust that the following rendering into English may convey to the non-Arabic speaker and modern reader something of their magnificent and beautiful power.

38. *Fut.* IV:552–3.

39. As opposed to the specific requests which are recorded at the beginning of this section, which are prayers for particular circumstances.

THE PRAYERS

TRANSLATION AND NOTES

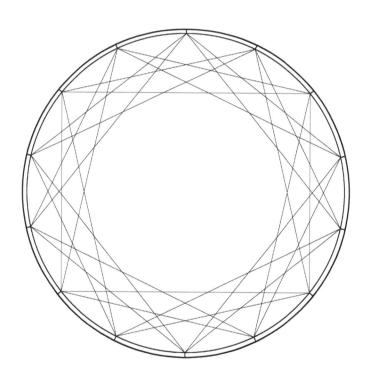

The Preface Prayer

IN THE NAME OF GOD,
THE ALL-COMPASSIONATE AND MOST MERCIFUL

Praise be to God for His bringing the most excellent success! I ask Him for:

guidance to follow His Path;

inspiration that is based upon the verification
of His Reality;

a heart of certainty that is orientated to confirming
His Truth;

a mind that is illumined by the providential grace
of recognising His Foreknowledge;

a spirit refreshed and gladdened by ardent desire
of Him;

a *soul at peace* from ignorance and being enveloped
in its clouds;

an understanding radiating with the flashes of
thought and its brilliance;

an innermost heart flourishing with the *spring-*
waters of illumination and its pure *nectar*;

speech strewn upon the carpet of expansion and its clarification;

thought exalted above the apparent finery of the ephemeral and its embellishment;

insight able to witness the secret mystery of Being in the setting of creation and its rising;

senses maintained in full health by the refreshing breeze of the Spirit and its smoothing the way;

a primordial natural constitution purified from the ailment of falling short and its veiling conditioning;

a disposition completely responsive to the reins of Divine Law and its authority;

a [state at each] moment conducive to His uniting and His distinguishing;

And a blessing-prayer and peace-greetings upon Muhammad and his family and his company, and the successors who came after him and the community of those who follow his path – may they all be greeted with peace.

The One desired is God, both in Being and in witnessing. He is the One intended, without any [possibility of] denial or disclaimer.

For *He is sufficient for me, the most excellent Trustee.*

Sunday Eve Prayer

IN THE NAME OF GOD,
THE ALL-COMPASSIONATE AND MOST MERCIFUL

O my God, You are the One who encompasses what is unseen by every seer, and the One who occupies and holds sway over the interior of every exterior. I ask of You by Your Face, before which all foreheads prostrate, to which *all faces submit*, and by Your Light at which *all eyes gaze*, that You guide me on Your private path, turning my face to You away from whatever is other than You.

O You who is the Unlimited 'He', while I am the limited 'He'! There is no He but He.

O my God, it is Your business to vanquish enemies and quell oppressors. I ask of You full backing from Your Exalted Might, that it may protect me from all that wish me ill, so that I can thereby *restrain the claws* of the covetous and *cut off the last remnant of the wrongdoers*. Grant me possession of my soul, as a dominion which sanctifies me from every disfiguring characteristic; and guide me to You, O Guide, for it is to You that all things return.

You *encompass all things. He has Supreme Power over His servants and He is the Wise, the Fully Aware.*

O my God, You are the Existent, *standing over every soul*, and the Self-Standing, subsisting in every meaning and every perception. You possess [all] Power, so You subjugate, and You possess [all] Knowledge, so You foreordain. To You belongs Ordaining Power and Subjugating Might, and in Your Hands are *the Creation and the Command.* You are with each thing, in the closest proximity, and You are its Master; by encompassing it You are its Director and its Guide.

O my God, I ask of You full backing from Your Subjugating Names, that You may thereby strengthen all my faculties of heart and soul, so that no possessor of a heart comes into direct contact with me without being *turned back upon their heels* [and rendered] powerless.

I ask of You, O my God, an expressive tongue and truthful speech; appropriate understanding and an innermost centre of taste; a truly receptive heart and a discerning mind; radiant thought and insatiable yearning; a lowered gaze and a burning longing. Grant me a powerful hand and a strength that brooks no resistance; a *soul at peace* and supple limbs for obeying You. Purify me that I may come to You, and grant that I may be brought near [in honour and esteem] to You.

O my God, gift me with a heart by which I may be devoted to You in utter poverty, led by yearning and driven by longing, [a heart] whose provision is fear [of You] and whose companion is restlessness, whose aim is [Your] closeness and acceptance! In Your Nearness lies the consummation of those who aim, and the fulfilment of the desire of those who search.

O my God, bestow upon me the presence of tranquillity and dignity. Keep me from self-aggrandisement and haughtiness. Let me stand in the station of being accepted as Your delegate, and may my words meet with positive response.

O my Lord, bring me close to You with the closeness of those who truly know [You]. Purify me from the attachments of the natural constitution. Eliminate the blood-clot of blameworthiness from my heart, that I may be one of *the completely purified ones.*

May God's blessing be upon our master Muhammad, and upon all his family and companions. *And praise be to God, Lord of the worlds.*

Sunday Morning Prayer

IN THE NAME OF GOD,
THE ALL-COMPASSIONATE AND MOST MERCIFUL

In the Name of God, the opener of existence!

Praise be to God, the manifester of every existent!

There is no god but God, the absolute Unity far beyond any unveiling or contemplation!

God is greater, from Him the order originates and to Him it returns!

Glory be to God, there is none other than Him to be contemplated! There is none with Him but Him to be worshipped!

One, Unique, He *is as He has [always] been* before the letters of limitation!

He has in every thing a Sign, pointing to the fact that He is One Existent.

His mystery is His veiling Himself from being perceived [by any other] or being limited in any way!

There is no power nor strength save through God, the Most High, the Most Magnificent, a treasure with which He has specially favoured us, from among the treasures of the Unseen in all Its Generosity. By it may I call upon all good to descend, by it may I repel all evil and harm, and by it may I unstitch all that which is sewn up and closed off!

Indeed we belong to God and to Him we return in all that has descended or is descending, in every state and station, in every thought and inspiration, and in all that arises from the interior or is received from the exterior.

God is the One wished for every thing, and in every thing He is the One hoped for and intended!

Inspiration and understanding come from Him, and that which is found to be is Him, without any [possibility of] denial or disclaimer.

When He unveils, there is no other. When He veils, all is other, and each one is concealed, distanced.

[He is] Inward in Uniqueness and Outward in Oneness. From Him and through Him is the existence of everything, so there is no thing. If there is a thing, in reality it is devoid and bereft of existence.

For He is the First and the Last, the Outwardly Manifest and the Inwardly Hidden, and He is Knower and Known of everything, before the existence of anything and after its existence.

To Him belongs the all-embracing Grasp, the unifying Reality and the eternally subsistent Mystery, the permanent Sovereignty and the inherent Authority! Deserving of all praise and glorification, He is *such that He extols Himself*, for He is both Praiser and Praised.

[He is] Unique of Essence, One in [all] Names and Qualities! Knowledgeable of all universals and particulars! Encompassing of all that is above and all that is below! It is before Him that *the faces bow* from all directions!

O God, O You who are the all-englobing Encompasser, who cannot be prevented from effusing gifts! O You whose treasuries are never exhausted, and whose generosity and support to the whole of creation is unfailingly extended!

O God, open for me the locks of these treasures; unveil for me the realities of these symbols. Be the One who faces me and my facing. By vision of You veil me from vision of me! By the manifestation of Your Self-revelation efface all my attributes, so that I have no orientation except towards You, so that my eyes alight upon none but You!

O God, look upon me with the eye of compassion and concern, of safeguarding and safekeeping, of election and direction, in every circumstance, so that nothing veils me from my vision of You and that I may look upon You through what You have accorded me of Your regard in everything. Render me completely conforming to Your Self-revelation, completely suitable to Your election and direction, place of Your regard in Your creation and channel for the effusion of Your gifts and favours towards them.

O You to whom belongs absolute Richness beyond need, whilst His servants possess [only] poverty beyond question!

O You who is Rich beyond need of anything, whilst each thing is in need of Him!

O You in whose hand lies the destiny of everything and to whom everything returns!

O You who possesses absolute Being, such that none knows what He truly is except Him, and none can be informed of Him except through His Guidance!

O You who commands that righteous actions be subject to the servant, so that all their benefit accrues to him! I have no goal other than You, and nothing suffices me except Your generosity and Your goodness.

O You who bestows most generously far in excess of any desire! O You who bestows favours before any asking! O You before whom the footsteps of every petitioner [always] stop short! O You who is all-powerful in His Command and all-triumphant! O You who gives freely to everything, but if He so wishes may deprive!

I strive towards You requesting, that I may find myself to be servant to You in every state. Direct me, my Master – indeed that is Your prerogative rather than mine.

How am I to aim at You when You are beyond reach? How am I to seek You when seeking itself signifies distance? Can One who is ever-close, ever-present, be sought? Can One be striven for when the one who strives for Him is in Him lost and perplexed? Seeking does not bring one to You; striving does not bring one back to You.

The revelations of Your Exteriorising cannot be caught hold of or grasped; the enigmas of Your Mysteries cannot be unravelled or undone. Is the one who is given existence capable of knowing the true nature of One who has bestowed existence on him? Is the one who is servant capable of attaining the reality of One who has subjected him to servanthood?

Seeking and aspiring, nearness and farness, these are [all] qualities of the servant: so what can the servant attain through his own qualities with respect to One who is Incomparable and Transcendent in His Essence? The [true] place of every creature is [total] incapacity, standing in true humility before the door of Exalted Glory, without any ability to grasp this Treasure.

How can I know You when You are the Inwardly Hidden who is not known?

How can I not know You when You are the Outwardly Manifest, making Yourself known to me in every thing?

How can I realise Your Unity when in Uniqueness I have no existence?

How can I not realise Your Unity when affirmation of Unity is the very secret of servanthood?

Glory be to You! There is no god but You! No-one but You can realise Your Unity, for You are as You are in pre-eternity without beginning and post-eternity without end. In reality no other than You can realise Your Unity, and in sum, none knows You except You.

You hide and You manifest – yet You do not hide from Yourself nor do You manifest to other than Yourself, for You are You. There is no god but You. How is this paradox to be resolved, when the First is Last and the Last is First? O You who causes the order to be ambiguous and the secret to be hidden, and plunges [other] into perplexity when [really] there is no other than He!

I ask of You, O God, that You unveil for me the mystery of Unity, that I may verify true servanthood and that I may fully accomplish the service of Your Lordship, according to what is suitable to its highest presence. For I am in existence only through You, being of ephemera and of non-existence, while You are Existent, Permanent, Living, Self-Subsisting, Ancient of Days, Eternal, Knower and Known. O You, whom none knows what He truly is except Him!

I ask of You, O God, that I may flee from me to You and that my whole totality may be integrated in You, so that [the sense of] my existence ceases to veil me from my witnessing. O You who are my aim and aspiration, O You whom I worship and adore! Nothing is lost to me when I have found You! Nothing is unknown to me when I have known You! Nothing is missing for me when I have witnessed You! My annihilation is in You; my subsistence is through You; and You are the object of my contemplation. There is no god but You. You are as I witness, and as I have been ordered [to realise].

My witnessing is my very existence, and I have not witnessed aught but me in my annihilation and my subsistence. The allusion is to me; the judgement is both for me and against me; the relationships are my relations; all these are my degrees. The [whole] affair is [truly] my affair, in manifestation and in non-manifestation, and in the permeating of the guarded Secret: Ipseity that pervades unseen, and places of manifestation that render visible, being and not-being, light and dark, pen and tablet, hearing and not-hearing, knowing and not-knowing, peace and war, silence and speech, separating and restoring, essential Truth and immediate Truth, concealment of interior eternity and permanence of exterior everlastingness.

Say: He, God, is Unique, God is the Universal Support and Refuge. He does not beget nor is He begotten, and there is no single one like Him.

May the blessing of God be upon the one who is first in coming into existence and first in Existence; the one who opens up for every witnesser [access to] the two presences of *witness and witnessed*; the one who is the hidden secret and the manifest light, the true aim and purpose; the one who distinguishes the two handfuls of precedence in the domain of creation, amongst those who are favoured and those who are far; the spirit most holy and sublime and the light most perfect and resplendent, who has realised the [condition of] perfect adoration in the presence of the Adored; whose spirit has received the overflowing from the presence of His Most Holy Spirit; whose heart is as a niche illumined by the rays of His [Divine] Light – for he is the greatest Envoy, the ennobled Prophet and the Friend brought close and made blessed.

And may the blessing be upon his family and his companions, [who are] the depositories of his secrets, the places where his lights shine and his full moons rise; treasures of truths and guides for creatures; [bright] stars of guidance for all who would follow [the Way]. And may He give greetings of great peace to them [all] up to the Day of Reckoning.

Glory be to God, for I am not among those who associate. God is sufficient for us and a most excellent Guardian. There is no power nor strength save through God, the Most High, the Most Magnificent! And praise be to God, Lord of the worlds.

Monday Eve Prayer

IN THE NAME OF GOD,
THE ALL-COMPASSIONATE AND MOST MERCIFUL

O my God, Your Knowledge embraces all that is knowable. Your Awareness encompasses the interior [meaning] of all that is understandable. You are sanctified in Your exaltedness from all that is blameable. The spiritual aspirations ascend to You, and *the words soar* to You.

You are the Supremely Exalted in Your eminence, so that the closest we can reach in our ascension to You is condescension [on Your part]. You are the Most Glorious in Your exaltedness, so that the noblest of our qualities with regard to You is self-abasement.

You have manifested in the interior and exterior of everything. You are permanent before every beginning and after every ending. Glory be to You! There is no god but You – the foreheads prostrate before Your Magnificence, and the lips are delighted by Your remembrance.

I ask of You, by Your Magnificent Name, to whom is elevated everyone who rises up [towards You] and from whom comes the great welcome for all who are received [by You], to grant me a secret concerning which the sublime aspirations request of me and the disdainful souls are led to me.

I ask of You, O my Lord, that You let Your condescension be a ladder by which I may rise to You and that You make my lowliness and abasement the means by which I may ascend to You. Envelop me in the protective covering of Your Light, by which You unveil for me everything that is veiled, and by which You conceal me from all the envious and the deluded. Grant me a character by which I embrace all that is created, and by which I establish all that is real and satisfy every right, just as *You have embraced everything in compassion and knowledge.*

There is no god but You. *O Living One, O Self-Subsisting One*!

O my Lord, instruct me with the subtle benevolence of Your Lordliness, as one who is conscious of being in total need of You should be instructed, as one who never claims to be independent of You. Watch over me with the eye of Your Providence, protecting me from all the knocks that may befall me, or anything that may afflict me or cause me to be troubled at any moment or in any perception, or that may inscribe one of the lines upon the tablet of my own will. Provide me with the ease of intimacy with You, and raise me to the station of Closeness to You. Revive my spirit with Your remembrance, and draw me on, now with *hopeful longing* for You, and now with *reverent fear* of You.

Restore to me the cloak of satisfaction, and bring me to the wellsprings of the welcome. Grant me compassion from You, re-establishing harmony in my disorder, perfecting where I am lacking, rectifying where I am deviating, restraining me when I am astray and guiding me when I am perplexed.

Indeed You are *Lord of every thing* and its instructor. You mercify the essences [of all beings] and You elevate the degrees. Your Closeness is the joy of the spirits, and the perfumed sweetness of rejoicing; the epitome of true prosperity, and the repose of all those who are at ease.

May You be blessed, Lord of lords! Liberator of slaves! Lifter of suffering! You *embrace everything in compassion and in knowledge*. You cover and forgive wrongdoing with loving tenderness and clemency. You are the Forgiving, the Merciful, the Clement, the All-Knowing, the High, the Magnificent.

And may the blessing of God be upon our master Muhammad, and upon all his family and companions. *And praise be to God, Lord of the worlds.*

Monday Morning Prayer

IN THE NAME OF GOD,
THE ALL-COMPASSIONATE AND MOST MERCIFUL

O God, I ask of You light and guidance, and good behaviour in [my] conformity. I seek refuge in You from the evil of my soul, and from the evil of everything that separates me from You. There is no god but You. Purify my soul from doubt and bad character, from misfortune and negligence. Bestow upon me true servanthood, that I may be obedient to You in all my states.

O Knowing One, instruct me in Your Knowledge! O Wise Judge, confirm me with the wisdom of Your Judgement! O Hearing One, let me hear from You! O Seeing One, let me see Your Favours! O Fully Aware One, grant me awareness of You! O Living One, vivify me with Your Remembrance! O Willing One, purify my will through Your Infinite Power and Magnificence! *Indeed You have power over everything.*

O God, I ask You for a governing divine nature, and a subservient human nature, and incisiveness of mind, embracing all in totality and in differentiation, in both form and measure.

O my God, I beseech You by Your Essence, which none can perceive and none can neglect; and by Your Uniqueness, wherein those who imagine there to be something with You have associated [others with You]; and by Your All-Encompassing, wherein those who suppose there to be another in Eternity have lied and have turned away and been separated themselves from the harmony of True Purity.

O You in whose transcendence whatever has no existence in His Ancientness is stripped away! O You who ordains all things through His all-encompassing Knowledge and incomparable Greatness! O You who brings out the light of everything's existence from the darkness of its non-existence! O You who forms the individuations of the spheres according to whatever Knowledge He has filled His Pen with! O You who empowers His Determinations through the secrets of His Wisdoms!

I am crying out to You, as one who is distant calls out for help from one who is close! I am beseeching You, as a lover yearning for their beloved! I am entreating You, as one constrained petitions one who favourably responds to their need!

O God, I ask You to lift up the veil of the Unseen and to untie the knots of doubt! O God, make me living through You with a life that is necessarily existing! Make me knowing with an equally essential knowledge that embraces the mysteries of all that is knowable! By Your Infinite Power, open up for me the treasure of the Garden of Paradise and the Throne and the Essence, and make my moon disappear beneath the lights of [Your] Qualities! By Your Gracious Benevolence liberate me from all the shackles of limited belief!

Glory be to You in Your transcendence! [You are] Glorified as absolutely transcendent of any marks of the recent or properties of invalidation; and [You are] Sanctified as utterly pure of all resemblance to what is blameworthy or all reason for rejection.

Glory be to You! You have made every seeker incapable of reaching You except through You.

Glory be to You! None may know who You are except You.

Glory be to You! How utterly Close You are, despite the supreme elevation of Your Sublimity!

O God, invest me in the garment of Glorious Praise! Clothe me in the robe of Supreme Might! Crown me with the diadem of Majesty and Glorification! Divest me of the attributes of dispersive frivolousness and constrictive rigorousness. Liberate me from the shackles of reckoning and limiting, and from the pursuit of difference, contradiction and opposition.

O my God, my non-existence in You is my very existence; my remaining with You is my very non-existence. Instead of the situation where I am imagining I exist along with You, let me realise my true non-existence in You, and make me whole by annihilating me in You!

There is no god but You! You are far above any like.

There is no god but You! You are elevated beyond any similar.

There is no god but You! You are without any need of minister or counsellor.

There is no god but You! O Unique One! O Universal Support and Refuge!

There is no god but You! Existence is through You alone! Prostration is to You alone! You are the One Real Truth that is adored!

I seek refuge in You from myself, and I beg You for annihilation from myself. I implore You to cover with Your Forgiveness whatever remains in me of [the illusion of] distance or lowness, or is still subject to a name or relative designation.

You are the One who establishes and elevates, the One who originates and finalises, the One who differentiates and unifies.

O Establisher! O Elevator! O Originator! O Finaliser! O Differentiator! O Unifier!

Protection and Refuge! Help and Succour! O my Protector! O my Helper!

Deliverance and Salvation! Sanctuary and Asylum! O You in whom lies my deliverance and sanctuary!

I ask of You that You may grant all that I have requested and entreated You for, through the one who is the very first of existence, the most perfect light of knowledge, the most excellent spirit of life, the eternal extension of compassion and the greatest elevation of character, the one who is foremost in spirit and excellence, and who has completed and sealed the [Divine] form and [the cycle of] prophecy, the light who brings guidance and clarification, the compassion who brings knowledge, establishment and security, Muhammad the chosen one, the elected envoy.

May God's blessing be upon him, and upon his family and companions, and may He give them greetings of great peace up to the Day of Reckoning.

And praise be to God, Lord of the worlds.

Tuesday Eve Prayer

IN THE NAME OF GOD,
THE ALL-COMPASSIONATE AND MOST MERCIFUL

O my God, You are the Most Forceful in assault, the Most Painful in seizing, the Most Tremendous in conquering. [You are] the sublimely Exalted above all opponents or rivals and the utterly Transcendent from *any consort or offspring*. It is for You to take on the vanquishing of enemies and the quelling of oppressors. You trick whoever You wish *and You are the best of tricksters.*

O my God, I ask of You, by Your Name with which You *seize the forelocks*, with which You *bring down the enemy from the fortresses and cast terror in their hearts*, with which You make the people of suffering wretched, that You extend help to me with one of the connecting threads of Your Name the Forceful. May [this Name] pervade my total and partial powers, so that I am enabled to accomplish what I desire, that the dark oppression of the wrongdoer may not reach me nor the arrogantly unjust assail me. Let my anger in defence of You and on Your behalf be coupled to Your Anger for Your Own Self. *Obliterate* the faces of my enemies, *transform them where they stand, harden their hearts* and *set up between* me and *them a wall with a door in it, the inner side of which is compassion and the outer of which is chastisement.* You are Most Forceful in assault, Most Painful in seizing, Most Tremendous in punishing.

Such is the seizing of Thy Lord when He seizes the cities that do wrong. Surely His seizing is grievously painful.

O my Lord, make me rich through You, beyond need of other than You, so that this pure sufficiency leaves me free of all conditions that might make me dependent on any creaturial need or spiritual requirement. Make me reach the utmost ease in my prosperity [in You], and elevate me to the *lote-tree of* my *extreme limit.* Let me witness existence as a cycle and the journey as an orbit, so that I may behold the mystery of Divine Descent to the ultimate ends and the Return to the very beginnings, where speech comes to an end and the vowel of the *lām* is silent, where the dot of the *ghayn* is removed from me and the One returns to the two.

O my God, grant me the facility of that secret which You have accorded to many of Your saints, a facility which will dispel from me the fog of my [apparent] self-sufficiency. Support me in all this by a radiant light, *dazzling the eyes* of *every envier among jinn and mankind.* Grant me the gift of an aptitude which brings success in every station. Make me rich beyond need of other than You, with a richness that establishes my complete poverty towards You.

Indeed You are the Rich, the Praiseworthy, the Friend, the Illustrious, the Generous, the Discerning Director!

And may the blessing of God be upon our master
Muhammad, and upon all his family and companions, and may He greet them with great peace up 55
to the Day of Judgment. *And praise be to God, Lord
of the worlds.*

Tuesday Morning Prayer

IN THE NAME OF GOD,
THE ALL-COMPASSIONATE AND MOST MERCIFUL

O my Lord, immerse me in the *fathomless ocean* of Your Uniqueness and in the open waters of the *sea* of Your Oneness, and fortify me with the sovereign power and *authority* of Your Singularity. Thus may I emerge into the vast expanse of Your Compassion, with my face illuminated by the lightning-flashes of Closeness, which are among the marks of Your Compassion. [May I be] revered through Your awe-inspiring Dignity; eminent and cherished through Your providential Grace; esteemed and honoured through Your instruction and purification.

Invest me with the robe of high rank and acceptance. Clear for me paths that lead to joining and attaining. Crown me with the diadem of high nobility and dignity. Bring me together with Your loved ones in this lower world and in the world of eternal repose. Through the Light of Your Name, grant me from the Light of Your Name an authoritative power and awesome grandeur that hearts and spirits may be guided to me, and souls and bodies be brought to submission before me.

O You before whom the oppressors bend their necks in submission, to whom the rapacious yield in contrition! O King of this world and the other!

There is no shelter or safe-hold *from You except in You.* There is no aid except from You. There is none to put trust in except You.

Drive away from me the machinations of the envious, and the dark evils of the obdurate! Shelter me beneath the canopy of Your Mighty Dearness, O You the Most Generous of the generous!

O my God, grant aid to my exterior that I may attain Your Satisfaction, and grant light to my heart and innermost secret that I may be thoroughly aware of the ways of Your working.

O my God, how can I be turned away from Your Door as a failure to You when I have arrived at it with complete confidence in You?

And how can You make me despair of Your Giving when You have ordered me to ask of You? Here am I, devoted to You, seeking refuge in You!

O my God, put a distance between me and my enemies, just as You have put distance between the East and the West. *Dazzle their eyes*, make their feet quake and drive away from me their evil and harm, through the light of Your Holiness and the majesty of Your Glory.

Indeed You are God, the One who bestows gifts, granting the greatest of blessings, Most Esteemed,

Most Venerated by the one who exchanges intimacies with You regarding the subtleties of benevolence and compassion.

O Living One! O Self-Subsistent! O Unveiler of the secrets of mystical and sacred knowledge!

May God's blessing be upon our master Muhammad, and upon all his family and companions.

Glory be to your Lord, the Lord of Eminent Might, beyond what they qualify Him with. Peace be upon the messengers. And praise be to God, Lord of the worlds.

Wednesday Eve Prayer

IN THE NAME OF GOD,
THE ALL-COMPASSIONATE AND MOST MERCIFUL

O my God, Your Name is master of the Names. In Your Hand is the kingdom of the earth and the heaven. You are the Self-Existent, who stands in every thing, *watching over every thing.* Richness beyond need is firmly established for You, and every thing that is other than You, all 'he' and 'I', is in need of the Most Holy Effusion of Your Generosity.

I ask of You, by Your Name with which You unite the complementary oppositions and divisions of the [two realms of] Creation and Command, and with which You appoint the non-manifestation of all that appears and make appear the manifestation of all the non-manifest: bestow upon me the condition of Universal Support, by which I may still the motions of Your Power and Might, so that everything that is motionless be put into motion in me, and everything that is put into motion be motionless in me. Then I may find myself the *qibla* of every facing, and the unifier of each separated differentiation, by virtue of Your Name, towards which my facing is orientated and in the face of which my own will and word are cleared away. Thus everyone shall take from me the *firebrand* of complete guidance, which will illuminate for him what Muhammad, the chosen one, has led him to. Were it not for him, the singular one, the I-ness of the Fire-bringer would not have been thrice affirmed for Moses.

O He who is He! and there is no I!

I ask of You, by every Name which derives from the *Alif* of the Unseen, which encompasses the reality of all that is witnessed, that I may witness the unity of each multiple in the interior of every immediate truth, and the multiplicity of each unit in the exterior of every ultimate reality. Then let me witness the unity of the exterior and the interior, so that whatever is unseen of that which is exterior is not concealed from me, and whatever is concealed of that which is interior is not unseen to me. Let me witness the totality in all [things], O You *in whose Hand is the kingdom of all things.*

Verily You, You are You!

Say: 'God' and then leave them to play in their discourse. Alif lām mīm. God, there is no god but He, the Living, the Self-Standing.

O my Master, *peace be upon me* from You, You are my support. For You it is the same whether I address You inwardly or outwardly, for You hear my call and answer my prayer. You have banished my darkness with Your Light. You have brought my lifeless body to life with Your Spirit. You are my Lord: my hearing, my seeing, my heart are in Your Hand. You have taken possession of all of me. You have conferred eminence upon my lowliness; You have elevated my rank; You have raised high my remembrance.

May You be ever-blessed! Light of lights! Unveiler of mysteries! Granter of life in all its span! Lowerer of the curtains of protection!

In the exaltedness of Your Majesty You are transcendentally far above the characteristics of the contingent. The rank of Your Perfection surpasses any attempt to gain access [to It] by means of inclinations [coloured] by desires, shortcomings, and imperfections. The earths and the heavens are illuminated by the pure vision of Your Essence. To You belongs the loftiest Glory, the most encompassing Honour, the most inaccessible Might.

Ever-Praised and Holy is our Lord, Lord of the angels and the spirit! It is He who illuminates the shadowy *fortresses* and the dark substances; it is He who delivers those who are drowned in the sea of matter. *I take refuge in You from the twilight when it becomes dark and the envious* as they watch and wait.

O my Sovereign Possessor, I call out to You and entreat You, secretly confiding [in You] as a broken servant, who knows that You are listening and who firmly believes that You will respond, one who stands at Your door, *constrained in utter need*, finding no-one *to put trust in, other than You.*

I ask of You, my God, by that Name with which You pour forth good things, bring down blessings and confer increase upon those who are grateful, and with which You bring forth from the darkness, and with which You dismiss people of association and baseness: may You spread over me the garments of Your Lights, striking enemies blind and rendering them powerless. Grant me my portion from You, as a radiance that discloses to me every hidden matter, unveils to me every high mystery and burns up every enticing satan.

O Light of light! O Unveiler of all that is veiled! *Unto You are all things returned.* Through You is all evil repelled. O Lord, O Merciful One, O Forgiving One!

May the blessing of God be upon our master Muhammad, and upon all his family and companions. *Peace be upon the messengers. And praise be to God, Lord of the worlds.*

Wednesday Morning Prayer

IN THE NAME OF GOD,
THE ALL-COMPASSIONATE AND MOST MERCIFUL

O my Lord, confer upon me the honour of contemplating the lights of Your Pure Holiness, and the support of manifesting the power and authority of Your Intimacy, so that I may be turned according to the glories of the knowledges [which flow] from Your Names, and that this variability may disclose to me the secrets of every atom of my being in every sphere that I contemplate. By this may I come to witness what You have placed within the seen and unseen realms, and may I behold how the mystery of Your Power permeates the evidences of Divine nature and human nature.

Grant me complete gnosis and universal wisdom, so that there remains nothing knowable [in the universe] without me coming to know the subtle threads of its intricacies, which are spread throughout existence. By this may I drive away the darkness of coercion which prevents the perception of the realities of [Your] Signs, and by this may I dispose freely over the hearts and spirits, kindling true love and friendship, right conduct and guidance.

Indeed You are the Lover who is Beloved, and the Seeker who is Sought! O You *who makes all hearts turn and turn*! O You who removes all distress! You are the *One who knows all that is unseen*, the One who puts a veil over all imperfection!

O You who has never ceased to be All-Forgiving! O You who has never ceased to veil and protect! O Forgiving One! O Veiling One! O Preserver! O Protector! O Defender! O Benefactor! O Truly Affectionate One! O Graciously Indulgent One! O Most Subtle and Benevolent! O Most Mighty and Invincible! O Flawless, Boundless Peace!

Forgive me, veil me and preserve me. Protect me, and defend me. Bestow upon me beneficence, affection and indulgence. Be benevolent to me, make me invincible, and grant me peace and security.

Do not take me to task for the baseness of my actions, and do not requite me for the evil of my works. Correct me without delay through Your complete Benevolence and the purity of Your universal Compassion. Do not let me stand in need of any other than You! Protect me and pardon me. Make my whole affair righteous and proper [to You].

There is no god but You! Glory be to You, indeed I have been one of the wrongdoers. You are the Most Merciful of the mercifiers!

May the blessing of God be upon our master Muhammad, and upon his family and companions, salutations to them all. *Peace be upon the messengers. And praise be to God, Lord of the worlds.*

Thursday Eve Prayer

IN THE NAME OF GOD,
THE ALL-COMPASSIONATE AND MOST MERCIFUL

O my Master, You are the author of the causes and their orderer, and the director of the hearts and their turner. I ask of You, by the wisdom which determines the arrangement of the prime causes and the effect of the highest upon the lowest, that You cause me to witness the ordered arrangement of the causes, ascending and descending, so that I may thus witness the interior of them by witnessing the exterior, and the first of them in the last. Let me view the wisdom of the ordered arrangement by witnessing the Arranger and how space-time causation is preceded by the Author of the causes, so that I am not veiled from the *ʿayn* (Eye-Essence) by the [dot of the] *ghayn* (of otherness).

O my God, extend to me the key of the [listening] ear, which is the *Cave* of mystical knowledge, that I may be given to speak in every beginning through Your Name the Incomparable Inventor, by which You open every written *inscription*.

O You, through whose eminent Names every self-exalted one is brought low! Everything is through You and You are without [need of] us. You are the Original Inventor of everything and its Creator.

To You is the praise, O Faultless Originator, for every beginning! To You is the thanks, O Forever Enduring One, for every ending! You are the One who brings forth all good, the interior of all interiors who extends to the furthest reaches of things, the expansive provider of nourishment for all beings.

O God, shower me with blessings unto the very end forever, just as You have blessed Muhammad and Abraham.

Indeed it is from You and to You, *and it is in the Name of God, the All-Compassionate and Most Merciful, the Incomparable Inventor of the heavens and the earth! When He orders a thing, He says to it 'Be' and it becomes.*

O my God, You are the firmly Established Ground prior to all constants, and the eternally Enduring Continuant after all speakers and non-speakers. There is no god but You, and there is no existent other than You!

To You belongs the grandeur, the power, the glory and the kingdom! You overwhelm the oppressors and destroy the deception of the unjust; You break up the gathering of those who stray and humble the necks of the arrogant.

I ask of You, O You who overcomes every victor, O You who overtakes every fugitive: [grant me] the *mantle* of Your *Pride*, the *girdle* of Your *Majesty* and the canopy of Your Awesomeness and all that is beyond this, which no-one knows but You, so that I may be clothed in awe from Your Awesomeness, to which hearts give honour and magnification and before which *eyes are downcast* in dread. Make me master of the forelock of *every obstinate tyrant* and *rebellious satan*, whose *forelocks* are in Your hand. Keep me in the lowliness of servanthood in all of this, safeguard me from deviating [from the truth] and lapsing, and support me in word and deed.

You are the One who reassures the hearts and grants relief from worries! There is no god but You.

May the blessing of God be upon our master Muhammad, and upon all his family and his companions. *And praise be to God, Lord of the worlds.*

Thursday Morning Prayer

IN THE NAME OF GOD,
THE ALL-COMPASSIONATE AND MOST MERCIFUL

O my God, You are Self-Standing through Your own Essence; Revealed through Your Qualities; Encompassing through Your Names; Manifest through Your Acts; and Hidden through what is only known to You! You are Alone in Your Majesty, as You are the One, the Unique; and You have singularised Yourself, as You permanently endure in eternity without beginning or end. You, You are God, who by virtue of Oneness is the Only One referred to in *iyyāka*. With You there is none other than You; in You there is none but You.

I ask of You, O God, for annihilation in Your Subsistence, and for subsistence through You, not with You.

There is no god but You!

O my God, cause me to be absent [from myself] in Your Presence, annihilated in Your Being and extinguished in Your Contemplation. Sever me from all that severs me from You; occupy me with You alone by turning me away from all that distracts me from You.

There is no god but You!

O my God, You are the Truly Existent, while I am the fundamentally non-existent. Your Subsistence is by virtue of Your Essence; mine is only accidental. So, my God, lavish Your True Existence upon my fundamental non-existence, that I may be as I was when I was not at all, and You may be as You are, as You always have been!

There is no god but You!

You are the One who *accomplishes whatever You desire*, while I am a servant for You, *one* among some *of the servants*. O my God, You have desired me and You have desired through me – thus I am the desired and You the Desirer. May You be what is desired through me, so that You Yourself become the Desired and I the desirer!

There is no god but You!

O my God, You are unmanifest in all that is unseen; manifest in every eye-entity; heard in every account, be it true or false; known in the degree of Unity and Duality. You are the One named by the Names which have been brought down in revelation, so that You are veiled from being seen by the eye, and concealed from being grasped by the intelligence.

O my God, You have revealed Yourself in the particular revelations of Your Qualities, so that all the degrees of created existence have become diversified. In each degree You are named by the realities of all that is named, appointing the intelligences as witnesses to the intricate unseen realities of [all that is] knowable. You have released the primordial spirits upon the plains of Divine Knowledge, where they become bewildered and wander about amidst the allusions of their 'Syriac' subtleties. When You have withdrawn them from all 'whole and part', removed them from all 'where and when', and stripped them of all 'how much and what'; when You have made known to them the essential knowledge in the places of their non-recognition, liberated them by announcing Yourself as the Lord in the Divine places of annunciation, and caused all sense of separation to fall from them by removing the veil of the *ghayn*, then they are strung according to the primordial Harmony [of Eternity] upon the thread of *Bismillāhi l-Raḥmāni l-Raḥīm.*

O my God, how often do I cry out to You as one who calls, when [in truth] You are the One who calls for the caller! How often do I secretly whisper to You as one who confides intimacies, when You are the One who confides for the confider!

O my God, if union is the essence of separateness, and closeness the very soul of distance, if knowledge be the site of ignorance, and recognition the seat of non-recognition, what then is the destination and where the starting-point of the path?

O my God, You are what is sought behind the aim of every seeker, what is acknowledged in the eye of the denier, what is truly close in the separation of the one who distances [himself]. Yet here conjecture has supplanted understanding – who is distanced from whom? Who is favoured by whom? Beauty says '*You alone*', without any limitation, while Baseness cries '*the One who rendered good and beautiful all that He has created*'. The former is an end at which journeying comes to a halt, and the latter is a veil by virtue of imagining there is other [than You].

O my God, when will intellect be free from the bonds of constraint? And when shall thought's eye be able to glimpse the fair beauties of essential realities? When will understanding be severed from the root of untruth? And when shall imagination be unfettered from the cloying cords which tie it to associating? When will conceptualising be safe from the schism of separating? And when shall the precious soul be detached from the characteristics of its creaturial nature?

O my God, acts of obedience do not profit You, nor do acts of disobedience harm You. In the hand of Your Almighty Sovereignty lies the command of hearts and forelocks, and *to You is returned the whole affair*, without distinguishing between obedient or disobedient.

O my God, for You no matter distracts You from any other!

O my God, for You necessity does not restrict You nor possibility limit You. Obscurity does not hide You, nor clarification explain You!

O my God, for You rational evidence does not substantiate You, nor logical proof verify You!

O my God, for You Eternity without beginning and without end coincide in Your Reality!

O my God, what is this 'You' and 'I'? What is this 'He' and 'She'?

O my God, should I search for You in plurality or in unity? How long will I have to wait for You? And how can this be done when a servant has no preparedness nor support without You?

O my God, my subsistence through You lies in my annihilation, [but is my annihilation] from myself, or in You or through You? Is my annihilation thus realised through You, or imagined through me, or conversely, or even both at once? And is my subsistence in You likewise?

O my God, my silence is a dumbness necessitating deafness, and my speaking is a deafness necessitating dumbness! Perplexity in all, yet there is no perplexity [in You].

In the Name of God, *God suffices me*. In the Name of God, *I place my trust in God*. In the Name of God, *I ask of God*. In the Name of God, *there is no power nor strength save through God*.

Our Lord, in You we place our trust; to You we turn; to You is the homecoming.

O God, I ask You through the mystery of Your Order and the grandeur of Your Decree; through the all-embracing grasp of Your Knowledge; through the special prerogatives of Your Will; through the efficacy of Your Power; through the permeation of Your Hearing and Sight; through the self-subsistent presence of Your Life; and through the necessary character of Your Essence and Qualities.

O God, O God, O God! O First, O Last! O Manifest, O Hidden! O Light, O Truth, O Most Evident!

O God, distinguish my secret heart with the secrets of Your Oneness! Sanctify my spirit with the sanctified revelations of Your Qualities! Purify my heart with the pure knowledges of Your Divinity!

O God, instruct my intellect in the sciences of Your Private Knowledge, and perfume my soul with the virtues of Your Lordship! Assure my senses by extending illuminating rays from the Presences of Your Radiant Light! Liberate the quintessential gemstones of my corporeality from the constraints of gross nature, from the condensity of sense-perception and from the confinement of place and [phenomenal] world!

O God, transport me from the descending steps of my created being and nature to the ascending flight of Your Truth and essential Reality. You are my Friend and Master: in You I die and from You I take life. *It is*

You alone whom we adore and it is You alone we ask for aid.

Look upon me, O God, with that regard by which You arrange all my stages in a harmonious progression, and by which You purify the inner heart where my secrets appear, by which You elevate the spirits of my remembrance to the Highest Assembly, and by which You intensify the shining of my light.

O God, make me absent from the whole of Your creation and unite me to You through Your True Reality. Preserve me in the contemplation of the dispositions of Your Order in the myriad worlds of Your Differentiation.

O God, it is You that I turn to for aid; You that I turn my face to; You that I ask of; and You, and no other than You, that I truly desire! I do not ask of You other than You; nor do I seek of You aught but You alone!

O God, I beseech You to respond to that through the most august intercessor, the greatest excellency, the nearest beloved, the most protective friend, Muhammad the elect, the serenely pure and completely agreed to [by God], the chosen prophet.

For him I ask that You bless him with a Blessing-prayer that is everlasting, permanent, self-standing, divine and lordly. Let me witness in that [Blessing] the reality of his perfection, and let me be consumed in the contemplation of the knowledges of his essential nature. [And may this Blessing] be likewise upon his family and companions, for You are the Master of that!

There is no power nor strength save through God, the High, the Magnificent. And praise be to God, Lord of the worlds.

Friday Eve Prayer

IN THE NAME OF GOD,
THE ALL-COMPASSIONATE AND MOST MERCIFUL

O my God, all the high fathers are Your servants, and You are Lord [of all] absolutely. You unite the complementary contraries, for You are both the Majestic and the Beautiful. There is no end to Your sheer delight in Your Essence, as there is no end to Your Contemplation of It. You are too Majestic and Perfect for us to contemplate, and You are too Sublime and Beautiful for us to describe You. You are Transcendent in Your Majesty far beyond the distinguishing marks of contingencies, and Your Sublime Beauty is Sanctified from being assailed by inclinations towards It through passions.

I ask of You, by the mystery with which You unite the complementary contraries, that You bring together for me all that is disunited of my being, in such a union that I may contemplate and witness the oneness of my being. Invest me with the robe of Your Beauty, and crown me with the diadem of Your Majesty, so that human souls may humble themselves before me, disdainful hearts be led to me, and the secrets of the Most Holy [Effusion] be extended to me.

Elevate my rank before You so that everyone who elevates themselves and wields power is brought low and humbled before me. Lead me to You by my forelock, and grant me mastery of the forelock of every [living thing] endowed with spirit, whose forelock is in Your Hand.

Grant me a tongue of veracity regarding [the two realms of] Your Creation and Your Command. Fill me with You, and preserve me *upon Your land and sea. Bring* me *forth from the city* of gross nature, *whose inhabitants are oppressors*, and free me from the bondage of created things.

Grant me from You an evident proof that bequeaths security, and do not grant power over me to any other than You. In my poverty towards You, grant me richness beyond need of anything sought, and safeguard me through Your Grace and Providential Support from anything desired.

You are my goal and my glory; to You the returning and the ultimate end. You comfort and mend the broken, and You shatter the tyrants; You take the fearful under Your wing, and You put fear into the oppressors. Yours is the Most Sublime Glory, the Most Complete Revelation and the Most Impenetrable Veil!

Glory be to You, there is no god but You: You are *my Reckoner and the best Trustee.*

Such is the seizing of your Lord when He seizes the cities that do wrong. Surely His seizing is grievously painful.

Then We took vengeance upon those who sinned; and it was ever incumbent upon Us to help the believers.

O God! O Creator of all that is created! O Vivifier of all that is dead! O You who gathers together all that is dispersed, and pours forth light upon the essences of all things! Yours is the Kingdom infinitely vast, Yours the Rank of most sublime honour! Lords are Your slaves, monarchs Your servants, and the wealthy are the poor towards You, for You are Rich in Yourself beyond need of any other than You.

I ask of You, by Your Name with which You have *created each thing, ordaining its destiny*, and with which You bestow upon whomsoever You wish *a garden and a raiment of silk*, and the power of vicegerency and *a great kingdom*: take away my covetousness, and perfect my imperfection; grace me with the garments of Your Favour, and teach me of Your Names what is most appropriate for Divine permission and dictation; fill my interior with godfearing and compassion and my exterior with awe and grandeur, so that the hearts of the enemies be in dread of me, and the spirits of the friends find pleasure and ease with me.

They fear their Lord above them and they do what they are commanded.

O my Lord, grant me the gift of the most perfect aptitude to receive Your Most Holy Effusion, that I may be Your appointed regent in Your lands and by that keep Your displeasure away from Your servants.

Indeed You appoint as regent whomsoever You wish and You *have power over all things*. You are *the Fully*
80 *Aware, the Seer.*

May the blessing of God be upon our master Muhammad, and upon his family and companions – salutations to them all. He is *my Reckoner and the Best Trustee.*

Friday Morning Prayer

IN THE NAME OF GOD,
THE ALL-COMPASSIONATE AND MOST MERCIFUL

O my Lord, make me advance on and on up the steps of the sciences. Make me turn round and round in the degrees of the mysteries of the realities. Protect me within the pavilion of Your Protection and the hidden secret of Your Veil from the arrival of those thoughts which do not befit the glories of Your Majesty.

O my Lord, let me stand through You in every affair. Let me witness Your Subtle Benevolence in every far and near. Open the eye of my insight within the decreeing of the arena of Union, so that I may witness the standing of all things through You, in such a contemplation that my vision is severed from all existents.

O Master of Grace and Generosity!

O my Lord, from the seas of pure detachment of the *Alif* of the most Holy Essence, bathe me with that which detaches me from all attachments that punctuate my awareness, and that close the chapter on my quest. With the primordial matter of Its Universal Dot, which appears from the Sovereign Unseen of Your Essence, fill me so that I may provide ink for the letters of created things, [and that I may be] safeguarded in that from deficiency or disfiguring.

O You, who have encompassed everything in compassion and knowledge, O Lord of the worlds!

O my Lord, purify me externally and internally from the stain of otherness and from stopping at the stages, by means of an effusion from Your Pure Holiness. Absent me from them by contemplating the lightning-flashes of Your Intimacy and Familiarity. Give me clear insight into the essential realities of things and the fine details of forms. Let me hear the speech of created beings in purest proclamation of Your Unity in every realm. Display Yourself in my mirror with a complete Self-Revelation of the jewels of the Names of Your Majesty and Subjugating Might, so that no oppressor among men and jinn may look upon me without there being reflected back upon them, through the radiance of that jewel [which is manifested in the mirror], that which burns up *the self that commands to wrongdoing*, thrusting them back in abased submissiveness, *turning their sight away from me in enfeebled* powerlessness.

O You to whom *all faces submit* and to whom the stiff-necked bow in total surrender! O Lord of lords!

O my Lord, distance me from any separation that severs me from the presences of Your Closeness. Strip me of whatever of my qualities is inappropriate through being overwhelmed by the lights of Your

Qualities. Banish the darkness of my natural and human condition by revealing one of the lightning-flashes of the Light of Your Essence.

Assist me with an angelic power, by which I may dominate whatever of the low nature and base characteristics hold sway over me. Erase the appearances of created things from the tablet of my mind, and through the hand of Your Grace inscribe therein the mystery which is kept within Your Prior Closeness, [a secret] which is hidden between the *kāf* and the *nūn*.

So glory be to Him in whose hand is the Kingdom of all things and to whom they are brought back.

O Light of Light! O You who deluges all with the rain-clouds of His Effusion! O Holy One! O Universal Support! O Protective Preserver! O Subtle Benevolence! O Lord of the worlds!

May the blessing of God be upon our master Muhammad, and upon all his family and companions. *And praise be to God, Lord of the worlds.*

Saturday Eve Prayer

IN THE NAME OF GOD,
THE ALL-COMPASSIONATE AND MOST MERCIFUL

O my Master, Your Subsistence endures forever; Your Decree is executed throughout creation. You have sanctified Yourself in Your Sublimity; You have elevated Yourself in Your Holiness. *Preserving* created beings *does not burden You*, and what is unveiled to the eye of [each being] is never hidden from You. You invite whomsoever You wish to Yourself, and through Yourself You direct them to Yourself. To You belongs eternal Praise and most glorious Everlastingness.

I ask of You for a pure 'moment' [of Being] through what You desire, in an appropriate and conforming manner, whose aim and end is Your Closeness, coming from the fruits of works [of adoration] that are dedicated to Your Satisfaction. Grant me the gift of a radiant secret which will unveil to me the realities of works. Distinguish me with a wisdom coupled with authority, and an ability to allude accompanied by understanding.

Indeed You are the Friend and Patron of one who entrusts their affairs to You; and the Answerer of one who calls upon You!

O my God, Your Bounty towards me continues forever, so make my contemplation of You continue [likewise]. Let me contemplate my essence from Your standpoint, not from mine, so that I may be through You, and not me. Grant me from Your own Presence a total knowledge in which all the knowledgeable spirits are guided to me. Indeed You are All-Knowing, the Knower [of the Unseen]!

Blessed be the Name of Your Lord, Lord of Majesty and Generosity! With Him are the keys of the Unseen, which none knows except He.

O my Lord, bathe me in the radiance of Your Light, unveiling for me all that is concealed within me, so that I may witness my existence in all its true perfection from Your standpoint, not from mine. Let me thus come close to You by my own attribute being dispelled from me, as You come close to me by the effulgence of Your Light upon me.

O my Lord, possibility is my true attribute, nonexistence my very substance, and poverty my true value; Your Existence is my sole cause, Your Power my very agent and You my only goal! Your Knowledge is all that I need from You in my not-knowing. You are just as I know You and yet far beyond what

I know! You are with every thing, and yet with You there is no thing!

You have *ordained stations* for the spiritual journey, arranged degrees for the beneficial and the harmful, and established the paths of Goodness. In all of this we are by virtue of You, while You are without [need of] us. For You are pure Good, sheer Generosity, unlimited Perfection.

I ask of You, by Your Name with which You pour forth light upon the receptacles and with which You dispel the darkness of obscurities: fill my being with light from Your Light, which is the substance of every light and the true goal of every desire, so that nothing may obscure me from what You have deposited in the essence of my being.

Grant me the gift of *a tongue of veracity* that can give expression to the witnessing of Truth, and distinguish me with clarity and the [ability of clear] communication from the *all-inclusive Words.* Protect me in all my utterances from claiming that which is not mine by rights, and make me speak *according to inner vision* of You, *I and those who follow me.*

O God, I take refuge in You from any speech that creates confusion or results in discord or sows doubt. It is from You that all words are received; it is from You that all wisdoms are obtained.

You are the One who *upholds the heavens*, the One who teaches the Names. There is no god but You, the

One, the *Unique*, the Singular, the *Universal Support*, who *neither begets nor is He begotten, nor is there a single one like Him.*

May the blessing of God be upon our master Muhammad, and upon all his family and companions. *And praise be to God, Lord of the worlds.*

Saturday Morning Prayer

IN THE NAME OF GOD,
THE ALL-COMPASSIONATE AND MOST MERCIFUL

Whosoever holds fast to God is guided to a straight path.

Praise be to God who has allowed me into the preserve of God's Benevolence!

Praise be to God who has brought me into the garden of God's Compassion!

Praise be to God who has seated me in the station of God's Love!

Praise be to God who has made me taste [the delicacies] from the tables which are spread with God's Provision!

Praise be to God who has bestowed upon me the testimony of being connected to God's Preference!

Praise be to God who has made me drink from wells wherein can be found God's Promise fulfilled!

Praise be to God who has clothed me in the robe of true servanthood to God!

All this despite *what I have squandered of the Divine side*, and neglected of the Divine entitlements. *That is superabundant grace from God. And who can forgive sins except God?*

O my God, You have shown Gracious Favour to me by bringing me into being, without any struggle or effort. And out of Your abundant Generosity, You have encouraged my hopes so that they reach their goal, without any deserving or predisposition [in me].

I ask You, by the One of all units and by the Witnessed of all witnesses, for the perfect security of the gift of love against the tribulation of distance; for the dispelling of the darkness of stubborn opposition, through the light of the sun of right guidance; and for the opening of the doors of proper action, through the helping hand of [the saying] *Indeed God is full of benevolence to the servants.*

O my Lord, I ask of You that the I-ness of my being be annihilated, and that the security of my witnessing remain; and that the distinction between me as a witness and me as a witnessed be preserved, through the union of my condition as [created] existent with my [real] being.

O my Master, through Your True Reality save my servanthood from the blinding clouds of conjecture of seeing otherness. Make me inheritor of Your prior Word given to *the chosen, the best.* Take possession of my power of command, choosing for me in every state and every desire. Help me through the affirmation of Your Unity and with well-seatedness, whether in movement or in rest.

O my Beloved, I ask You for a swift reunion, with creative Beauty, impregnable Majesty and exalted Perfection, in every state and in every outcome.

O You who is He, O He, O You apart from whom there is none but He!

I ask of You for the most Unfathomable Unseen through the Most Holy Essence, and for the most precious Spirit *in the night when it closes in, and the dawn when it streams out; truly this is the word of a noble messenger, endowed with power and firmly established with the Lord of the Throne, completely obedient and trustworthy, in an Arabic tongue most clear; and truly it is a bringing-down by the Lord of the worlds* – a decisive ruling that establishes the order [of things] through its own spirit, coloured in the forms of clarification with the dye of assignment.

And I ask of You, O God, that this be brought for me, with all the capacity of my life's breath, through the spirits that animate my greetings, [when I address You] with Your blessed prayers and Your everlasting salutations upon the one who is the means by which quests are fulfilled, the uniting link by which lovers attain, and also upon all those who are related to him in all the degrees. *Indeed* he is *according to the most Clear Truth*. Make us one of their special company. Amen.

May the blessing of God be upon our master Muhammad, and upon all his family and companions.

Glory to your Lord, Lord of Eminent Might, beyond all that they qualify Him with. Peace be upon the messengers. And praise be to God, Lord of the worlds.

Notes to the Prayers

THE PREFACE PRAYER

The preface prayer (*muqaddima*), which is only in three manuscript copies, is unlike the other prayers in having a consistent rhyming pattern throughout (in -*īqih*, = 7, the same value as the opening word *ḥamd*). This structural element and the fact that this prayer is not commonly found might possibly indicate that it is a later addition.

Line 4 Ibn 'Arabī makes a distinction between the descent of Revelation (*wahy*), which ended with the Prophet Muhammad, and the coming of divine 'inspiration' (*ilhām*), which 'is never cut off from the hearts of His Friends (*awliyā'*) ... because the Real (*al-ḥaqq*) has not ceased, and will not cease, to inspire them with His mysteries and to make the suns and moons of His Knowledge rise in the sky of their hearts' (*Contemplations*, p. 112; Taher, 'Sainthood and Prophecy', p. 20). Almost all the following sentences end in a noun of the second form, which has an active causative meaning: here *taḥqīq*, 'verification', can have the sense of 'giving Him His right (*ḥaqq*)' or 'making Him real'.

Line 6 'a heart ...' (*qalb*) here is related to the primary quality of 'certainty' (*yaqīn*) in confirming or assenting to Truth (*taṣdīq*).

Line 9 '... recognising His Foreknowledge' (*tasbīq*) refers to the Divine foreknowledge of creation: 'God ordains no decree except through the precedent decree of the Book, for His Knowledge in things is the same as His *Word* in His giving existence. *The Word is not changed with* Him, so no creator or created possess any authority except by virtue of what the *Divine* Book foreordains. This is why He says: *I am not one who does wrong to [His] servants* (Q 50:29). That is to say, "We bring about for them only what is precedent in knowledge, and I judge them only through what precedes"' (*Fut.* IV:15). This recognition is here related to the highest degree of 'mind', the intellect (*'aql*).

Line 12 See Q 89:27: *O soul at peace, return to your Lord, pleased and pleasing.*

Lines 16–7 '... the spring-waters of illumination', literally the '*Salsabīl* of Opening' (*salsabīl al-fatḥ*). This is a reference to the people of virtue (*al-abrār*) mentioned in the Quran: *There they are given a drink in a cup tempered with ginger, from a spring there, named Salsabīl* (Q 76:18). The same group *drink from a pure nectar* (*raḥīq*), *sealed* (Q 83:25).

Lines 24–5 '... the refreshing breeze of the Spirit': the vowelling in the manuscripts is not marked, and so this could be read as *rūḥ* (spirit) and as *rawḥ* (refreshing breeze, ease). We have tried to reflect this in our translation.

Line 26 The 'primordial natural constitution' (*fiṭra*) is what each human being is born with, prior to any addition from upbringing or education, in the security of faith in God. According to a hadith, 'every child born is born according to the natural [human] constitution', which for Ibn 'Arabī means 'being established in servanthood to the Lord' (*Fut.* I:381) and 'knowing that God is' (*Fut.* I:34). The veiling effects (*taṭbīq*) of 'falling short' in relation to one's true potential suggest that a person remains limited by particular conditioning, unless their heart is purified. The same word is used in line 9, there translated in its graphic image as 'being enveloped in its clouds'.

Line 41 See Q 3:173: *Those to who the people said: 'The people have gathered against you, so fear them', yet this only increased them in their faith and they said: 'God is sufficient for us, the most excellent Trustee.'*

SUNDAY EVE PRAYER

The two letters of this prayer are: *hā'*, as in *hū* (He) and *hādī* (guide); and *qāf*, as in *qāhir* (subjugating), *qā'im* (existent), *qayyūm* (self-subsisting), *qadr* (power), *qurb* (closeness), *quds* (holiness) and *qalb* (heart). As an example of the importance of sound in the prayers, we might mention that the letter *qāf* is repeated more than seventy times in the second half of the prayer.

Throughout this prayer Ibn 'Arabī is making use of many contrasting expressions and we have tried to keep the sense of these contrasts in the translation: seen and unseen, exterior and interior, unlimited and limited, His Face and His Light, the One who is prior to creation and the One who preserves all creation, the Divine Power in this world and in the next, and so on.

Lines 1–19 In contrast to most of the other letter-prayers, the first part does not begin with a word containing the specific letter in question (*hā'*), but with an allusion to its written form (ه), which is a circle that encompasses (*muḥīṭ*) all things, and can be divided into two sides, the unseen interior and the seen exterior.

Line 5 See the *verse: All faces submit to the Living, the Self-Subsisting* (Q 20:111).

Line 6 See the verse: … *He is only giving them respite to a day on which the eyes will gaze* (Q 14:42), in other words the Day of Reckoning (*yawm al-dīn*), when everyone is brought face to face with their Lord. It is the Day on which the King requites His subjects for their actions.

Lines 5–7 There is here another allusion to the circle: any point on the circumference is connected and 'prostrates' to the central point according to the 'private face' (*al-wajh al-khāṣṣ*), via a line that extends from the centre and is called 'Your private path'.

Lines 9–10 The letter *hā'* stands for the 'He-ness' or Ipseity (*huwiyya*), which preserves Itself as Unseen and preserves the creation (*kawn*). The Perfect Human Being, who mirrors God completely, is thus simultaneously preserved as 'He' and 'not-He'. See Appendix D.

Line 10 'There is no He but He' mirrors the testimony 'there is no god but God'.

Line 14 '... restrain the claws', an unusual phrase that alludes to the verse: *If they do not keep aloof from you, and do not offer you peace, nor restrain their hands, take them and kill them wherever you find them; against these We have given you a clear authority* (Q 4:91).

Line 15 Referring to the verse: *So the last remnant of the people who did wrong was cut off* (Q 6:45).

Line 20 Referring to the verse: *Truly He encompasses all things* (Q 41:54), again returning to the nature of the circle as all-inclusive.

Lines 20–1 Referring to the verse: *He has Supreme Power over His servants and He is the Wise, the Fully Aware* (Q 6:18), emphasizing the relationship between the upper semi-circle of the Divine Names and the lower of the servant who is their place of manifestation.

Line 22 Referring to the verse: *What, He who stands over every soul with what it has earned? And yet they associate others with God* (Q 13:33). Here the author is playing with the two forms, *qāʾim* and *qayyūm*, of the root *q-w-m*, which carries meanings of existing, rising and standing, but also denotes being in charge of, watching over and persisting. It seems that he is making a correlation between the way God stands over every soul, calling it to account and His irresistible Power, on the one hand, and between His subsistence in all comprehension and His Knowledge, on the other.

Line 28 *The Creation and the Command* (*al-khalq wa-l-amr*): in other words, the two worlds, one of matter, within which His Might is irresistible, and the other of spirit, within which He has the Power of ordainment or destiny. See the verse: *Your Lord is Allāh, who created the heavens and the earth in six days, and then settled Himself upon the Throne, covering the day with the night, pursuing it swiftly – with the sun and moon and stars, subject to His Command. His indeed is the Creation and the Command. Blessed be God, Lord of the worlds* (Q 7:54). As Ibn ʿArabī remarks in his discussion of this verse, 'God specified these (creation and command) for the Name Lord (*rabb*), apart from any other. The world of creation and composition requires [the existence of] evil by its very essence, while the world of command is the good in which there is no evil.' (*Fut.* II:575, translated in *SDG*, p. 310)

Line 28 An implicit reference to *He is with you wherever you are* (Q 57:4).

Line 35 See the following verse which has an implied warning to the believers: *If [Muhammad] dies or is killed, will you turn back upon your heels?* (Q 3:144). The word 'turning back' (*inqalaba*) is derived from the same root as 'heart' (*qalb*).

Line 38 The 'innermost centre' (*sirr*) denotes the heart of the human being, the fundamental ground of awareness which is 'above' or beyond all qualification. 'Taste' is a technical term denoting direct experience of Reality.

Line 48 The phrase 'a truly receptive heart' (*qalban qābilan*) can be found in the famous line in the *Tarjumān al-ashwāq* (poem XI, p. 67): 'My heart has become capable of all forms'.

Line 41 The phrase 'a powerful hand' (*yadan qādiratan*) establishes the connection of the hand to the Name *al-Qādir*, which is explained in the following passage: 'When the hand of the servant becomes the Hand of the Real (*al-ḥaqq*) – exalted is He – then that is the ability and power which is referred to in: *Those who swear allegiance to you, are swearing allegiance to God. The Hand of God is above their hands* (Q 48:10). God, exalted is He, also said: 'And when I love him, I become his hearing by which and within which he hears, and his hand with which he takes'... [The person who adopts these qualities] does not need to bring the action into existence as a condition of this Name, but simply has the ability to carry it out whenever he wishes, without anything preventing it' (*Kashf*, 69–3).

Line 42 Referring to the verse: *O soul at peace, return to your Lord, well-pleased, well-pleasing!* (Q 89:27–8).

Line 44 See the verse: *It is not your wealth nor your children that shall bring you close in nearness to Us* (*'indanā zulfā*)*; only the one who has faith and acts righteously* (Q 34:37).

Line 60 This refers to the famous story about the Prophet when he was a small boy: 'There came unto me two men, clothed in white, with a gold basin of snow. Then they laid hold upon me, and splitting open my breast they brought forth my heart. This likewise they split open and took from it a black clot which they cast away. Then they washed my heart and my breast with the snow... Satan toucheth every son of Adam the day his mother beareth him, save only Mary and her son.' (Lings, *Muhammad*, p. 26; see also Schimmel, *And Muhammad is His Messenger*, p. 68). As Ibn 'Arabī clarifies in the *Fuṣūṣ* (p. 33), 'the whole affair is [necessarily] disparagement and praise' (*dhamm wa-ḥamd*), so be His protection in the disparagement and make Him your protection in the praise, that you may be both tactful and knowledgeable'. This suggests that the removal of 'the blood-clot of blameworthiness [or disparagement] (*dhamm*)' restores a human being to the fullest condition of being 'praiseworthy [or capable of praise]' (*ḥamīd* or *muḥammad*). In other words, it means the realisation of pure servanthood, or the Muhammad-ness of one's own purified being.

Line 61 In the Quran purity and purification are specifically coupled with the first day, which is Sunday. See Q 9:108: *A mosque founded on mindfulness of God from the first day is more worthy for you to stand in: in it there are men who love to keep themselves pure, and God loves those who are purified* (*al-muṭahharūn*). Only Mary and Jesus are regarded by tradition as being completely purified from birth.

SUNDAY MORNING PRAYER

In Arabic, Sunday is named *yawm al-aḥad*. This is usually taken to mean the first day of the week, but it may equally be translated more literally as 'the Day of the One', pertaining to the Divine Name *al-Aḥad* (the One or Unique). Ibn 'Arabī refers to this second meaning, for example, in the following passage: 'Some gnostics fast on Sunday specifically because it is the Day of the One, for the One is an attribute that asserts the incomparability of the Real.' (*Fut.* II:647, translated in *SDG*, p. 315) The emphasis in this prayer on *aḥad* and related terms such as *wāḥid* (One), *aḥadiyya* (Uniqueness) and *tawḥīd* (Union) is entirely consonant with this reading, as is the association of Sunday with the prophet Idrīs (whose message according to the Shaykh is primarily concerned with the meaning of *tawḥīd*). It opens with a series of seven well-known devotional expressions, each linked by a *wāw* ('and'), beginning with *Bismi Llāh* which 'opens existence' and ending with the Quranic verse associated with the return after death, corresponding to the completed cycle of seven days.

Line 1 'In the Name of God' opens the Quran and every sura except the ninth (*al-Tawba*).

Line 2 'Praise be to God' is the first verse of the first sura, the Fātiḥa. As the origin of existence is God, the principle of each thing in existence is praise of Him.

Line 10 Allusion to the hadith: 'God is (*kāna*) and there is with Him no thing', more commonly translated or understood as 'God was ...'. To this were added the words referred to here, 'He is now as He was (*huwa l-ān ʿalā mā ʿalayhi kāna*), which again can be translated as 'He is now as He has always been'. In his discussion of this hadith, Ibn ʿArabī specifies: 'He is not accompanied by thingness nor do we ascribe it to Him. Know that the word *kāna* generally refers to a temporal limitation [hence the translation 'was'], but that is not the case here. What is meant here is the apparent existence (*kawn*), in the sense of Being (*wujūd*), and so *kāna* here acts not as a verb demanding temporality but as a sign indicating being (*ḥarf wujūdī*)' (*Fut.* II:56). See also *Fut.* I:41 or II:592 for further discussion of this saying.

Line 12 'He has in every thing a Sign pointing to the fact that He is One' is a verse by the ʿAbbasid poet Abū al-ʿAtāhiya (d. 211/826) often quoted in Ibn ʿArabī's writings (see *Fut.* I:491). A 'Sign' (*āya*) also has the meaning of a 'Verse' of the Quran. 'Existence is entirely letters, words, suras and verses, and it is the macrocosmic Quran, which falsehood cannot enter into either from in front or from behind' (*Fut.* IV:167).

Line 15 'Limited in any way', literally 'being used up or exhausted' (*nufūd*), alluding to the Quranic verse: *the ocean would be used up before the Words of my Lord are exhausted* (18:109; see *Fut.* I:29).

Lines 16–7 According to a hadith, this formula is described as 'one of the treasures of the Throne', and is also said to have been the attribute of Adam. See *Fut.* II:436 (translated in *UM*, pp. 143–4) for the vision that Ibn ʿArabī had of the Divine Throne, in which this formula was uttered by the 'treasure beneath the Throne', which was Adam.

Line 22 Allusion to the verse: *Have those who do not believe not seen that the heavens and the earth were closed up together, and We split them apart, and We made every living thing of water?* (Q 21:30)

Line 23 *Indeed we belong to God and to Him we return* (Q 2:156), known as the verse of *istirjāʿ* ('seeking return'), is traditionally recited in the face of affliction or on hearing the news of someone's death: the first part affirms servanthood and acceptance of His decree ('we belong to God') and the second part completion in His Unity after annihilation ('to Him we return').

Lines 39–41 *He is the First and the Last ...* (Q 57:3), the verse quoted by Abū Saʿīd al-Kharrāz when asked how he had come to know God, to which he replied 'By His uniting the opposites'. Ibn ʿArabī points out that in this verse God is referred to as *ʿalīm*, normally translated as 'All-Knowing', but which for him denotes both the knower (*ʿālim*) and the known (*maʿlūm*) (*Fut.* III:300). So this final phrase indicates that God is both the

Knower and the Known of everything. He applies this understanding to all Names that have this form (for example, *ḥamīd*), which can be understood as both active ('praising') and passive ('praised').

Lines 46–7 In reference to the hadith: 'I am not able to enumerate all Your praises; You are such that You extol Yourself.' The word 'extol' (*athnā*) comes from a root which means 'to double'. Praise can be understood as being doubled since He is both Praiser and Praised.

Line 48 The whole section of the prayer up to this point rhymes in *-ūd* (= 6 + 4 = 10 = 1), affirming the Unity which forms the primary subject of this prayer. The same rhyme is repeated at the end of the prayer in the blessing upon the Prophet.

Line 52 Referring to the verse: *He is knowing of all that is before them and all that is behind them, but they cannot encompass Him in knowledge. The faces bow before the Living One, the Self-Subsisting* (Q 20:110). This line indicates the process of 'descent' from the Essence to manifestation, encompassing both the vertical dimension (above and below) and the horizontal (in front and behind).

Line 61 Allusion to the verse: *Wherever you turn, there is the Face of God* (Q 2:115).

Line 66 The emphasis on 'looking' with the 'eye' is reflected in the numerical equivalence of the terms *naẓar* and the letter *ʿayn,* both of which equal 7 in the *abjad* system.

Line 74 See the Chapter on Adam in the *Fuṣūṣ al-ḥikam*, where Ibn ʿArabī gives a similar description of the Perfect Human (*insān kāmil*): 'As for being Man, that is due to the universality of his formation and his embracing all the realities. He is for God as the pupil is for the eye, [a hole or channel] by which the act of seeing takes place... Through him God looks upon His creatures and bestows Compassionate Mercy upon them.' (*Fuṣ*, p. 27; *Fusus*, pp. 110–2; *Bezels*, p. 51)

Lines 80–1 See the verse: *O people, you are the poor towards God, while God is the Rich beyond need, the Praiseworthy* (Q 35:15).

Lines 105–6 Ibn ʿArabī explains these two apparently negative qualities (lost/straying, confused/perplexed) in a remarkably positive light: 'those who go astray (*al-ḍāllūn*) are those who are lost and perplexed (*al-tāʾihūn al-ḥāʾirūn*) in the Majesty and Grandeur of Allah: whenever they want to rest, He opens for them a knowledge of Him that brings them perplexity and causes them to perish (*atlafahum*)' (*Fut.*II.137; see also III.506, IV.43, 279).

Lines 124–28 See the Chapter on Idrīs in the *Fuṣūṣ al-ḥikam* where, in his comment on the Quranic verse *He is the First and the Last, the Manifest and the Hidden* (57:3), Ibn ʿArabī writes: 'He is the same as that which manifests, and the same as that which is hidden when He manifests. There is no-one who can see Him other than Him, and there is no-one from whom He is hidden! He is the Manifest to Himself and the Hidden from Himself!' (*Fuṣ*, p. 55; *Fusus*, pp. 339–40; *Bezels*, pp. 85–6)

Lines 164–65 'You are as I witness...' refers first of all to the verbal attestation (*shahāda*) that 'there is no god but God'. It also points to the fact that He has established this in His Knowledge from all eternity and that He has ordered mankind to have faith in and realise the meaning of this attestation, as in *I have not created men and jinn except to worship Me*

(Q 51:56). The second phrase 'and as I have been ordered' alludes to *So stand firm [on the straight path] as you have been ordered (istaqim kamā umirta)* (Q 11:112).

Lines 170–1 'Affair' (*sha'n*) alludes to the verse: *Every day He is at work (kulli yawm huwa fī sha'n)* (Q 55:29), which can also be translated as *Every day He is engaged in some labour.*

Line 177 'Separating and restoring' (*fatq wa-ratq*) are Quranic terms that could also be translated as 'unstitching and sewing up'.

Lines 177–8 When one of his companions declared that he was a true believer, the Prophet responded: 'To every [immediate] truth belongs an essential reality' (*li-kulli ḥaqq ḥaqīqa*), and asked him what was the 'reality' of his faith.

Lines 180–2 Sūrat al-Ikhlāṣ, the Chapter of Purity (Q 112).

Line 183 This, and all the following epithets, evidently refer to the Prophet Muhammad. Ibn 'Arabī considers him to be both the first to be given existence in potential, the primordial Man, and the first in rank in actual existence, the complete Perfection of the Human Being. The first aspect is summarised by the hadith 'I was a prophet while Adam was between water and clay', while the second corresponds to his saying 'I will be the master of mankind on the Day of Resurrection, without boasting'. See *Fut.* III:141.

Line 186 Referring to the verse: *By the heaven of the constellations, by the promised day, by the witness and the witnessed, slain were the Men of the Pit* (Q 85:1–3).

Lines 188–90 'The two handfuls' refers to a hadith (Ibn Ḥanbal, 17660) according to which God grasps all the human souls in His two handfuls and says: 'This group belong to the Fire, and they shall perform the deeds of the people of the Fire; this group belong to Paradise, and they shall perform the deeds of the people of Paradise – and I shall not disapprove!' In the *Futūḥāt* Ibn 'Arabī comments: 'He brought forth the world as two handfuls, to which He gave two ranks: 'These are for Paradise, and I shall not disapprove; these are for the Fire, and I shall not disapprove.' No one raised the least objection at that time, since there was no existent other than Him. Everyone is under the authority of His Names: one handful stands under the Names of His Trial, and one handful stands under the Names of His Favour' (*Fut.* I:37). In Chapter 320, based on the first two verses of Q 64 (*All that is in the heavens and on earth glorifies God ... It is He who has created you. Some of you are unbelievers, and some of you are believers*), Ibn 'Arabī discusses 'the glorification of the two handfuls' and how both are under the order and precedence of Mercy (*raḥma*) (*Fut.* III:75–8).

Lines 195–6 An allusion to the famous verse of Light: *His Light is like a niche in which there is a lamp – the lamp in a glass, and the glass like a brilliant star – lit from a blessed tree, an olive that is neither of the East nor of the West, whose oil almost glows, even though no fire has touched it; Light upon light* (Q 24:35).

Line 205 See Q 82:17–9: *What will give you knowledge of the Day of Reckoning (yawm al-dīn)? Again, what will give you knowledge of the Day of Reckoning? A day when no soul will have anything to help another soul, and the command on that day will be God's.*

Lines 206–7 Q 12:108.

Lines 207–8 Q 3:173.

MONDAY EVE PRAYER

The two letters of this prayer are: *wāw*, as in *wāsiʿ* (embracing), *sumuww* (eminence) and *ʿuluww* (exaltedness); and *rāʾ*, as in *rabb* (lord), *raqīb* (watching over), *razzāq* (nourishing), *raḥma* (compassion), *rāḥa* (ease) and *rūḥ* (spirit).

Lines 1–6 The first word of the prayer *wāsiʿ* ('embraces'), which begins with the letter *wāw*, alludes to the all-inclusive quality of the Perfect Human Being, who is symbolized by the *wāw*. The rhyme letters of these initial lines are *-ūm* (*wāw* + *mīm*, as in 'knowable', 'understandable', 'blameable'), whose numerical value is 6 + 4 = 1(0), emphasizing the Unity of His Knowledge and Praiseworthiness. For the specific link between sanctification and Divine Height, see the Chapter of Idrīs in the *Fuṣūṣ al-ḥikam* and the Saturday Eve prayer.

Line 6 See the verse: *Good words soar to Him, and He raises the righteous deed* (Q 35:10).

Line 21 '... grant me a secret', referring to the meaning of the human being as *khalīfa* who is 'the secret of Allāh' (*Fut.*IV.268). It could also be understood as 'a secret heart', referring to the *ḥadīth qudsī*: '... the heart of My faithful servant contains Me'.

Lines 26–7 'lowliness and abasement...' Compare this with Ibn 'Arabī's account of Abū Yazīd al-Bisṭāmī. 'When he asked God: 'O my Lord, with what can I draw close to You?', God replied: 'You may only draw close to Me by that which does not belong to Me.' 'And what is it that does not belong to You?' God replied: '[The qualities of] abasement (*dhilla*) and neediness (*iftiqār*)' (*Fut.* III:316).

Lines 32–3 'all that is real... every right' (*kulla ḥaqq*). The word *ḥaqq* has both meanings, so that the character (*khuluq*) that is asked for is one that establishes the Real in everything and gives each thing its right.

Lines 33–4 Q 40:7.

Lines 35–6 A reference to the *Verse* of the Throne, the Āyat al-Kursī: *God, there is no god but He, the Living, the Self-Subsisting* (Q 2:255). Some copies insert here the full verse.

Lines 44–5 '... inscribe one of the lines...'. We may understand this as an allusion to the tradition that the actions which spring from one's personal will are recorded, as if on a tablet of stone or scroll, and on the Day of Reckoning when the person stands before God, they are called to account for them.

Lines 48–9 Referring to the verse: *So We heard [Zachariah's] prayer, and bestowed John upon him and made his wife right for him. They used to vie in doing good deeds, and used to call to Us in hopeful longing* (*raghba*) *and reverent fear* (*raḥba*) (Q 21:90).

Line 56 Referring to the verse: *Say: shall I seek a lord other than God, when He is Lord of everything* (Q 6:164).

Line 58 Allusion to the verse: *Elevator of degrees is He, the Lord of the Throne, casting the Spirit by His bidding upon those of His servants whom He wishes, to warn of the Day of Meeting* (Q 40:15).

Lines 58–61 This is an allusion to the verse: *If he be one of those brought close, there will be joy and sweetness* (or: *rest and fragrance; rawḥ wa-rayḥān*) *and a garden of delight* (Q 56:89). Literally, *rayḥān* signifies the aromatic plant, sweet basil, which grows wild throughout the Mediterranean. In these lines Ibn ʿArabī plays on the many forms of the root *r-w-ḥ: rawḥ* (joy or rest), *rūḥ* (spirit), *rayḥān* (sweetness or scent), *rāḥa* (repose or ease) *and murtāḥ* (one given ease). See *Fuṣūṣ al-ḥikam*, Chapter of Jesus: 'Nourish His creation through Him, and thou wilt be a reviving rest and a scent of life (*rawḥān wa-rayḥān*).' (*Fuṣ*, p. 131; *Fusus*, p. 715; *Bezels*, p. 179)

Line 63 Allusion to the prayer: *O our Lord, lift from us the suffering; truly we are believers* (Q 44:12).

Lines 63–4 Q 40:7.

Line 66 These Divine Names, 'the Forgiving, the Merciful' (*al-Ghafūr al-Raḥīm*), which contain both the letters of this prayer (*wāw* and *rāʾ*), occur together many times in the Quran. See for example the verse: *Say: O my servants, who have been prodigal against yourselves, do not despair of God's Mercy; surely God can forgive sins altogether; indeed He is the Forgiving, the Merciful* (Q 39:53).

Lines 66–7 See for example: *God knows what is in your hearts; God is All-Knowing, Clement* (*ʿAlīm Ḥalīm*) (Q 33:51).

Lines 66–7 This pair of Names, 'the High, the Magnificent', also appears several times. For example: *To Him belongs whatsoever is in the heavens and whatsoever is in earth, and He is the High, the Magnificent* (*al-ʿAlī al-ʿAẓīm*) (Q 42:4).

MONDAY MORNING PRAYER

Although the week traditionally begins with Sunday, Ibn ʿArabī considers it to be a special case because it is the Day of the Unique (*aḥad*). Since 'unique' is not a number, he does not consider it to be the start of the days of the week. He therefore describes Monday as 'the beginning of the days' (*ṣadr al-ayyām*; *Fut.* II:652).

Line 2 Conformity to God (*iqtidāʾ*) normally refers to following the model and guidance of the prophets. See for example the verse in reference to the prophets, eighteen of whom are explicitly mentioned: *These are the ones whom God has guided; so follow their guidance* (Q 6:90). The coupling of Divine guidance and conformity is also attested in the following hadith: 'God has thus guided us and we conform to Him.'

Line 16 Q 3:26.

Lines 34–6 All creatures are considered as letters written by the Pen, which symbolises the First Intellect.

Lines 41–3 Allusion to the verse: *Is He not the One who answers the constrained* (*al-muḍṭarr*) *when he calls to Him, and removes evil, and appoints you to be regents of the earth. Is there a god with God? Little indeed do you remember* (Q 27:62).

Lines 51–2 Literally, 'efface me or make me disappear' (*amḥaqnī*). The root *m-ḥ-q* carries the basic meaning of effacement or obliteration, but is typically used of the waning or disappearance of the moon. This latter meaning seems more appropriate here because of the imagery of light.

Line 61 The word *wuṣūl* ('reaching') is very difficult to translate precisely: to reach God implies a 'distance' to be overcome, and yet there can be no real distance, only an imagined chasm. When He removes this illusion, then the seeker may see through His Sight that he is already in Union.

Lines 86–8 Allusion to *Your Lord has decreed that you should adore none but Him* (Q 17:23). This for Ibn 'Arabī signifies that we cannot adore any but God, since He is the only Existent.

Line 87 Allusion to the hadith: 'I seek refuge in You from You.' In his commentary on this hadith, Ibn 'Arabī notes that the second person ('in You from You') is repeated without specifying who it refers to: 'The one who seeks refuge sees himself according to His Form and so he says: 'from You', meaning that he takes refuge in God from Himself/himself (*min nafsihi*). This self (*nafs*) is the [Divine] Likeness ... You can thus consider both pronouns to be one [referring to the same subject] or that the pronoun 'from You' refers [only] to the Likeness which is the self that takes refuge from the hidden Divine ruse. [And that only applies to] the representative (*khalīfa*) who attains the Divine Form in the most complete manner' (*Fut.* III:183).

Lines 92–3 Or 'which gives me a name (*ism*) or a surname (*kunya*)'. Literally, *kunya* denotes having children (while *nisba* denotes the place a person is from). Compare this to the following extract from a poem in the *Dīwān* (no. 94, p. 44):

> I am the Reviver – I have no *kunya*
> and no *nisba*. I am the Hatimite Arab, Muḥammad!
> To every age is one who is its Eye-entity, and I
> alone am now that Individual.

Lines 97–100 The aim of this invocation is the actualisation of the properties of these Divine Names in the servant.

Lines 106–7 'The extension (or robe) of compassion' (*bisāṭ al-raḥma*) is an idiom for the winding sheet or shroud in which a corpse is laid, which is traditionally the white robe of purity worn by the pilgrim in Mecca during the pilgrimage. This phrase can be understood figuratively as 'the one who from pre-eternity extends compassion to the whole of creation'. The term *bisāṭ* ('robe, carpet', which extends horizontally) is contrasted with *samā'* ('sky, heaven, elevation', which extends vertically).

TUESDAY EVE PRAYER

The two letters of this prayer are: *shīn*, as in *shadīd* (forceful), *baṭsh* (assault) and *sha'n* (business); and *ghayn*, as in *ghanī* (rich), *ghayma* (fog) and *ghalaba* (victory). Both letters occupy the final place in the two *abjad* alphabetical orders (see Appendix C), *shīn* being last in the Western system, *ghayn* in the Eastern. This gives this prayer a special quality of finality within the prayers of the week (see Introduction: the seven days and seven nights).

Line 1 Allusion to the verse: *Surely your Lord's assault is most forceful* (Q 85:12). This combination is found elsewhere in the Quran in reference to earlier peoples who thought themselves mighty: *How many generations have We destroyed before them, who had greater strength than they did (ashadda minhum baṭshan)* (Q 50:36). This Name also appears in a positive meaning in the prayer of Lot: *Would that I had the power to deal with you or that I could take refuge with a firm support (rukn shadīd)*! (Q 11:80). In the Chapter on Lot in the *Fuṣūṣ al-ḥikam*, Ibn 'Arabī writes: 'The Envoy of God said: 'May God have mercy upon my brother Lot, for he had recourse to a firm support', and he meant by this that he was with God in respect of [His Name] the Forceful. By the words 'firm support' Lot meant his own people, and by the words 'would that I had the power to deal with you' he meant [the power of] resistance, which refers to that power of concentration peculiar to man.' (*Fuṣ*, p. 113–4; *Fusus*, p. 629; *Bezels*, pp. 157–8)

Lines 1–2 Both these epithets, the Forceful (*shadīd*) and the Painful (*alīm*), are found together in the Sura of Hūd, in the context of previous generations who have spurned the Divine invitation brought by the prophets: *Surely His seizing is painful, forceful* (Q 11:102).

Line 5 Referring to: *He, glory be to Him, has not taken for Himself any consort or son* (Q 72:3).

Lines 7–8 Q 8:30.

Line 10 Referring to the verse: *The sinners will be known by their marks, and they will be seized by their feet and forelocks* (Q 55:41).

Lines 10–12 See the verse: *And He brought down those of the People of the Book who supported them from their fortresses and cast terror into their hearts* (Q 33:26). This refers to the War of the Trench in 5H, when the Jews of Banū Qurayẓa withdrew to their strongholds but were forced to surrender to the Muslim army from Medina.

Line 14 'Connecting threads' (*raqā'iq*) is a technical term in Ibn 'Arabī's writing, denoting the network which ties together different levels of existence: 'Between the two worlds there are 'threads' which extend from each [spiritual] form to its likeness [in the lower world], connecting them together so they are not disconnected. Ascent and descent take place upon these threads, so that they are as ascending and descending ladders' (*Fut.* III:260).

Lines 20–1 There are two allusions in these lines, combined for emphasis. One is to a part of the prayer of Moses when faced with the oppression and opposition of Pharaoh and his people in Egypt: *Our Lord, obliterate their wealth and harden their hearts, so that they do not believe [in You] until they see the painful punishment* (Q 10:88). The second allusion is to the verse: *If We so wished, We would obliterate their eyes, then they would rush to the Path but how could they see? If We so wished, We could transform them where they stand, then they would not be able to go forward nor could they return* (Q 36:67).

Lines 22–4 See the verse: *[The hypocrites] will be told: Go back and seek light. Then a wall will be set up between them, with a door in it, the inner side of which is compassion and the outer of which is chastisement* (Q 57:13).

Lines 27–8 Q 11:102.

Lines 34–5 The Quranic expression 'the lote-tree of the extreme limit' (*sidrat al-muntahā*) indicates for Ibn ʿArabī the furthest point, in the ascent to God (*miʿrāj*), which the soul as such can reach. It is situated at the limit of the seventh heaven. *He saw him in another descent, at the Lote-Tree of the Extreme Limit, close to which lies the Garden of Abode, when the lote-tree was enveloped by that which envelops* (*yaghshā*) (Q 53:14). See Ibn ʿArabī, *The Alchemy of Human Happiness*, pp. 123–5.

Line 39 The silence of the *lām* alludes to Ibn ʿArabī's complex understanding of the phrase *li-llāh* (as in *al-ḥamdu li-llāh*, praise belongs to God). In Arabic, the first part of this phrase, *li*, is a particle written with the letter *lām*, meaning 'belonging to' or 'for'; the vowel, 'i', is called *kasra*, which is 'separated' or written below the letter and is therefore in a subordinate position. The ending in *kasra* is called 'lowering' (*khafdh*) by the grammarians, and was interpreted by the Sufi tradition as a symbol of servanthood. See, for example, al-Qushayrī's *Naḥw al-qulūb al-kabīr* ('Grammar of the Hearts'), p. 40.

The letter *lām* thus symbolises the servant, who is 'separated' or subordinate to God, and when his vowel is silenced (literally, 'when his movement ceases'), then he is reunited with Him, and all that remains is God (*Allāh*). For the symbolical meaning of this *li*, see *Fut.* I:111ff., translated by Gerald Elmore in *Praise*, pp. 80ff.

Line 40 In Ibn ʿArabī's writings, *ghayn* is taken as the symbol of separation or distance from reality, since it is the first letter of *ghayr* ('other'). If the dot is removed from the letter *ghayn*, it becomes the letter *ʿayn*, which signifies 'Essence'. It may refer here to the One Reality or Eye-entity (*al-ʿayn al-wāḥida*).

Lines 40–1 The relation between the One and the two is beautifully described in the following passage: 'The utmost purpose of the servant is that he praises his own Self which he beholds in the [Divine] Mirror, since there is no aptitude for the originated to bear the Pre-Existent.' (*Fut.* I:112, translated in *Praise*, p. 86)

Lines 46–7 Referring to the verse: *God encompasses the unbelievers; the lightning dazzles their eyes; whenever it gives them light, they walk in it, and when the darkness is over them, they stand still* (Q 2:19–20).

Lines 46–7 Allusions to the two 'Refuge' suras at the end of the Quran: *I take refuge in the Lord of the daybreak ... from the evil of an envier when he is envious* (Q 113:5); and *I take refuge in the Lord of mankind ... from the evil of the whisperer who whispers into the breasts of men, among jinn and mankind* (Q 114:5).

Line 51 This combination of Names 'the Rich, the Praiseworthy' (*ghanī ḥamīd*) occurs often in the Quran. For example: *O mankind, you are the poor towards God, and He is the Rich, the Praiseworthy* (Q 35:15). Note that all these Names are in the *faʿīl* pattern, which is both active and passive.

TUESDAY MORNING PRAYER

Four manuscripts record what we take to be an oral commentary by Ibn ʿArabī himself on the writing of this prayer. In the margin of [R], we find the following details: 'The shaykh Muḥyī al-Dīn Ibn ʿArabī, may God sanctify his secret, said: "Two men of awesome mien, dressed in white, appeared to me during a retreat, and they told me to pray with this prayer, which is called the Prayer of Unveiling (*duʿāʾ al-kashf*)."' In [C], [K] and [P] this is corroborated with the following information: 'Two shaykhs of awesome mien appeared to me during a retreat on the Mountain of Opening (*jabal al-fatḥ*) in the year 610H. One of them said to me: "Transmit this from me to all sincere seekers and agreeing aspirants."'

Bearing in mind the correspondence between Tuesday and the prophet Aaron, we may infer that the two awesome-looking men could have been Moses and Aaron, the latter taking his customary role as 'public' speaker – certainly this prayer has many Mosaic references. Alternatively, as Tuesday is also associated with the prophet Yaḥyā (John the Baptist), we might also take these figures to be Aaron and John. As for the mountain, there are several possibilities: it might denote somewhere near Mecca or Medina, such as Mount Hira where Muhammad was inspired by the Angel Gabriel, or it could perhaps refer to Mount Sinai, although we have no other evidence that Ibn ʿArabī ever visited the site. Equally, it could refer to other sacred mountains such as Mount Qāsiyūn, which dominates Damascus, or Mount Tabor, scene of the Transfiguration. What is clear is that those who heard Ibn ʿArabī's words knew which place he was referring to.

Lines 1–4 It is noteworthy that this prayer for Tuesday, which is the 'Day of the Three' in Arabic, opens with three words that convey Unity: *aḥadiyya, wāḥidiyya and fardiyya.* Each of them are framed as a threesome: *lujjati baḥri aḥadiyya* ('fathomless ocean of Uniqueness'), *ṭamṭāmi yammi wāḥidiyya* ('open water of the sea of Oneness') and *ṣatwati sulṭāni fardiyya* ('sovereign power and authority of Singularity').

Line 1 Allusion to the verse: *They are like the layers of darkness upon a fathomless ocean (fī baḥri lujjiyyin), wave upon wave covering its surface, above which are clouds, and darkness layer upon layer; when he puts out his hand, he can hardly see it* (Q 24:40).

Line 2 Allusion to the following passages in the Quran where the 'sea' (*yamm*) both destroyed the Pharaoh and his hosts and washed away the ashes of the Golden Calf: *We revealed unto Moses, 'Go with My servants by night; strike for them a dry path in the sea, not fearing that you will be overtaken, nor being afraid.' Pharaoh followed them with his armies, but they were overwhelmed by the sea; Pharaoh led his people astray, and did not guide them* (Q 20:77–9), and *We shall burn it and scatter its ashes into the sea. Your God is only One God; there is no god but He alone, He embraces everything in His Knowledge* (Q 20:97–8).

Lines 3–4 Allusion to the verse where God addresses Moses: *We shall strengthen your arm through your brother* (Aaron), *and We shall give to the two of you an authority* (*sulṭān*) (Q 28:35). The Mosaic connection to the term *sulṭān* is also evident in Q 11:96 and 23:45, where it is coupled with the adjective *mubīn* ('clear'): *We sent Moses [and his brother Aaron] with Our signs and a clear authority to Pharaoh and his nobles …*

Lines 8–10 We may also note the three qualities or adjectives that characterize the marks of Compassion: *mahīb* ('revered'), *ʿazīz* ('eminent and cherished') and *mubajjal/mukarram* ('esteemed and honoured').

Lines 17–8 '*Your* Name' refers to *Allāh*, the all-inclusive Name which unites all the Names. The two qualities mentioned here, 'authoritative power' (*saṭwa*) and 'awesome grandeur' (*hayba*), are specifically linked by Ibn ʿArabī to the Divine Name 'the All-Compeller' (*al-jabbār*) which rules over the people of devotion (*taqwā*). Here the request is to be the place of manifestation of this Name in relation to others. See his comments on Q 22:34 (*On the day when We will gather the devoted ones to the All-Compassionate*) in *Fuṣūṣ al-ḥikam* (chapter of Noah), ed. Kılıç, p. 50, and *Fut.* I:210 and 269.

Lines 25–7 Alluding to: *And towards the three who were left behind, when … they thought that the only shelter from God was to Him, then He turned to them, that they might also turn [to Him]; surely God is Relenting and Merciful* (Q 9:118). The other phrases allude to: *It is You we ask for aid* (Q 1:4) and *In Him I put my trust* (Q 9:129).

Line 44 See the verses: *God encompasses the unbelievers; the lightning dazzles their eyes; whenever it gives them light, they walk in it, and when the darkness is over them, they stand still. If God wished, He could have taken away their hearing and sight. God has power over all things* (Q 2:19–20).

Line 51 Some manuscripts add here: 'Preserve me with the majesty of Your Holiness and Your Glory! Indeed You are God, there is no god but You, You alone without partner! And I bear witness that our master Muhammad is Your servant and messenger, Your truly loving and intimate friend.'

Lines 57–9 Q 37:180–2.

WEDNESDAY EVE PRAYER

The two letters of this prayer are: *alif*, as in *Allāh*, *ism* (name), *ana* (I) and *anta* (you); and *sīn*, as in *sayyid* (master), *salām* (peace), *sanad* (support), *subbūḥ* (glorifying) and *ism* (name).

Line 1 'Your Name' is Allāh, the Name which unites all the Names.

Lines 2–3 Allusion to the verse: *Glory be to Him, in whose Hand is dominion over all things and to whom you are returned* (Q 36:84).

Lines 3–4 The word *qāʾim* ('Self-Existent') comes from the root *q-w-m*, which has a basic meaning of 'to stand erect', from which it comes to mean 'to be existent' *and* 'to subsist'. Here it is followed by two prepositions: with *bi-* ('through') it means 'standing in the place of, subsisting through, managing, maintaining'; and with *ʿalā* ('over') it has the meaning of 'taking care of, watching over, being occupied with'. This quality of self-standing corresponds to the verticality of the *alif*, which subsists in every letter. We may also note that in the first few lines, the letter *alif* is found in both its isolated form, at the beginning of almost every phrase or sentence (*ism*, *anta*, *aftaqara*), and its joined form (*asmā'*, *samā'*, *ghinā'*, *ana*).

Lines 13–4 This 'Universal Support' (*ṣamadiyya*) is the condition of being Support to all the Names. 'The *Ṣamad* is the presence where the effects of the Names are manifest' (*Kashf*, no. 68). '*This* is the Presence of Recourse and Reliance (*al-iltijā' wa-l-istinād*) which everyone *in* need falls back on for support' (*Fut.* IV:295). Here there is also an allusion to the Sūrat al-Ikhlāṣ (Q 112), where *Allāh* is described first as Unique (*aḥad*) and then as Universal Support (*ṣamad*).

Lines 15–7 The roots *ḥ-r-k* (motion) and *s-k-n* (motionless) also refer to the vowelling and non-vowelling of the letters. This passage is notable for the repeated use of doubled letters (with *shadda*) with verbs in Forms II and V, indicating the dynamic activity of putting into motion (*taḥarraka*) and making motionless (*sakkana*), facing (*tawajjuh*) and differentiating (*tafarraqa*). We may also note the insistence on the word *kull* ('all, every'), which appears no less than sixteen times in these lines, emphasising the totalising all-inclusive nature of 'Your Name' (*Allāh*).

Line 18 Just as the *qibla* in a mosque defines the direction in which all Muslims pray, so the Name *Allāh* can be considered the *qibla* of the Names, for each Name refers to or is orientated to Him. *Allāh* is also the unifier or synthesiser (*jāmiʿ*) of all the Names, in that they are ultimately identical with Him. Similarly, the *alif* is both *qibla* and unifier of the letters.

Line 22 Allusion to the story of Moses on Mount Sinai: *Have you heard of the story of Moses? When he saw a fire and said to his family: 'Wait, I have spotted a fire. Perhaps I can bring you a firebrand* (*qabaṣ*) *from it or find guidance* (*hudā*) *at the fire'. When he reached it, a voice called out: 'Moses, I am your Lord. Take off your shoes. You are in the holy valley, Ṭuwā. I have chosen you, so listen to what is revealed. Verily I, I am God, there is no god except I. So worship Me and perform prayer for My Remembrance'* (Q 20:9ff.). See also Q 28:29, where the specific term *jadhwa* ('firebrand') is used: '*I have seen a fire. Perhaps I shall bring you news from it or a firebrand, so that you may warm yourselves.*' It is worth noting that the account in the Quran indicates that Moses' staff, which he took up the mountain with him, was transmuted in the Divine fire into a living thing. After removing it from the fire, he brought it down as the 'firebrand' which would demonstrate to Pharaoh the meaning of the One Living God. Moses' staff is, for Ibn ʿArabī, a direct symbol of the *alif* (see Appendix D). This seems to have been the subject of a lost work mentioned in Ibn ʿArabī's *Fihrist* (no. 7) called *K. al-Jadhwa al-muqtabasa* ('The Book of the Firebrand taken from the fire').

Lines 25–7 This refers to the Divine Speech to Moses from the Burning Bush (Q 20:12–4): three times the Divine 'I' is mentioned (*I am your Lord*; *I have chosen you*; *I am God*), and three times in one sentence (*Verily I, I am God, there is no god but I, innanī ana Allāh lā ilāha illā ana*). According to Ibn ʿArabī, three is the first 'singular' or odd number (*fard*), and is directly linked to Muhammad. See the Chapter of the Wisdom of Singularity (*fardāniyya*) in the Word of Muhammad in the *Fuṣūṣ al-ḥikam*.

Lines 39–40 *Glory be to Him, in whose Hand is the kingdom of all things, and to whom you are returned* (Q 36:83).

Line 42 *Say: 'Who sent down the Book that Moses brought as a light and a guidance to the people? You put it on parchments, revealing them but concealing much; and you were taught what you did not know, neither you nor your forefathers.' Say: 'God.' Then leave them to play in their [vain] discourse* (Q 6:91). In *Fut.* IV: 141–2, Ibn 'Arabī describes this final phrase as being the invocation (*hijjīr*) peculiar to Abū Madyan, explaining that the word 'them' refers to the Divine Names. Each of them strives to manifest their own rulership (*ḥukm*) and discusses their own merits with the others. The verse then means: let the Names play with each other, and turn yourself exclusively to the Name *Allāh*, which unites all the Names.

Line 43 Q 3:2. Concerning the three initial letters of this Sura, see *Fut.* I:61 (translated by Gril in *Meccan Illuminations*, p. 461). The Quranic verses quoted here and in the above note give particular prominence to the Name *Allāh*.

Line 45 Referring to the words of Jesus reported in Q 19:33: *'Peace be upon me the day I was born, the day I die, and the day I shall be raised alive.'*

Lines 53–4 See Sūrat al-Inshirāḥ: *Have We not expanded your breast for you, and lifted from you your burden, the burden which weighed down your back? Have We not raised high your remembrance* (*rafaʿnā laka dhikraka*)? *Truly with every hardship comes ease, truly with every hardship comes ease* (Q 94:1–6).

Lines 62–4 Allusion to the hadith: 'I call the seven heavens and the seven earths as witness for You' (Ibn Ḥanbal V.135). The word *shuhūd* has both the meaning of 'witness' and 'vision-contemplation'.

Lines 67–8 Referring to the Night of Power in the Sūrat al-Qadr: *The angels and the spirit descend during it by permission of their Lord, with every command* (Q 97:4). This line is said to be a formula for recitation, given by the Prophet to his daughter Fatima. It is the Islamic counterpart of the biblical Trisagion, the thrice-repeated invocation of holiness which is sung in the Eastern Church: 'Holy, holy, holy, Lord God Almighty, which was, is and is to come.' (Rev. 4:8; see also Isa. 6:3)

Line 69 This imagery recalls the verse: *He brought down those of the People of the Book who supported them from their fortresses and cast terror into their hearts* (Q 33:26).

Line 70 The phrase 'drowned in the sea...' alludes to the story of Moses: ... *when We divided the sea for you and delivered you, and drowned the hosts of Pharaoh as you watched* (Q 2:50).

Lines 70–2 Q 113:3 and 5.

Lines 77–8 This line is a kind of commentary on Q 27:62: *He who answers the constrained when he calls to Him, and removes evil and appoints you to be regents of the earth. Is there a god with God? Little indeed do you remember.* The last part also quotes the verse: *We gave Moses the Book and made it a guidance for the Children of Israel, saying: do not choose anyone to put trust in other than Me* (Q 17:2).

Lines 80–3 These terms are all allusions to Quranic passages that specifically mention the Name *Allāh*: for example, see Q 4:113 ('bring down', *anzala*), Q 14:7 ('grateful', *shukr*), Q 14:5 and 5:16 ('darkness', *ẓulumāt*) and Q 22:52 ('dismiss', *nasakha*).

Lines 89–90 Allusion to the verse: *To Him belongs the Kingdom of the heavens and the earth; to Him are all things returned. He makes the night enter into the day, and the day enter into the night* (Q 57:5–6).

Lines 90–1 See the verse: *We are able to show you what We promise them. Repel the evil with what is better* (Q 23:95–6).

WEDNESDAY MORNING PRAYER

Lines 1–2 Allusion to the verse: *They say: 'the All-Compassionate has taken a son'. Glory be to Him! No, they are only honoured servants ('ibād mukramūn). They do not speak until He has spoken, and they act by His command* (Q 21:26–7). This is a clear reference to Jesus, whose day this is. Throughout this prayer we find many instances drawn from Sura 21 (al-Anbiyā', 'The Prophets'). It concerns the message delivered by the messengers and the subsequent judgement of God over their peoples, delivering the people of faith and destroying the unbelievers. This Divine judgement is particularly associated with the function of Jesus at his Second Coming.

Line 4 The word 'turned' or 'turned about' (*taqallab*) is often used by Ibn 'Arabī to mean the way the heart (*qalb*, from the same root) is moved according to the *way* God reveals Himself. It is this fluctuation or variability which is the primary characteristic of the heart (see *Fut.* II:198 and *Fuṣ*, pp. 104–5; *Fusus*, pp. 608–9; *Bezels*, pp. 149–50).

Line 9 'the seen and unseen realms' literally, 'the worlds of the kingdom and the kingship' (*mulk wa-malakūt*).

Line 11 These two aspects, Divine nature and human nature, are precisely what has given rise to confusion in the manifestation of Jesus. See the chapter of the Wisdom of Elevation in the Word of Jesus in the *Fuṣūṣ al-ḥikam*.

Line 12 An allusion to the fact that Jesus is the Seal of Universal Sainthood, whose wisdom encompasses all the conditions of saintliness. See, for example, *Fut.* II:9, and Chodkiewicz, *Seal of the Saints*, Chapter 8.

Line 17 The word 'Signs' (*āyāt*) has a general meaning as in *We shall show them Our Signs to the horizons and in themselves …* (Q 41:53), as well as a specific sense of a prophetic proof. See the verse where people complained: '*Let him [Muhammad] bring us a Sign, just like the former prophets were sent*' (Q 21:5), and also the verse: *We breathed into her [Mary] of Our Spirit and We made of her and her son a Sign for all beings* (verse 91).

Line 19 Alluding to the verse: *We bestowed upon Abraham his right conduct before* (Q 21:51).

Lines 21–2 Hadith (*Concordance*, vol. V, p. 459).

Line 22 Sura 21 refers to no less than four prophets, who after being in great distress had their prayers answered. For example, Noah: *We answered him, and delivered him and his people from the great distress* (*al-karb al-ʿaẓīm*).

Line 23 This phrase is found twice in Sūrat al-Māʾida. The first time it is uttered by all the messengers when questioned on the Day of Judgement: *On the day when God gathers the messengers and says: 'What answer were you given?', they will say: 'We have no knowledge; You are the One who knows all that is unseen'* (Q 5:109). The second time it is uttered by Jesus himself when questioned by God: *'You are the One who knows all that is unseen; I said to them only what You ordered me to say'* (Q 5:116).

Line 36 This part of the prayer recalls the closing verses of the Sūrat al-Baqara (Q 2:286), where it is affirmed that no distinction should be made between any of His messengers and where the following prayer is given for all people of faith: '*Our Lord, do not take us to task if we forget, or make a mistake. Our Lord, do not lay on us a burden like that You laid on those who were before us. Our Lord, do not lay on us such a burden as we are incapable of bearing. Pardon us, and forgive us, and have mercy on us.*'

Lines 39–40 See the verse in reference to Abraham, Isaac and Jacob: *Indeed We purified them with a pure quality, the remembrance of the Abode* (Q 38:46).

Lines 41–2 Throughout Sura 21, there are numerous references to the prophets being righteous (*ṣāliḥ*). In addition, there are two verses referring the same quality to others: *Those who do righteous deeds and are people of faith – there will be no rejection for their efforts. We record it for them* (verse 94) and *The earth will be inherited by My righteous servants* (verse 105).

Lines 43–4 *And Dhū'l-Nūn [Jonah] – when he departed in anger and thought that We had no power over him; but he cried out in the darkness: 'There is no god but You. Glory be to You, I have been one of the wrongdoers.' So We responded to him, and delivered him from his grief. Thus We deliver the believers* (Q 21:87–8).

Lines 44–5 Referring to the verse: *And Job – when he called out to his Lord, saying: 'Harm has touched me, and You are the Most Merciful of the mercifiers. We responded to him and removed the harm that was upon him, and We gave him his household and their like with them, as a mercy from Us and as a reminder for the adorers* (Q 21:83). This phrase is also found in the prayer of Moses: *He said: 'My Lord, forgive me and my brother [Aaron], and admit us to Your Mercy; You are the Most Merciful of the mercifiers'* (Q 7:151).

THURSDAY EVE PRAYER

The two letters of this prayer are: *bāʾ*, as in *sabab* (cause), *qalb* (heart), *tartīb* (arranging), *badīʿ* (inventor), *bāqī* (enduring), *bāʿith* (instigating), *bāṭin* (interior), *bāsiṭ* (expander) and *baraka* (blessing); and *thāʾ*, as in *thābit* (firmly established) and *muthabbit* (reassuring).

Lines 12–3 This is a beautiful example of Ibn ʿArabī's complex understanding of letters and their symbolism. The word *ʿayn* can mean either 'essence', 'source' or 'eye', or refer to the letter of the alphabet of the same name. Here it stands for the essential reality or vision of the contemplative. The only difference in writing between the letter *ʿayn* (ع) and the letter *ghayn* (غ) is the dot above the letter. The *ghayn* may be viewed as an *ʿayn* ('eye') which is 'veiled' by a dot, where the dot symbolizes a 'separation' (*ghayr*) from Reality, or as a 'cloud' (another meaning of *ghayn*) which obscures vision. In other words, the true knowledge of causation allows the eye of the contemplative to see clearly without any obscurity.

Lines 14–8 This part of the prayer is an allusion to the famous story of the Sleepers in the verses: *Do you think that the Men of the Cave (kahf) and of the Inscription (raqīm) were a wonder among Our Signs? When the youths took refuge in the Cave, they said: 'Our Lord, give us Mercy from You and prepare for us a way in our affair.' Then We sealed up their ears (ādhān) for many years* (Q 18:8–11). These youths are traditionally associated with the Sleepers of Ephesus, the early followers of Jesus who took refuge in the Cave from the mass persecutions of Christians at their time. They are reputed to have remained there asleep for hundreds of years. The physical detachment of the Sleepers from this world is thus a potent symbol of the complete inner detachment of the contemplative. As Ibn ʿArabī points out in Chapter 205 of the *Futūḥāt*: 'The seekers, not knowing who is the Manifest and the Witnessed and who is the world, have chosen retreat in order to be alone with God. Since the multiplicity witnessed in existence veils them from God, they have inclined to withdrawal' (*Fut.* II:484). He adds that if they knew the real situation, they would witness Him in all things.

Lines 15–7 '...that I may be given to speak...' (*unṭiqa* from the same root as *nāṭiq* as in the phrase *al-nafs al-nāṭiqa*, 'the speaking or expressive self'), alluding to: *God who gave speech to everything gave us speech* (Q 41:21). The total receptivity of the contemplative, symbolized by the 'ear', allows God to 'speak' through the Divine Name *Badīʿ*, 'the Incomparable Inventor' which initiates creation. This is the Name which corresponds to the first articulation (*hamza*) and the degree of the Supreme Pen and Intellect (see *Fut.* II.397; *Alchemy of Human Happiness*, p. 170).

Lines 19–31 These lines contain a plethora of Names, words and phrases beginning with the letter *bāʾ*, such as *bika*, *bi-lā*, *bāriʾ*, *bidāya*, *bāqī*, *bāʿith* and so on, emphasizing the initiating quality of this letter.

Lines 20–1 Allusion to the hadith: 'We are through Him and for Him' (*naḥnu bihi wa lahu*). See *SDG*, p. 441.

Line 29 'shower me with blessings' (*bārik lī wa-ʿalayya*), where the author's use of two prepositions (*li-* and *ʿalā*) give particular emphasis to the continuing of the blessing and goodness in the manner of that received by Muhammad and Abraham.

Lines 32–3 See the verse: *[Bilqis, Queen of Sheba,] said: O notables, a noble letter has been brought to me. It is from Solomon and it is 'In the Name of God, the All-Compassionate and Most Merciful. Do not exalt yourselves against me, but come to me in surrender'* (Q 27:30). The word 'it' in the Quranic account refers to Solomon's letter (*kitāb*), a word that in other contexts usually means the Book (of the Quran). The use of this quotation here indicates that the Divine blessing is from God and to God, as well as from your 'Solomon' to your 'Bilqis'.

Lines 35–6 Q 2:117. Ibn 'Arabī explains the creation of things in the following way: 'A thing's being brought into existence means that it becomes a place of manifestation for God. This is what is meant by 'and it becomes'. It does not mean that it acquires existence; it only acquires the property of being a place of manifestation' (*Fut.* II:484).

Line 37 '...the firmly Established Ground' (*thābit*), which could equally be translated as 'the One who stands firm', i.e. as fact and truth, in comparison to those who are firm of heart in battle or firm in intellect, for example. Many Arabic words that begin with the letter *thā'* (whose numerical value is 5 in correspondence with Thursday Eve as 'the night of the Five', *laylat al-khamīs*) have negative connotations such as destruction (*thubūr*), blame (*tharaba*) or heaviness (*thaqāla*), whereas those used or implied in this prayer are all positive: for example, *thābit*, *thawb*, 'clothing', *muthabbit*, 'reassuring' or *thany*, 'doubling'.

Lines 48–9 Allusion to the *ḥadīth qudsī* in which God Himself says: 'Grandeur is My mantle, and Majesty My girdle. Whoever wrestles with Me over either of these, I shall cast into the fire' (*Mishkāt*, no. 15). This alludes to the Divine clothing (*thawb*).

Line 54 Referring to: *On the day when the shuddering shudders, followed by the one who rides behind, there are hearts on that day that will beat painfully, their eyes downcast* (Q 79:6–9).

Lines 55–6 See the verse: *That was 'Ad who denied the signs of their Lord, and rebelled against His Messengers, and followed the command of every obstinate tyrant* (Q 11:59). See also: *Among the people is he who disputes about God without knowledge and who follows every rebellious satan. Against him it has been prescribed that whosoever takes him as a friend will be misled by him, and guided by him to the chastisement of the burning* (Q 22:3).

THURSDAY MORNING PRAYER

Lines 1–4 The Arabic text here uses only one preposition (*bi-*) after each of the Names, and we have reflected this in our translation, even though in English such repetition is not usually favoured. The repeating of *bi-* five times not only alludes to Thursday as the fifth day but also to the insistence on Unity which is prominent in this prayer (*bā'* = 2; 2 × 5 = 10 = 1).

Line 6 The words 'You have singularised Yourself' (*tafarradta*) are used here in contrast to the Aloneness (*aḥadiyya*) of the Divine Unity. The root-word *fard* in Ibn 'Arabī's thought corresponds to the number 3, and implies a triplicity of aspects within Oneness: for example, knower, known and knowledge, or lover, beloved and love. See *K. al-Mīm wa-l-Wāw wa-l-Nūn*, 2/78.

Line 9 The expression *iyyāka* occurs twice in the Quran, in the fifth verse of the Fātiḥa, referring to the Divine You: *It is You alone whom we adore; and it is You alone whom we ask for aid* (*iyyāka na'budu wa iyyāka nasta'īn*). The two *iyyāka*-s may correspond to the two expressions in the next phrase of the prayer ('with You' and 'in You').

Lines 16–7 This is reminiscent of the Quranic account where Moses prayed: *'Lord, cause me to see that I may look upon You', to which God replied: "You will not see Me, but look at the mountain: if it stays still in its place, you will see Me.' And when his Lord revealed Himself to the mountain, He turned it into a flattened surface; and Moses fell down thunderstruck* (Q 7:143). This constitutes the extinction in contemplation par excellence. For a full discussion of this, see 'The Vision of God according to Ibn 'Arabī' by Michel Chodkiewicz in *Prayer & Contemplation*, pp. 53–67.

Line 30 See the verse: *It is He who originates and restores, and He is the Forgiving, the Loving, Lord of the Throne, the Glorious, the One who accomplishes what He desires* (Q 85:*13*–6).

Lines 31–2 Referring to the verse: *[then they found] one of Our servants, to whom We had given Mercy from Us, and taught him knowledge from Our private Knowledge* (Q 18:65). This is a reference to Khiḍr, whom tradition takes as the companion of Moses in the Quranic story (Q 18:60ff.).

Line 39 Or 'manifest in every essence' (*'ayn*). The contrast here is between the non-manifest (*ghayb*), which implies being veiled from perception, and the perceptible or perceiving reality.

Lines 41–2 Literally, the 'Names of descent' (*asmā' al-nuzūl*), which signify the Names by which God has named Himself in revelation. These Names are not established arbitrarily by human intelligence or reasoning (*Fut.* II:232). Ibn 'Arabī distinguishes two kinds of Divine Names: the primordial Names themselves and the Names of the Names, composed of letters. See, for example, *Fut.* II:122, II:684 and IV:214.

Line 54 The word 'Syriac' (*suryānī*) here refers not to the historical Syriac language, but to a primordial 'solar' language, considered by Islamic tradition to have been the one spoken by Adam in Paradise and which is known to the prophets and saints of all ages. In terms of its Arabic root, it includes the *ideas* of permeation and diffusion (*sarayān*) and the night-journey (*isrā'*), as well as secret or mystery (*sirr*). It equally derives from the Sanskrit *surya*, which means 'sun'. Ibn 'Arabī links the Syriac station (*al-maqām al-suryānī*) to the original Adamic nature of Man (*Fut.* II:690ff.). There is also a direct etymological connection between 'allusion' (*ishāra*, from *sh-w-r*), the Assyrian god Ashshūr represented as a sun with wings (as in the name of the ruler Ashurbanipal, Ashshur-bani-apli, = *al-shūr*, and in the later name of Syria), and the *Suryāniyya* language (connected to the roots *s-r-y* and *s-y-r*). This suggests that *Suryāniyya*, which is associated with the language of human beings prior to the Tower of Babel, is a universal subtle allusive language permeating all existence. Its link to the numerical values 1–9 is implied in the following passage from *K. al-Ḥaqq*, where Ibn 'Arabī expresses the fundamental principle of going beyond all allusion to the Reality of Unity: 'They know Him when knowledge of the divine relations is raised up for [the people of realisation] in their Syriac seeking (*al-ṭalab al-suryānī*), and they cut it in two: so in annihilation they find Him, and in remaining they worship Him' (*Rasā'il*, 3/405). See our book, *Patterns of Contemplation*.

Lines 57–9 This alludes to the hadith concerning God's Self-transmutation in forms. In his commentary on this hadith, Ibn 'Arabī writes: 'At the Resurrection the Truth will reveal Himself and say: 'I am your Lord.' They will see Him, but nevertheless they will deny Him and not acknowledge Him as their Lord, despite the fact that they are actually seeing Him because the veil has been lifted. When He transmutes Himself for them into the sign by which they do recognise Him, they will say to Him: 'Thou art our Lord.' And yet He is the very One whom they were denying and seeking refuge from, just as much as He is the One whom they acknowledged and recognised' (*Fut.* III:540–1, translated in *SDG*, p. 215).

Line 62 The 'veil of the *ghayn*' refers to the dot over the letter (غ): if it is removed, it is the letter *ʿayn* (ع), meaning 'eye-entity', indicating vision of the essential reality without the obscurity of 'otherness' (*ghayr*). For a similar phrasing, see also Thursday Eve prayer.

Lines 62–4 The imagery here suggests a necklace made up of the letters of the *basmala*, representing the original divine harmony of all things.

Lines 66–9 See the verse: *And listen thou for the day (yawm) when the Caller shall call from a near place* (Q 50:42). The root *n-d-w* ('to call') implies an open address or announcement from a distance, and this Quranic verse refers to the day when this 'normal' situation is reversed. The root *n-j-w* ('to confide'), on the other hand, suggests a private, intimate converse in the security of closeness. These two aspects form Moses' question to God in a well-known hadith (quoted in *Mishkāt*, no. 43):

> 'O Lord, are You distant that I should call out to You? Or are You near that I should confide in you?'
>
> God replied: 'I keep company with him who remembers Me, and I am with him.'
>
> [Moses] asked: 'What is the work You love most, O Lord?'
>
> He replied, 'That you propagate My Remembrance in every state.'

Lines 70–4 Compare this with the following passage from the Chapter on Noah in the *Fuṣūṣ al-ḥikam*: 'For the person of perplexity and wonderment (*ḥayra*) there is turning, and the circular movement of turning is always around the Pole [or centre of the circle] from which he never departs. The person of the protracted Way [on the other hand] is always turning aside from the [true] aim and intention, seeking [elsewhere] what is [actually already] within him, taking what he has imagined as his goal. Such a one has a starting-point [a 'from'] and a destination [a 'to'] and whatever lies between them, while for the man of circular movement there is no beginning that he has to keep to nor end that can impose upon him, since he possesses the most complete being and has been granted the totality of the Words and Wisdoms.' (*Fuṣ*, p. 51; *Fusus*, pp. 314–6; *Bezels*, p. 79)

Line 72 'And recognition the seat of non-recognition.' This also may be translated as 'the definite is the seat of the indefinite', referring to a grammatical contrast.

Lines 81–3 Referring to Q 1:5 and Q 32:7.

Lines 86–7 There is a play in the original Arabic on two words from the same root, intellect (*ʿaql*) and bonds (*ʿiqāl*). The intellect is the faculty that 'binds' things together.

Lines 98–9 Q 11:123.

Lines 126–7 See the verse: *Say, God suffices me. There is no God but Him. I place my trust in God ...* (Q 9:129).

Lines 130–1 Q 604. This is a prayer of Abraham and his people.

Lines 132–9 It should be noted that this passage refers to all the seven essential attributes of the Divine Self: Life, Knowledge, Power, Will, Speech (here mentioned as Order and Decree, as in the word 'Be'), Seeing and Hearing.

Lines 136–7 In his *Kashf* (nos. 27–8) Ibn 'Arabī asks for the permeation (*nufūdh*) of the two faculties of hearing and seeing in an unlimited manner (*iṭlāq*).

Lines 140–1 The combination of Names here suggest two Quranic passages: *He is the First and the Last, the Manifest and the Hidden* (Q 57:3), and *On that day God will pay them in full their just due, and they will know that God is the Truth, the Most Evident* (Q 24:25).

Line 142 The 'secret heart' (*sirr*) suggests both secret/mystery and the innermost heart, the 'place' where God Himself truly resides since there is no longer anyone else to receive Him but He Himself. The word 'distinguish' (*khaṣṣiṣ*) alludes to the 'private face' (*al-wajh al-khāṣṣ*), which is the Face of God in each being, the intimate private relation of the Real with Itself which always remains as it is. Each of the seven levels delineated here, of which the secret heart is the first, correspond in a certain sense to the seven essential attributes.

Line 144 The heart here (*qalb*) implies a place of reception or 'turning' (*taqallub*), which is in constant change in accordance with the revelations of the Name Allāh (cognate with Divinity, *ulūhiyya*), which includes all the Names.

Lines 146–7 This kind of science is specific to Khiḍr.

Lines 154–6 There is an implicit reference in the Arabic terms *darakāt* (descending steps) and *darajāt* (ascending steps) to the idiomatic expression: *darajāt al-ḥayāt wa darakāt al-mawt* ('the ascent of life and the descent of death').

Lines 157–9 Q 1:5.

Line 164 The 'Highest Assembly' is that of the Angels round the Throne, described in the verse: *We have adorned the nearest heaven with the adornment of the stars, and as a protection against every rebellious satan. They cannot listen to the High Assembly* (Q 37:6-8). There is also an implicit reference to the famous hadith: 'If someone remembers Me in himself, I remember him in Myself; if someone remembers me in a company (assembly), I remember him in a better company than that' (*Mishkāt*, no. 27).

Line 165 Literally: '... by which You fortify the oil of my lamplight'.

Line 182 We may note the five qualifications of the Blessing-prayer (*ṣalāt*) that end this morning prayer for the fifth day. Some manuscripts add two further qualities at the beginning: *sarmadiyya* ('without beginning or end') and *azaliyya* ('eternal').

FRIDAY EVE PRAYER

The two letters of this prayer are: *jīm* as in *jamʿ* (uniting), *jalāl* (majesty) and *jamāl* (beauty); and *khāʾ*, as in *khāliq* (creator), *khadama* (attendants), *khilāfa* (vicegerency), *khawf* (fear) and *khabīr* (fully aware). *Jīm* is also associated with the Arabic term for Friday, *yawm al-jumʿa* (the day of coming-together), when the community gathers for prayer. It is worth noting that Friday is the 6th day of the week, and since the number 6 contains the qualities of its divisors, 2 and 3, this may partly explain the choice of *jīm* (= 3) and *khāʾ* (= 6) in this prayer.

Line 1 The letter *jīm*, the third of the letters in *abjad* order, is specifically linked to *jumuʿa* (Friday), from the same root as *jamʿ*, 'gathering together' (as the Islamic community does on Friday). It is also associated by Ibn 'Arabī with the starless sphere, the highest of the celestial spheres, which are collectively known as 'the high fathers' (see *Futūḥāt*, Chapter 11: 'On the knowledge of our high fathers and low mothers'). This letter manifests the Divine Name *al-Ghanī* (the Rich, the Independent), and is considered to be the first of the stations of Singularity (*fardāniyya*) since it has the numerical value of 3 (see *Futūḥāt*, Chapter 198, summarised in *SDG*, pp. xxixff.).

Lines 2–12 The principle of 'uniting' (*jamʿ*) at its highest level is the union of Majesty (*jalāl*) and Beauty (*jamāl*) within the Perfection (*kamāl*) of His Essence.

Lines 16–7 The manuscripts read this line in two ways: '[witness] the oneness of my being' (*waḥdat wujūdī*) or 'the oneness of Your Being' (*waḥdat wujūdika*). Although the second is preferred in some manuscripts and apparently refers to the principle of the Unity of Being (*waḥdat al-wujūd*), with which Ibn 'Arabī would famously become associated, ultimately there is no difference between the two expressions since this 'oneness' indicates the uniting of all 'I' and 'You'. We have chosen the first form as it seems to fit the rhyme and rhythm of the sentence better.

Lines 25–7 Allusion to the words of Hūd: *I have put my trust in God, my Lord and your Lord; there is no creature that crawls, but He takes it by the forelock. My Lord is on a straight Path* (Q 11:56).

Line 28 'Grant me ...', the first of three requests beginning *wa-jʿal* (from the root *j-ʿ-l*). See the verse: *My Lord, grant me judgement, and join me with the righteous, and grant me a tongue of veracity among those who come later* (Q 26:83–4).

Lines 30–1 A reference to: *We have honoured the children of Adam and carried them on land and sea* (Q 17:70).

Lines 31–2 See the verse: *Our Lord, take us out of this city whose people are wrongdoers, and appoint for us a protector from You, and appoint for us a helper* (Q 4:75). This was the plea of the Muslims in Mecca at the time of great persecution, when they asked for help from the Prophet and the people of Medina.

Lines 41–4 These two sentences taken together have three words beginning with *jīm*. 'You comfort and mend ...' (*tajburu*) and 'tyrants' (*jabbārūn*), which both come from the same root. In the *Kashf* (no. 10:2), Ibn 'Arabī explains that the Divine Name *al-Jabbār* (the One who compels one to recognise the Source) derives from the first form of the root *j-b-r*, rather than from the fourth form. Thus he takes it to mean 'the One who re-establishes, brings together, restores, mends and comforts' as well as 'the One who forces and compels'. The latter meaning is also used to describe those who force others, the oppressors, the unjust and tyrannical who are vilified in the Quran. The same root is found in the name of the Angel of Revelation, Gabriel (*Jibrīl*), who may be understood as the one who 'mends' the previous revelations by re-establishing the original message. The primary meaning here is 'to bring back the one who is broken and humbled to their original nature'. The third *jīm* word is 'You take... under Your wing' (*tujīru*), where again the best meaning of the root is emphasized: the fourth form means 'to grant asylum, protect', while the first form means 'to persecute, tyrannise' and is equivalent to the more usual 'oppressors' (*ẓālimūn*) used at the end of the sentence.

Lines 44–5 We may observe a further set of three words with *jīm: majd* ('glory'), *tajallī* ('revelation') and *ḥijāb* ('veil').

Lines 46–7 Q 3:173.

Lines 48–51 Q 11:103 and 30:48.

Lines 52–3 In these three phrases we may observe the descending movement of the dot from above the letter (خ) in *khāliq* ('Creator') to disappearing (ح) in *muḥyī* ('Vivifier') only to reappear below the letter (ج) in *jāmiʿ* ('Gatherer').

Line 61 Referring to *The One to whom belongs the kingdom of the heavens and the earth, has not taken a son nor has He a partner in the kingdom. He has created each thing, ordaining its destiny* (Q 25:2). See *Kashf*, no. 12:2 (and n. 3, p. 78) for a discussion of the three stages of ordainment (*taqdīr*) in the process of creation.

Lines 62–3 Referring to: *God has protected them from the evil of that day, and granted them a radiance and joy. He has recompensed them for their patience God with a garden and a raiment of silk* (Q 76:11–2).

Lines 63–4 Referring to the verse: *When you see them, then you see bliss and a great kingdom. The clothes they wear will be of green silk and brocade, and they are adorned with bracelets of silver, and their Lord gives them a pure draught to drink* (Q 76:20–1).

Lines 66–7 An allusion to the verse: *He taught Adam all the Names* (Q 2:31). Compare with the following: 'When the angel came to the Prophet with a ruling (of Law) or knowledge given through notification, the human spirit encountered this [angelic] form and they met, with one giving ear and the other dictating (*ilqāʾ*), and these are two lights' (*Fut.* III:39).

Lines 72–3 Q 16:51.

Lines 76–7 'Your appointed regent' (*khalīfa*) and 'Your displeasure' (*sakhaṭ*) both contain the letter *khāʾ*.

Line 79 Q 3:26.

Lines 79–80 *God is Fully Aware* (*khabīr*), *All-Seeing of His servants* (Q 35:31).

FRIDAY MORNING PRAYER

Unlike the other prayers, the mode of address on Friday is simply 'O my Lord' (*rabbi*), reiterated five times, along with the expressions 'Lord of the worlds' (*rabb al-ʿālamīn*) and 'Lord of lords' (*rabb al-arbāb*).

Line 6 'There are four kinds of thought (*khawāṭir*): lordly, psychic, angelic and satanic. Lordly thought gives you knowledge of secrets, sciences and states. Psychic thought incites you to accomplish that which involves neither good nor evil for you ... Satanic thought will drive you to perpetrate that which will cause you sorrow in the dwelling-place of the Hereafter, whereas angelic thought prescribes for you that which will be the cause of happiness in your final resting-place.' These are the words of Ibn ʿArabī reported by his disciple, al-Ḥabashī (*JMIAS*, 15, 1994, p. 13).

Lines 5–6 Allusion to the famous hadith of the veils: 'God has seventy veils of light and darkness; were they to be removed, the Glories of His Face would burn away whatever His Sight perceives of His creatures.' See *Fut.* II:80; for other references, see *SPK*, p. 401 (ch. 11, n. 19).

Lines 15–6 Allusion to the verse: *If all the trees on earth were pens, and the sea [ink] – with seven seas after it to replenish it, the Words of God would not be used up* (Q 31:27). The *alif* is detached in written Arabic from any succeeding letter, and this graphic isolation symbolises the detachment and sanctity of the Divine Essence from all manifestation. The *alif* also represents the Pen of the First Intellect, which 'writes' upon the Tablet of the Universal Soul.

Lines 16–7 *ʿAjama* means 'to punctuate' or 'to provide with diacritical points', as well as 'to obscure'. Attachments punctuate and obscure awareness.

Line 18 Literally, '... closes the door (*bāb*)'. As the general tone of this passage is describing the idiom of writing, it seems more appropriate to speak of 'chapter', which is another meaning of *bāb*.

Line 19 *Hayūlā* usually means 'primordial matter', but here it also suggests the unlimited ink (*midād*) which fills the Pen and is the means for the letters to come into existence. The Perfect Human is the inkwell, through whom the Pen gives form to the letters of created beings.

Lines 24–5 Q 40:7.

Line 32 '... speech' (*nuṭq*), alluding to: *God who gave speech to everything gave us speech* (Q 41:21). The term shares the same letters as *nuqṭa* ('dot'), suggesting that through the Universal Dot of the Divine Image all things have speech.

Line 40 Referring to the verse where Joseph is apparently speaking: *'Yet I do not declare that my soul was innocent. The soul always enjoins wrongdoing, except so far as my Lord has mercy. My Lord is All-Forgiving, Most Merciful'* (Q 12:53).

Lines 41–2 See the verse: *You cannot see any fault in the All-Compassionate's creation. Look again: do you see any cracks? Look again and again, and your sight will be turned back to you, dim and weary* (Q 67:4).

Line 43 *All faces submit to the Living, the Self-Subsisting* (Q 20:111).

Line 58 In the Arabic word *kun* ('Be') the two letters *kāf* and *nūn* are linked together, and the *wāw* of the lexical root (*k-w-n*) is hidden and implicit – it only appears as a vowel. In the word *yakūnu* ('it becomes', in the Quranic quotation) the *wāw* (as '*ū*') appears in writing explicitly. In the same way, the *wāw* also appears when things are created through the Divine Command (creation = *kawn*). Elsewhere he refers to the *wāw* as the symbol of the Perfect Human, uniting God and His Creation. See Appendix D for a more detailed description of the secrets of the *wāw*. For this particular phrase, see *Fut.* II:632 (poem) and the poem of Abū Madyan (translated in Cornell, *The Way of Abū Madyan*, p. 150):

> Your Command subsists between the *kāf* and the *nūn*,
> executed more swiftly and easily than the blink of an eye.

Lines 59–60 Q 36:82.

Lines 61–2 The Effusion of the Essence into manifestation is here characterized as 'rain-clouds' (*midrār*), from the root *d-r-r* which suggests flowing copiously and abundantly and is particularly used in reference to rain or to she-camels, ewes or goats that have too much milk.

SATURDAY EVE PRAYER

The two letters of this prayer are *dāl*, as in *dāma* (endure, be permanent), *daʿwa* (invite), *dalla* (indicate) and *ḥamd* (praise); and *ṣād*, as in *ṣifa* (attribute), *ṣirf* (sheer), *ṣidq* (truthfulness) and *ṣamad* (universal support), as well as in the Quranic chapter of Ikhlāṣ.

Lines 3–4 The specific association of sanctified holiness (*quds*) with height and elevation (*ʿuluww*) can be seen in the Chapter of Idrīs in the *Fuṣūṣ al-ḥikam*, which expounds the wisdom of *quddūs* (holiness) in terms of the meaning of the Divine Name *ʿAlī* ('The Most High').

Lines 4–5 Allusion to part of the famous Āyat al-Kursī: *His Footstool extends over the heavens and the earth, and preserving them does not burden Him* (Q 2:255).

Line 20 A possible allusion to the verse: *My Friend and Patron is God, who has sent down the Book and has taken charge of the righteous* (Q 7:196).

Lines 21–2 Referring to the verse: *Your Lord has said: 'Call upon me and I shall answer you'* (Q 40:60).

Lines 31–3 Q 55:78 and 6:60.

Line 34 As with the Sunday Eve prayer, this final part of the prayer does not begin with the actual letter *ṣād* (ص) but with its sister, the *ḍād* (ض), as in the word *afiḍ* ('bathe', 'effuse'), whose numerical value is 9, the last of the digits. The *ṣād* denotes the level of earth and the Divine Name *al-mumīt*, the bringer of death, in contrast to the first letter *hā'* of Sunday Eve, which denotes the level of the Guarded Tablet and Spirit blown into forms (*Fut.* II.453 and 427). The *ṣād* also represents both the closed human heart (whole circle) and the fully open human heart (loop), as well as a human being in prostration (facing left) (see James Morris, 'Opening the Heart: Ibn 'Arabī on Suffering, Compassion and Atonement', *JMIAS*, 51, 2012, pp. 36–7).

Lines 37–40 The 'coming close' of the servant to God and God to the servant alludes to the *ḥadīth qudsī*: 'If [My servant] comes close to Me by a hand's breadth (*shibr*), I come close to him by an arm's length (*dhirāʿ*), and if he draws near to Me by an arm's length, I draw near to him by a fathom ...' (*Mishkāt*, no. 27). The two Arabic terms for measurement have subtle meanings: *shibr* ('span') has root-connotations of giving and marriage, and hence can be understood as that which dispels 'my own attribute' as single; the term *dhirāʿ* ('cubit') also designates a mansion of the moon associated particularly with dawn and the rising of the sun, hence the effulgence of Light.

Line 49 Allusion to the verse: *It is He who made the sun an illumination and the moon a light, and ordained for it mansions, that you might know the number of years and the reckoning [of time]* (Q 10:5). The stations or mansions (*manāzil*) of the moon correspond to the twenty-eight days of the lunar cycle, which are determined by the relation between the two lights of the sun and the moon. The degrees of the beneficial thus describe the visible aspect of the moon, reflected radiance of the sun, while the degrees of the harmful describe the dark side of the moon, that which is hidden from us. Each phase of the moon displays a different degree of light and absence of light. This passage can equally be read from the perspective of the individual: the 'stations' or 'spiritual abodes' are the stopping-places on the spiritual Path (this inspired the title of the famous *Manāzil al-sā'irīn* by 'Abdullāh al-Anṣārī al-Harawī). The word *manāzil* (abodes, stations) is for Ibn 'Arabī a complex term, to which he devotes a whole section in the *Futūḥāt* in correlation to the Suras of the Quran. See Chodkiewicz, *An Ocean without Shore*, p. 65.

Line 62 *My Lord, grant me judgement and join me with the righteous; give me a tongue of veracity among those who come later* (Q 26:84).

Line 65 Allusion to the hadith of the Prophet: 'I was sent with the all-inclusive Words' (al-Bukhārī, *Jihād* 122).

Lines 67–8 *Say: This is my way. I call to God according to inner vision, I and those who follow me* (Q 12:108).

Lines 73–4 See the verse: *Have you not seen that God has subjected to you all that is on the earth, and the ship that runs on the sea at His Command, and He upholds the heaven from falling onto the earth, except by His permission? God is Kind and Most Merciful to mankind* (Q 22:65). Also see: *He taught Adam all the Names* (Q 2:32).

Lines 75–7 From the Sūrat al-Ikhlāṣ (Q 112).

SATURDAY MORNING PRAYER

Lines 1–2 Q 3:101.

Lines 3–16 This is a set of seven praises on the seventh day, which is associated with Abraham, the intimate friend of God and model of hospitality. These seven praises describe how the servant is welcomed by God as an honoured guest, from being admitted into the presence of the Friend to being given spiritual food, drink and clothing. From an arithmosophical perspective, there is a special connection between the number seven and praise, since each of the seven sentences begins with the word *ḥamd,* whose value is 16 (1 + 6 = 7).

Lines 5–6 This may allude to the prayer of Moses: *'My Lord, forgive me and my brother, and admit us into Your Compassion, and You are the Most Merciful of those who show Mercy'* (Q 7:151). This is also referred to as a garden of Paradise in the verse: *He was told: 'Enter the Garden!' and he said: 'Would that my people knew how my Lord has forgiven me and made me one of the honoured'* (Q 36:26).

Lines 7–8 Divine Love (*maḥabba*) is mentioned only once in the Quran, in connection with Moses' being looked after when he was a baby: *I gave you Love from Me, that you might be brought up under My Eye* (Q 20:39).

Lines 9–10 Allusion to the prayer of Jesus: *Jesus son of Mary prayed: 'O God, our Lord, send a table down to us from heaven, to be a festival for us, the first of us and the last of us, and to be a Sign from You. Give us sustenance. You are the best of Providers'* (Q 5:114).

Lines 11–2 The Divine Preference or Choice is mentioned in various Quranic passages: *God preferred Adam, Noah, the family of Abraham and the family of Imran, exalting them above all created beings* (Q 3:33); *Say: 'Praise be to God and peace be upon His servants whom He has chosen'* (Q 27:59); and *Remember Our servants Abraham, Isaac and Jacob – men of power and vision. We purified them with the purity of the remembrance of the Abode. With Us they are of the chosen, the best* (Q 38:45–7). The 'testimony' (*biṭāqa*) literally means a piece of paper or card on which, according to a well-known hadith, is written the testimony of faith (*shahāda*) which will outweigh a person's deeds on the Day of Judgment (al-Tirmidhī, *Sunan*, Book 40, hadith 34; see *Fut.* IV:536).

Lines 13–4 The word *wafā'* (fulfilment) has the sense of redeeming a promise or discharging one's obligations. There may be an allusion here to the story of Moses watering the flocks of the women at the wells of Midian, and then fulfilling his pledges to Jethro (Shu'ayb). See Q 28:23ff.

Lines 17–8 Referring to: *Lest a soul say, 'Alas for me, in what I have squandered of the Divine side, and I was indeed one of those who scoffed* (Q 39:56).

Lines 18–20 Q 4:71 and 3:136.

Line 21 This final prayer of the week is remarkable for its inclusion of the different modes of address: *ilāhī* ('O my God'), *rabbi* ('O my Lord'), *sayyidī* ('O my Master'), *ḥabībī* ('O my Beloved'), *yā man hū* ('O You who is He') and *allāhumma* ('O God').

Lines 32–3 Q 42:20.

Line 43 See Q 38:47, quoted above in note on lines 11–2.

Lines 51–2 This form of invocation follows half of the manuscripts, with the others giving 'O You who is He' (*yā man huwa hū*). This may be compared with the invocation found in 'Umar al-Suhrawardī's Persian treatise on retreat: 'O He. O You who is He. O You whom there is no god but He' (*yā hū, yā man huwa hū, yā man lā ilāha illa hū*). Such an invocation is recommended in the third retreat to take the aspirant beyond the seven heavens to 'a station that no angel can ever attain' (see Aydogan Kars and Ashkan Bahrani, *'Umar al-Suhrawardī*, Leiden, forthcoming, pp. 258–61).

Lines 55–60 Q 81:17–22 and 26:195 and 192. Ibn 'Arabī understands Arabic to mean not simply a physical language but the language of clarity. See *Fut.* III:517.

Lines 60–4 This allusive sentence, which has several variants in the manuscripts, primarily signifies that what is revealed or 'brought down' as divine Word through the messenger is an unambiguously clear ruling for those who truly understand from God. The word *muḥkam* ('decisive', 'clear') is used to describe certain verses of the Quran, in contrast to *mutashābih* ('ambiguous' and subject to multiple interpretations). 'He is the One who has sent down to you the Book: part of it are decisive verses which are from the Mother of the Book, while others are ambiguous... those who are rooted in knowledge say: We believe in it. All is from our Lord.' (Q 3:7) '... the forms of clarification' (*tabyīn*) is an implicit reference to the Quran (which is known as the Clarification, *al-bayān*, from the same root). 'Dye' (*sibgha*) refers to: *The dye of God. And who gives better colouring than God? We are His servants* (Q 2:138). 'Assignment' (*tamkīn*) literally means to assign someone or something a particular place or abode, and hence to establish them with the power to act. In a technical sense it is also used by Ibn 'Arabī and others to mean 'stability' in contrast to 'colouring' (*talwīn*), which indicates constant change. He observes that *talwīn* is 'the passing of the servant through his states... and according to us is the most perfect of stations', while *tamkīn* means 'being established in constant change, and is called the state of those who have arrived' (*al-Iṣtilāḥāt al-Ṣūfiyya, Rasā'il*, 3/71).

Lines 72–3 See the verse: *Put your trust in God; you are according to the most clear Truth* (Q 27:79). Some manuscripts read: 'H/he is the most clear truth' (*inna-hu al-ḥaqq al-mubīn*), apparently referring to the Prophet.

Lines 76–8 Q 37:180–3.

The final lines of this prayer conceal a remarkable allusion to the first perfect number 6, which is the value of the letter *wāw*. There are 5 iterations of the word *Huwa* ('He', = 11) in lines 52–3, which emphasises Absolute Unity (11 × 5 = 55 = 10 = 1). These are followed by 5 iterations of the rhyme-letter *sīn* (= 3 × 5 = 15 = 6) in lines 54–6, pointing to the Perfect Human Being who is contained within the *Hu-wa* (5 + 6). If the succeeding extended rhyme-letters (*-īn*/6 × 8, *-tī*/6 × 3, *-t*/4 × 2, and *-b*/2 × 3) are included as far as the closing word *āmīn*, the total value is 48 + 18 + 8 + 6 = 78 – this not only adds up to 15 (= 6), but is also the value of the Name *Ḥakīm* as well as the sum of all the digits up to 12 (1 + 2 + 3 ... + 12). In addition, the sum of all the digits up to 14 (as in the nights and days of the week) is 105 (= 6). See our book, *Patterns of Contemplation.*

APPENDICES

A

Time according to Ibn ʿArabī's *Ayyām al-shaʾn*

The circle of Time

The most evident symbol of Unity is a circle or sphere. It is an undivided whole. Every point on the circumference of a circle or on the surface of a sphere is identical to every other, insofar as they have the same relationship to the centre. Ibn ʿArabī depicts the Divine Throne, which contains the whole of manifestation, and upon which the All-Compassionate is seated, as a circle encompassing all the degrees of existence.

Likewise, when we consider the passage of Time as circular, we are considering it as symbolic of Unity. Whether it be a year of 12 months, a lunar month of 28 days, a week of 7 days or a day of 24 hours, each of these is a complete cycle that endlessly repeats itself in a 'circular' movement. Each division, whether into 12 or 7 or 24, expresses specific truths about the Whole. Inaccuracies in the lunar or solar calendars, which require the addition of extra months or days every three or four years, do not affect the symbolic nature of the cycle.

Time-cycles, indeed all cycles insofar as they are whole, can also be considered in a sense totally equivalent to each other. It is this 'horizontal' correspondence that allows some of the most profound insights into the order of the universe. According to Ibn ʿArabī, there are 28 degrees of existence which correspond to the 28 mansions of the moon and the 28 letters of the Arabic alphabet. Described by 28 Divine Names, they are ranked in descending order from the very principle of order itself, which is called the Pen or the First Intellect, to the human being who englobes the whole in a synthetic manner (*al-jāmiʿ*), and the Perfect Human, who knows the entire structure of the hierarchy of existence (*rafīʿ al-darajāt*).[1]

1. For further details of this, see the chart drawn up by Titus Burckhardt in *Mystical*

Ibn ʿArabī's explanations of Time itself are presented to us, not as the result of a speculation, but primarily as insights from a contemplation of the revealed Word. His *K. Ayyām al-sha'n* is the most explicit about temporal cycles, and the interrelationship between the 24-hour day and the 7-day week. Explaining the various Quranic descriptions of day and night, Ibn ʿArabī depicts a highly original and complex view of Time. He considers the day under two fundamental aspects, physical and spiritual:

> What we mean by 'day' is one complete cycle of the cycles of the sphere of the fixed stars, which contains the heavens and the earth ... Every day is the final day of [a cycle of] 360 days [or 1 year] ... or we can equally well say that every day actualises everything that has taken place in the 6 [prior] days [of the week], from the beginning to the end. For in one day is the ending of each of those [other] 6 days, and it necessarily contains the property of each of them. However, this remains hidden because each of these days has a particular ending in it. A day thus spans 360 degrees, because the whole sphere [of the fixed stars] is manifest in it, moving through all the degrees. This constitutes the corporeal day (*al-yawm al-jismānī*).
>
> Within it there lies a spiritual day (*yawm rūḥānī*), during which the intellect receives its knowledge, the insight its contemplation and the spirit its secrets. This is just like the way that the body receives its nourishment, growth and development, health and sickness, life and death, during the corporeal day. From the point of view of their ruling properties which manifest in the cosmos due to the active power of the Universal Soul, there are seven different days (Sunday, Monday, Tuesday, etc.). To these [corporeal] days there correspond seven spiritual days, which are known [only] to the gnostics. These [spiritual] days have ruling properties as regards the spirits and intellects due to the all-knowing power that belongs to the Real, through whom exist the heavens and the earth, and that is the Divine Word (*al-kalima al-ilāhiyya*).[2]

Astrology according to Ibn ʿArabī.

2. *Ayyām al-Sha'n*, 2/57–8.

The seven spheres

Ibn 'Arabī speaks of seven spheres *(aflāk)* which correspond to the seven days of the week. Each of these spheres relates to a planet and a prophetic figure, whose interrelationship can be represented in the following sevenfold diagram. Although he may have had this in mind when writing, it is never explicitly mentioned and we must emphasise that what follows is our own graphic representation.

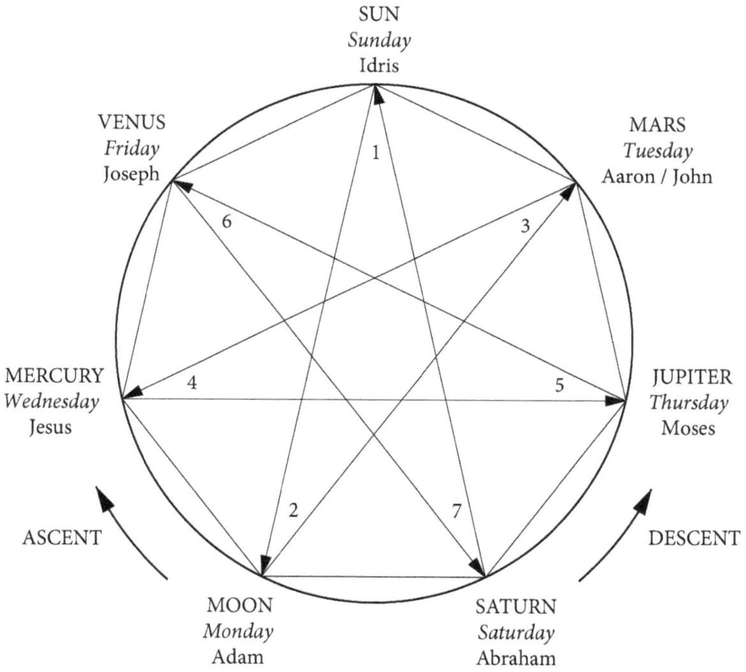

1. The seven spheres

In Diagram 1 the seven planets are arranged around the circumference according to their arrangement in physical space: clockwise in ascending order from the Moon, and anticlockwise in descending order from Saturn. The clockwise movement depicts the way in which the human being experiences the heavenly order, as a rising-up from earth, while the anticlockwise movement represents the way in which the universe comes into existence, as a descent from God.

The order of the days of the week follows the internal lines of the 7-pointed star, beginning with Sunday (Day 1). When we consider the order of the days around the circumference, we find a 14-day period, or a double cycle of 7. Each step equals two days (Sunday to Tuesday, Tuesday to Thursday and so on). Two successive cycles of 14 days, corresponding to the waxing and waning of the moon, would equal a full month of 28 days.

The seven prophets (or eight, if we include John), therefore, have two separate relationships: in the first case, they are related to the order of the planets in physical space, which corresponds to the heavenly ascension (*miʿrāj*) of the Prophet Muhammad; in the second case, they are related to the order of the days in temporal space, following the lines of the 7-pointed star within the circle.

The three kinds of day

I

He wraps (*yukawwiru*) the day-time around the night,
and the night-time around the day. (Q 39:5)

The first kind of day is the familiar, corporeal one, where Sunday eve is followed by Sunday morning, Monday eve followed by Monday morning and so on. He calls it the cyclical day (*yawm al-takwīr*), which is how we normally view the daily or weekly round. It is an endless succession of night and day, within the pattern of the seven days of the week. Ibn ʿArabī notes that those who give precedence to the day-time over the night-time are people of the solar calendar, whilst those who give the night primacy are people of the lunar calendar.

II

A Sign for them is the night: We detach the day-time from it and
lo, they are in darkness. (Q 36:37)

The second kind of day is called the detached day (*yawm al-salkh*), which is only known to the gnostics. The night is still the root or principle of the day, but here the night and day have become detached from each other. The night-time or eve of one day is connected to the day-time of another day: Sunday eve is attached to Wednesday morning, Monday eve to Thursday morning and so on. The interval between the night and its corresponding day-time is 7 units of 4 night-times and 3 day-times. These two kinds of day can again be represented on our diagram:

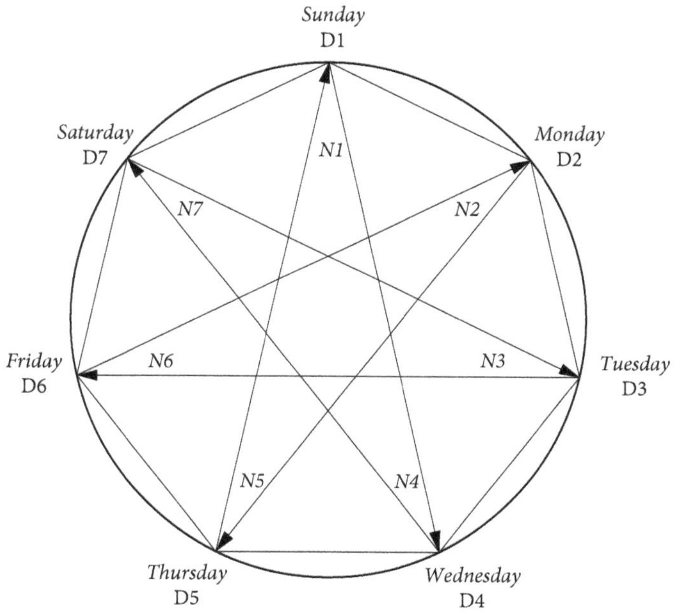

2. The cyclical day and the detached day

The ordinary, cyclical day is depicted around the circumference of the circle, starting from Sunday and moving clockwise, while the detached day may be found by following the lines of the 7-pointed star. Each night is placed within the line to show the connections, as the night is the invisible part of the day. It is thus connected to a different day along the arrowed lines. Sunday eve (N1) links with Wednesday (Day 4), and so on. The alchemical work (*sha'n*) of the first night appears and is completed at the end of another 7-fold cycle, in the day-time of the fourth day.

If we now split the nights and days of the week and represent them separately around the circumference of another circle, we shall find the same combinations of night and day as in the table above. We begin the cycle with Night 1 (Sunday eve), followed by Day 1 (Sunday) and

NIGHT		DAY
Thursday eve (N5)	⟶	Sunday (D1)
Friday eve (N6)	⟶	Monday (D2)
Saturday eve (N7)	⟶	Tuesday (D3)
Sunday eve (N1)	⟶	Wednesday (D4)
Monday eve (N2)	⟶	Thursday (D5)
Tuesday eve (N3)	⟶	Friday (D6)
Wednesday eve (N4)	⟶	Saturday (D7)

so on. The fourteen nights and days thus form two cycles of 7, with a night and day for each point on the circle.

These new combinations are the seven 'detached' days, the first of which is N5/D1 or Thursday eve and Sunday. The 'detached' days may thus be considered to form the interior pattern of the seven outer or 'cyclical' days. Days, like other creatures or things, have an interior and an exterior, a visible and invisible aspect, a spirit and a body. Ibn 'Arabī describes the day-time as 'the shadow of the night and according to its form'. The meaning of this beautiful and poetic expression can be represented graphically in the diagrams corresponding to the third kind of day.

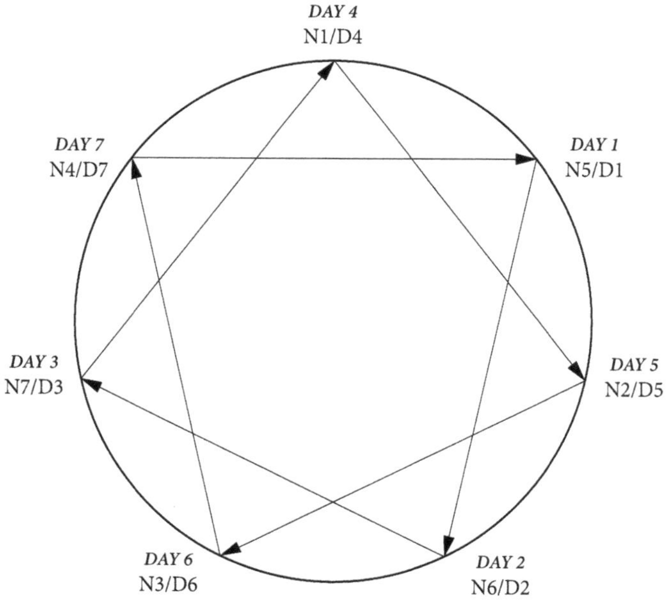

3. The detached days

III

'Have you not seen that God makes the night enter (interweave) into the day and makes the day enter into the night?' (Q 31:29)

The third kind of day is called the interwoven day (*yawm al-īlāj*). Here, at the level of the hours of a day, each hour of every night and day interlock in an intricate network with hours of succeeding nights and days.

The first hour of the first detached day connects with N5, the second hour N7, the next two day-time hours D5 and D7, the next two night-time hours N6 and N1, and the 7th hour with D6, before starting the cycle again from N5. Each night includes 4 night-hours and 3 day-hours in cycles of 7, while the day, its shadow, contains 4 day-hours and 3 night-hours. It would appear that some people have read the *Awrād* with these connections in mind: one manuscript specifies, for example, that the prayer for the 'first night' is to be read in the first hour of Thursday eve, or the prayer for the 'third night' is to be read in the first hour of Saturday eve.

Hours of the day and night

Hrs	N5	D1	N6	D2	N7	D3	N1	D4	N2	D5	N3	D6	N4	D7
1	n5	d1	n6	d2	n7	d3	n1	d4	n2	d5	n3	d6	n4	d7
2	n7	d3	n1	d4	n2	d5	n3	d6	n4	d7	n5	d1	n6	d2
3	d5	n2	d6	n3	d7	n4	d1	n5	d2	n6	d3	n7	d4	n1
4	d7	n4	d1	n5	d2	n6	d3	n7	d4	n1	d5	n2	d6	n3
5	n6	d2	n7	d3	n1	d4	n2	d5	n3	d6	n4	d7	n5	d1
6	n1	d4	n2	d5	n3	d6	n4	d7	n5	d1	n6	d2	n7	d3
7	d6	n3	d7	n4	d1	n5	d2	n6	d3	n7	d4	n1	d5	n2
8	n5	d1	n6	d2	n7	d3	n1	d4	n2	d5	n3	d6	n4	d7
9	n7	d3	n1	d4	n2	d5	n3	d6	n4	d7	n5	d1	n6	d2
10	d5	n2	d6	n3	d7	n4	d1	n5	d2	n6	d3	n7	d4	n1
11	d7	n4	d1	n5	d2	n6	d3	n7	d4	n1	d5	n2	d6	n3
12	n6	d2	n7	d3	n1	d4	n2	d5	n3	d6	n4	d7	n5	d1

By representing the fourteen nights and days around the circumference of a circle, we can see how these hours of the interwoven day relate to each other. Yet again we see that the hours of a particular night delineate a 7-pointed star (Diagram 4).

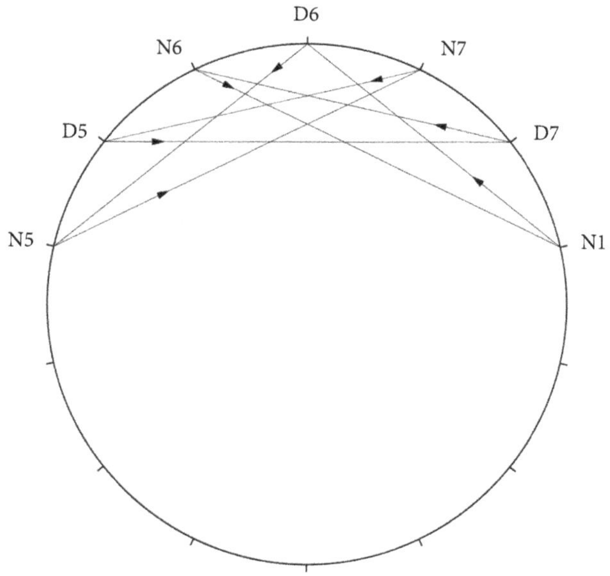

4. The interwoven hours of the 5th night (Thursday eve)

This represents the 'work' (*sha'n*) of the night, and the same applies to its corresponding day, which appears in perfect symmetry as 'the shadow of the night' (Diagram 5).

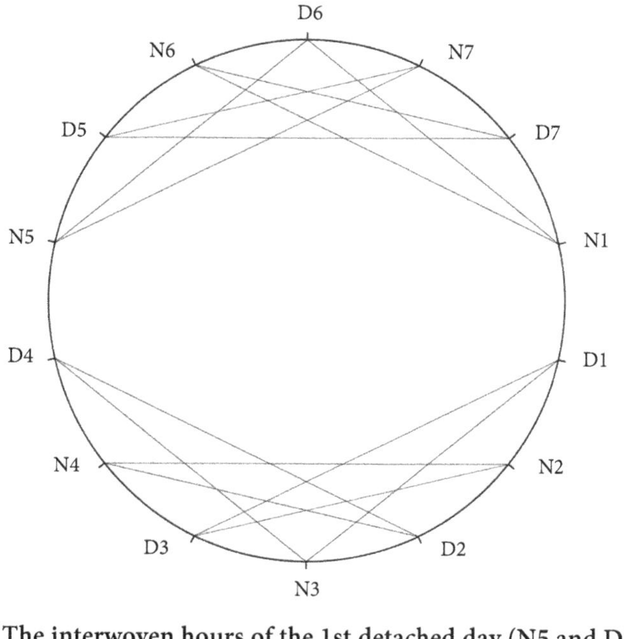

5. The interwoven hours of the 1st detached day (N5 and D1)

The 'work' of this whole interwoven day pervades and touches upon the entire week, so that every day interrelates with every other. Diagram 6 (see next page) thus depicts graphically the perfect harmony of the interweaving of hours and days, which symbolises the Divine Work. This final diagram is a beautiful representation of the harmony (*niẓām*) underlying the succession of temporal states. In his collection of poems dedicated to the woman called Niẓām whom he met in Mecca, Ibn 'Arabī celebrated the beauty manifest in 'the maid of fourteen':

> Between Adhri'āt and Buṣrā a maid of fourteen rose to my sight like a full moon.
> She was exalted in majesty above time and transcended it in pride and glory.
> Every full moon, when it reaches perfection, suffers a waning that it may make a complete month,
> Except this one: for she does not move through the zodiacal signs nor double what is single.
> Thou art a pyx containing blended odours and perfume; thou art a meadow producing spring-herbs and flowers.
> Beauty reached in thee her utmost limit: another like thee is impossible.[3]

3. *Tarjumān al-ashwāq*, XL, edited and translated by R. A. Nicholson (London, 1911).

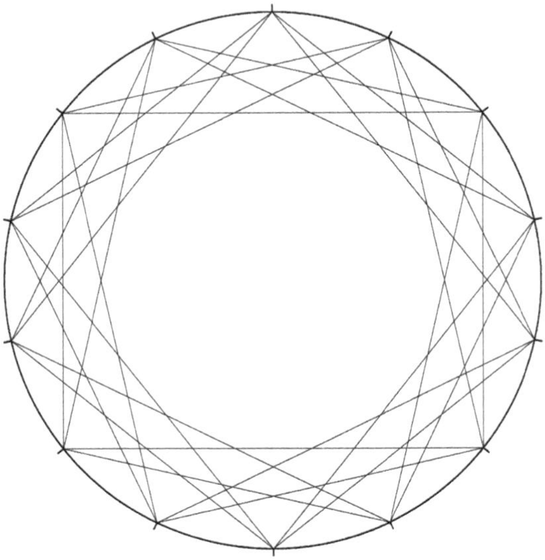

6. The interwoven hours of the 14 days and nights

B

The creative week of the Soul

The table on the next page has been constructed from Ibn ʿArabī's descriptions in 'The Days of God's Work', although some details (shown by parentheses) are not directly mentioned (even in the autograph copy) and have had to be deduced. It shows the strength of involvement of the spiritual realities of each sphere in the individual days of the Universal Soul. For example, on Sunday and Tuesday the spiritual reality of the 4th sphere or the Sun is involved in 'helping the Soul' at full strength, but only at half strength on Thursday and Saturday. The underlying pattern of the 'help' for the Soul is based upon an alchemical correlation between the planets of each sphere and the four elements (earth, air, fire and water), and their interactions on each day.[1] This alchemical work (*sha'n*) accounts for all the processes of transformation in the world. Each element may be considered to possess two characteristics: earth is cold and dry, water cold and moist, fire hot and dry, air hot and moist. In addition, cold causes a descending movement leading to the condensation of water, while heat causes an ascending movement leading to its evaporation.

(*continued on p. 138*)

1. This correlation is explained in Ibn ʿArabī's *Madkhal fī ʿilm al-ḥurūf* (an unedited text – see, for example, Shehit Ali 1341, fols. 167–73): 'Saturn is cold and dry; Jupiter is hot and moist; Mars is hot and dry; the Sun is hot and dry; Venus is cold and moist; Mercury is mixed; the Moon is cold and moist.' In addition, the text explains the relation between elements and astrological signs, physical directions, letters, numbers and spheres. 'The letters follow the nature of the number, and the nature of the number follows the nature of the sphere.' Thus, *alif* = 1 and has the action of the Sun; *bā'* = 2, Moon; *jīm* = 3, Mars; *dāl* = 4, Mercury; *hā'* = 5, Jupiter, *wāw* = 6, Venus; *zāy* = 7, Saturn.

Sphere	Element	Sunday	Monday	Tuesday	Wednesday[1]	Thursday	Friday	Saturday	Total
1. Sun (4th)	fire	***FULL***		FULL[4]	(quarter)	half		half	3.25
2. Moon (1st)	water		***FULL***		(half)	half	FULL	half	3.5
3. Mars (5th)	fire	FULL		(***FULL***)	(quarter)	half		half	3.25
4. Mercury (2nd)	mixed	quarter	two quarters[2] (descent)	quarter (ascent)	(***FULL***)	half	half[3] (descent)	half	3.5
5. Jupiter (6th)	air	half	half (descent)	half	(half)	***FULL***	half (descent)		3.5
6. Venus (3rd)	water		FULL		(half)	half	***FULL***	half	3.5
7. Saturn (7th)	earth	half	half (descent)	half	(half)		half (descent)	***FULL***	3.5
Total units or 'hours' of the day		3.25	3.5	(3.25)	(3.5)	3.5	3.5	3.5	24

Notes to the table

1. The autograph gives no details for the individual spheres' effect upon Wednesday, except to say: 'God charged the Soul with this compound [of Mercury] and ordered the spiritual realities of the spheres to help the Soul with the strength which they possess as appropriate to this spirituality. There was not a single one of them that did not help, and that is the basis of an immense knowledge.' In the *Futūḥāt* Ibn 'Arabī calls this the day of Light, occupying a central position in the week analogous to the Sun amongst the planets (*Fut*. I:155). We may note that Sunday eve (N1), the 'solar' night of firstness, is connected to Wednesday (D4) as a 'detached' day.

2. The text specifies that 'the 2nd sphere helps with one quarter of its strength in descent (*hubūṭ*), and one quarter in the move towards descent (*sayr li-hubūṭ*).' So Mercury, which contains all the elemental characteristics, adds one quarter cold (condensing) and one quarter wet (the precondition for condensation being water) to the day of the Moon (which is cold and wet).

3. The 2nd sphere, Mercury, is described as 'helping with the descent' on Friday, the day of Venus (which is cold and moist, like the Moon) – this means again two quarters, one in descent and one in the move towards descent. According to our understanding of the text, this descent also applies to the 6th and 7th spheres.

4. The text states: '… and the 4th sphere helped the Soul with all its strength' (the Sun, hot and dry, helping on the day of Mars, also hot and dry). 'It [i.e. 2nd sphere] helped her with a quarter of its strength in various ways, and with its quarter in ascent (*ṣuʿūd*).' In other words, Mercury helps with dryness and rising heat.

The table we have drawn up shows the relation between the individual sphere, element and the 7 days. As certain information is not made explicit in the text, we have assumed there to be an equivalence between the two fire-planets (Sun and Mars), and the two water-planets (Moon and Venus) on the one hand, and between the cycle of the 7-day week and the 24 hours of the day, on the other. The totals at the end of each row and column represent the 'hours' that make up the spiritual 'day', with one hour equalling 'full' help given to the Universal Soul. The table thus exhibits a perfect symmetry along the diagonal axis of 'full' strength. In terms of the days of the week, we may also derive the following qualities:

Sunday = hot / dry (Sun)

Monday = cold/moist (Moon)

Tuesday = hot / dry (Mars)

Wednesday = mixed (Mercury)

Thursday = hot / moist (Jupiter)

Friday = cold / moist (Venus)

Saturday = cold / dry (Saturn)

C

Abjad system

Ibn ʿArabī refers to different versions of the 'alpha-numerical' system, which fall into two basic categories: the Eastern and the Western systems. When discussing letters and their numerical value in Chapter 2 of the *Futūḥāt al-Makkiyya*, he mentions that the Eastern version is used by the 'people of lights' (*ahl al-anwār*) while the Western is preferred by the 'people of secrets' (*ahl al-asrār*). For Ibn ʿArabī this science is a means of direct contemplation, but he does not give it explicit prominence in the way that many other writers, like al-Būnī, have done.[1]

Eastern

The last letter of this system is *ghayn*, which indicates the West (*gharbī*), i.e. the point that is furthest from the East (*sharq*).[2]

It is worth noting that the letters for the eve-prayers in this book have been combined by selecting two from each of the 7 columns – these are highlighted in bold caps.

1	2	3	4	5	6	7
ALIF	***BĀʾ***	***JĪM***	***DĀL***	***HĀʾ***	***WĀW***	*zāy*
8	9	10	20	30	40	50
ḥāʾ	*ṭāʾ*	*yāʾ*	*kāf*	*lām*	*mīm*	*nūn*
60	70	80	90	100	200	300
SĪN	*ʿayn*	*fāʾ*	***ṢĀD***	***QĀF***	***RĀʾ***	***SHĪN***
400	500	600	700	800	900	1000
tāʾ	***THĀʾ***	***KHĀʾ***	*dhāl*	*ḍād*	*ẓāʾ*	***GHAYN***

1. Aḥmad b. ʿAlī al-Būnī, a native of Bejaia (Bougie) in Algeria (date of death uncertain, but most probably a few decades after Ibn ʿArabī) wrote voluminously on the symbolism and operative powers of numbers and letters. One can also find prayers devoted to each of the letters in his *Shams al-maʿārif al-kubrā* (pp. 363–81, Egypt, no date), but although their style is similar, they cannot be compared in terms of clarity or inspiration with those under consideration here.
2. See *Fut.* I:71, letter *ṣād*, or 73, letter *sīn*.

Western

The last letter of this system is *shīn*, which indicates the East (*sharqī*), i.e. the point that is furthest from the West (*gharb*).[3]

1	2	3	4	5	6	7
alif	*bāʾ*	*jīm*	*dāl*	*hāʾ*	*wāw*	*zāy*
8	9	10	20	30	40	50
ḥāʾ	*ṭāʾ*	*yāʾ*	*kāf*	*lām*	*mīm*	*nūn*
60	70	80	90	100	200	300
ṣād	*ʿayn*	*fāʾ*	*ḍād*	*qāf*	*rāʾ*	*sīn*
400	500	600	700	800	900	1000
tāʾ	*thāʾ*	*khāʾ*	*dhāl*	*ẓāʾ*	*ghayn*	*shīn*

The same values apply to the abridged versions (*ḥisāb ṣaghīr*) of these two systems, except that the zeros are omitted. Only unit numbers are considered: for example, *ʿayn* = 7 in both, and *ghayn* = 1 (Eastern) or 9 (Western).

As we have shown in the Introduction, the *Awrād* utilises the Eastern system for the eve-prayer combinations, rather than the Western which Ibn ʿArabī uses in his letter-poems in the *Futūḥāt*. For further details of the *abjad* systems employed by Ibn ʿArabī, see our book, *Patterns of Contemplation* (Oxford, 2021).

3. See *Fut.* I:67, letter *ghayn*.

D

On the meanings of the letters *Alif* and *Wāw*

The following extracts are a series of contemplations on the esoteric significance of the letters *alif* and *wāw*, and give an example of Ibn 'Arabī's complex understanding of the Arabic language. Letters are in themselves a field of Divine manifestation, revealing all the principles that are outwardly displayed in the cosmos. Each letter is accorded a numerical value, which may vary depending on the system used (see Appendix C). It may be written in different forms, according to whether it is joined to other letters or appears on its own.

In terms of sound, the letters are considered as points of articulation where the breath is 'stopped', this interruption causing the particular sound of each letter. The letter *alif*, which only appears as the support of the *hamza* or glottal stop, comes from the depth of the chest, without any interruption of its sound. As the sound closest to breath itself, the *alif-hamza* is thus a symbol of primordiality. While the letter *hā'* is produced at the most interior point, in the centre of the chest, the letter *wāw* is articulated at the most exterior point of the mouth, where the lips are pursed. Thus the *wāw* is considered to be the final letter in terms of articulation, including the properties of all the other 'previous' sounds that can be articulated. The breath has to pass over all these points of articulation in order to reach the 'place' of the *wāw*. It therefore incorporates and embodies the powers of all letters. For this reason, Ibn 'Arabī considers it to be the symbol par excellence of Man in perfection.

The symbolism of the Alif

The letter *alif* is not only the first letter of the Arabic alphabet but also the letter which 'unites' all the letters. Its written form is a straight vertical line, which is never linked to any following letter. This verticality stands as the most pertinent symbol of the Divinity.

All other letters are curved, or how the straight appears in myriad forms. In writing, the *alif* can be understood as the primordial letter, with all the other letters being its articulations. Likewise, in numerical terms, its value is 1, principle of all numbers. The first part of the Wednesday Eve prayer is devoted to a meditation on the *alif*. The following extracts from other works by Ibn 'Arabī bring out some of the allusions in the prayer. Ibn 'Arabī calls the *alif* the 'self-standing root of the letters' (*qayyūm al-ḥurūf*): 'everything is dependent on it, while it is dependent on nothing'.[1]

> He said to me: 'The *alif* is silent whilst the letters speak. The *alif* is pronounced in the letters, but the letters are not pronounced in the *alif*. The letters are constituted of the *alif*, and the *alif* always accompanies them without them being aware of it.' Then He said: 'The letters are Moses and the *alif* is the staff.'[2]

> If you ask 'How did the *alif* come to be the [self-subsistent] principle of the letters?', the answer is that the *alif* possesses a vertical movement, and due to its condition of subsistent Self-Standingness (*qayyūmiyya*) everything stands in existence. Now you might say that the world only comes into existence through horizontal movement, since it happens through 'ailment' (*maraḍ*) and this ailment is an inclination [towards the horizontal].
>
> And don't you see the way that philosophers describe the One who brought the world into existence as the Cause of the causes (*'illat al-'ilal*), whereas the cause [which necessarily entails its effect] is incompatible with the condition of subsistent Self-Standingness? In reply we will say: existence only happens through the self-standing condition of the Cause, and every spiritual reality (*amr*) possesses this self-subsistent condition. So understand! For the self-subsistent condition of divinity undoubtedly requires the existence of that over which divinity is exercised. 'What, He who stands and watches over every soul for what it has earned? And yet they ascribe partners to God!'[3]

1. *K. al-Alif*, *Rasā'il*, 3/396.
2. *Mashāhid al-asrār*, Chapter 5, p.50 Arabic text; Twinch and Beneito, *Contemplation of the Holy Mysteries*, p.56.
3. *Fut.* II:122. The Quranic quotation is from Q 13:33. For a fuller discussion of Ibn 'Arabī's doctrine of causality, see *SDG*, pp.18–9.

The symbolism of the Wāw

Beginning with a consideration of number symbolism, Ibn 'Arabī proceeds to describe the relationship between the Creator and the creation in terms of how the words *kun* ('Be', the Divine Command that gives existence) and *kawn* (the creation which is given existence) are written in Arabic. Turning his attention to the graphic forms of the letter, he relates the *wāw* to the letter *hā'* (as in *huwa* or 'He', the Divine Ipseity), finding a symbolic allusion to the essential connection between Man and God. The *wāw* here symbolises the Perfect Man who knows his reality according to the Divine Knowledge. The final section is a meditation on the spelling and internal form of the letter *wāw*, which again shows the fundamental distinction between Creator and created.

This extract presents one of Ibn 'Arabī's expositions on 'the secret between the *kāf* and the *nūn*', alluded to in the Friday Eve prayer. The headings are our own, not Ibn Arabī's.

Extract from *K. al-Mīm wa-l-Wāw wa-l-Nūn*[4]

As for the *wāw*, it is a noble letter with many different aspects and ways of considering it.

Wāw as number

It is the first perfect number.[5] It corresponds [in the alpha-numerical system] to the number 6, whose component parts are: a half which is 3 parts, a third which is 2 parts and a sixth which is 1 part, adding up to a total of 1 whole, which is 6 [parts].

In letter symbolism the *wāw* represents what the number 6 represents for schools of number symbolism, like the Pythagoreans. It is engendered from two noble letters, namely the *bā'* and the *jīm*. The

4. *Rasā'il*, 2/81–3.

5. A perfect number is one which is the sum of its divisors including unity: so 1 + 2 + 3 = 6, and 6 can be divided by 2 and 3. The second perfect number is 28: thus 1 + 2 + 4 + 7 + 14 = 28. The letter *wāw* has a numerical value of 6 and corresponds phonologically to 28 (as the last sound). The first four perfect numbers were known to the Greeks, and had been described in Arabic by Ibn Sīnā, known in the West as Avicenna (980–1037).

bāʾ [whose numerical value is 2] corresponds to the degree of the First Intellect, which is the second existent, or rather in the second degree of existence. This is the case with all the other written letters, whether isolated or linked. The *jīm* [whose numerical value is 3] represents the first of the odd numbers.[6]

If you multiply the *jīm* by the *bāʾ* [i.e. 3 × 2], the result is the *wāw* [i.e. 6], which possesses in equal measure the properties and tempers of both its factors. The *wāw* has the properties of the number 6, and it also includes the properties of the numbers 2 and 3. It is a letter which preserves itself particularly.7 This is why it can be found in the 'He-ness' (*huwiyya*) [from the pronoun *huwa*, which is made up of the letters *hāʾ* and *wāw*]. The Ipseity preserves the Unseen and never appears in manifestation. In this respect the *wāw* is more powerful than any other letter apart from the *hāʾ* [whose numerical value is 5]. The latter preserves itself and others,8 while the *wāw* only preserves itself. The *hāʾ* and the *wāw* [together] are the same as the 'He' (*huwa*, written as *h* + *w*), and that is 'He-ness' (*huwiyya*).

Kun and *kawn*

The other [letter] which is preserved by the *hāʾ* is the *kāf* [whose numerical value is 20] of the creation (*kawn*). This (*kawn*) is the shadow of the Divine Command 'Be' (*kun*): the essence of the *kun*'s shadow is the created world (*kawn*), because the light of the Divine Essence shines upon the essence of the *kun*, projecting from it a shadow, which is the creation (*kawn*) itself.

Between the creation and God the Most High lies the veil of *kun* [written in Arabic as two joined letters, *k* + *n*]. The *kāf* is joined to the *nūn*: the *nūn*'s numerical value is 50, which may be seen as 5 in the tens column. In like manner, the 5 ritual prayers preserve the 50 steps of prayer, as is reflected in the hadith transmitted by Bukhārī: 'They

6. Literally, 'the stations of singularity', 3 being the first singular or odd number.

7. In other words, 6 × 6 = 36; 6 × 36 = 216; etc. Hence the number 6 is always preserved.

8. 5 × 5 = 25; 5 × 25 = 125; 5 × 125 = 625; etc. Thus the *hāʾ* preserves the number 5 (= *hāʾ*) and the number 20 (= *kāf*).

are five and they are 50, and the word is not changed for Us.'[9] In this sense 5 [the *hā'*] is the same as 50 [the *nūn*].

As for the *kāf*, it is only preserved by the *hā'* [i.e. 20 is an off-shoot of multiplying by 5]. Although it has apparently become separated from it in the [command] *kun*, in fact it is supported by the *nūn*, which here stands for the *hā'* itself.[10] Its existence is preserved through it [the *nūn*], and through that preservation in the *kun*, the *kawn* is preserved from non-existence. For the imperative *kun* ('Be') cannot bring something out of existence into non-existence, as that would be contrary to its nature, which is essentially to bring into existence, and not to make non-existent ...

Wāw in graphic form

Due to its realisation in the *hā'*, the *wāw* was given existence in terms of form according to one of the forms of the *hā'*, whether it be linked or isolated. If isolated, the form of the *hā'* is ه, which is an inverted *wāw*, or like this ه, or like this ه, which would be the head of the *wāw*. Whichever way it is, its graphic form is contained in the *wāw*. How could it not be contained, when the number 6 naturally and necessarily includes 5? When the *hā'* is a joined letter, it has two possible forms, and again the *wāw* is present graphically in both: in one form, ﻫ, the *hā'* is only linked to the succeeding letter and the *wāw* appears in its natural position, whereas in the second form, ﻬ, it is linked to both preceding and succeeding letters, and the *wāw* appears inverted.

All this points to the intensity of its original spiritual relationship to the Divine Side (*janāb al-aʿlā*). For us the *wāw* indicates Him, and that is what the imam Abū al-Qāsim Ibn Qasī referred to in his *Khalʿ al-Naʿlayn*.[11] When someone attains knowledge of the secrets of the *wāw*,

9. This refers to the 50 prayers which God gave to the Prophet for the community, and which were subsequently reduced to 5. There is an equivalence between 5 and 50, in the sense that the same number has been transposed from the column of tens to the column of units. In the abridged *abjad* system, *nūn* equals 5.

10. *Kun* is written as two letters, *k–n* (*kāf–nūn*), where the second letter is seen as supporting the first.

11. Ibn Qasī (d.1151) was an Andalusian Sufi who organised a rebellion against the Almoravids in the Algarve. Ibn ʿArabī met his son and wrote a critical commentary on his book.

through it he makes the highest spirits descend in a noble revelation. This [letter] also points for us to the existence of the Divine form in us, according to His saying: 'God created Adam according to His Form'.

The elements of the letter *Wāw*

Between the two *wāws*[12] lies the veil of the Uniqueness (*aḥadiyya*), which is the *alif* [first letter of *Aḥad*]. Thus the creation (*kawn* = second *wāw*) appeared in the form of its Creator (*mukawwin* = first *wāw*), while between the two is placed the veil of Most Inaccessible Might and Most Superlative Uniqueness (*aḥadiyya* = *alif*), so that the essences [of the two sides] were distinguished. When you consider creation from the side of the [Divine] Form, you say it is non-existence, since the Form is the 'He' (*huwa* = the Ipseity). However, if you consider it from the side of its essence, then you say it is existence. Now nobody knows this except the one who knows what it is that separates the two *wāws*, which is the *alif.* It is the *alif* which shows you that this [first *wāw*] is not that [second *wāw*].

In the name of the letter *wāw*, the first *wāw* is the *wāw* of Ipseity and the *hā'* [of *huwa*, Ipseity] is implicit in it, just as the number 5 is contained within 6, and so there is no need for it to appear explicitly.

The second *wāw* is the *wāw* of creation (*kawn*). The *wāw* appears in both the creation (*kawn*) and the Creator (*mukawwin*), or the Ipseity (*huwiyya*) if you prefer. The *wāw* is also in that which lies between the Ipseity and the creation, which is the *kun* ('Be'): yet here it is invisible.[13] It is hidden because of the nature of the Divine Command. For if it had appeared in the Command itself, then the creation would not have manifested, for it has no capacity to witness the Ipseity and the reality of Ipseity would have disappeared. The Ipseity [the One who is absent and unseen] is completely opposed to witnessing [which implies presence and visibility], since He is the Absolute Unseen [or Absent One].

12. The name of the letter *wāw* is spelt: *wāw* (*w*) + *alif* (*ā*) + *wāw* (*w*).

13. It is not visible as a letter but appears as the vowel *ḍamma* (= *u*), which has the same graphic form as the *wāw*.

[Note: we can represent Ibn ʿArabī's explanation in the following way:]

Witnessing (*shuhūd*)	Uniqueness (*aḥadiyya*)	Ipseity (*huwiyya*) Unseen (*ghayb*)
و	ا	و
WĀW	*ALIF*	*WĀW*
كَوْن	كُنْ	مُكَوِّن
Creation (*k–w–n*)	'Be' (*k–n*)	Creator (*m–k–w–n*)

Bibliography

Austin, Ralph W. J., 'Aspects of Mystical Prayer in Ibn 'Arabi's thought'. In *Prayer & Contemplation*, ed. S. Hirtenstein, Oxford, 1993.

Beneito, Pablo, and Stephen Hirtenstein, *Patterns of Contemplation: Ibn ʿArabī, Abdullah Bosnevi and the Blessing-prayer of Effusion*, Oxford, 2021.

Brockelmann, Carl, *Geschichte der Arabischen Litteratur*, Leiden, 1945–49

Burckhardt, Titus, *Mystical Astrology according to Ibn ʿArabi*, Aldsworth, Glos.,1977.

Chittick, William, *The Sufi Path of Knowledge: Ibn al-ʿArabī's Metaphysics of Imagination*, Albany, NY, 1989.

—— *The Self-Disclosure of God: Principles of Ibn al-ʿArabī's Cosmology*, Albany, NY, 1998.

Chodkiewicz, Michel, *An Ocean without Shore*, Albany, NY, 1993.

—— *Seal of the Saints*, Cambridge, 1993.

—— 'The Vision of God according to Ibn 'Arabī'. In *Prayer & Contemplation*, ed. S. Hirtenstein, Oxford, 1993.

—— 'The Banner of Praise'. In *Praise*, ed. S. Hirtenstein, Oxford, 1997.

—— ed. *Meccan Illuminations.* Vol. I, New York, 2002; Vol. II, New York, 2004.

Cornell, Vincent J., *The Way of Abū Madyan: Doctrinal and Poetical Works of Abū Madyan Shuʿayb ibn al-Ḥusayn al-Anṣarī*, Cambridge, 1996.

Elmore, Gerald, 'Paradox of Praise'. In *Praise*, ed. S. Hirtenstein, Oxford, 1997.

al-Ḥakīm, Suʿād, *al-Muʿjam al-Ṣūfī*, Beirut, 1981.

Hirtenstein, Stephen, *The Unlimited Mercifier: The spiritual life and thought of Ibn ʿArabī*, Oxford, 1999.

Ibn 'Arabī, Muḥyiddīn, *Kitāb al-ʿAbādilah*, in *Rasāʾil Ibn al-ʿArabī.*

—— *Kitāb al-Alif.* In *Rasāʾil.*

—— *Kitāb ʿAnqāʾ mughrib*, ed. Abdelbaki Meftah, Beirut 1442/2020, and translated by Gerald Elmore as *Islamic Sainthood in the Fullness of Time*, Leiden, 1999.

—— *Risālat al-Anwār*, translated by R. T. Harris as *Journey to the Lord of Power*, London and The Hague, 1981.

—— *Ayyām al-shaʾn*, in *Rasāʾil.*

—— *Dhakhāʾir al-aʿlāq*, Cairo, 1995.

—— *Dīwān*, Būlāq, 1855.

—— *Fuṣūṣ al-ḥikam.* Critical Arabic edition by Mahmud Kılıç and Abdurrahim Alkış, Istanbul, 2016. Translated by R. W. J. Austin as *Bezels of Wisdom*, London, 1980, and by A. Culme-Seymour as *The Wisdom of the Prophets*, Aldsworth, Glos., 1988. *Ismail Hakki Bursevi's translation of and commentary on Fusus al-Hikam*, rendered into English by Bulent Rauf, 4 volumes, Oxford & Istanbul, 1986–91.

—— *al-Futūḥāt al-Makkiyya*, Cairo, 1911; reprinted Beirut, n.d. Selected passages translated in M. Chodkiewicz et al., *Meccan Illuminations*; W. C. Chittick, *The Sufi Path of Knowledge* and *The Self-Disclosure of God.*

—— *Ḥilyat al-abdāl*, edited and translated by S. Hirtenstein as *The Four Cornerstones of the Way*, Oxford, 2008.

—— *Kitāb al-Isrā'*, edited by S. Ḥakīm, Beirut, 1988.

—— *Kashf al-ma'nā*, edited and translated into Spanish by P. Beneito as *El secreto de los nombres de Dios*, Murcia, 1996, and into English by S. Hirtenstein and P. Beneito as *The Secret of God's Beautiful Names*, Oxford, forthcoming.

—— *Mashāhid al-asrār al-qudsiyya* (Arabic text), edited and translated into Spanish by P. Beneito and S. Hakim as *Las Contemplaciones de los Misterios*, Murcia, 1994; and into English by C. Twinch and P. Beneito as *Contemplation of the Holy Mysteries*, Oxford, 2001.

—— *Mawāqi' al-nujūm*, Cairo, 1965.

—— *Kitāb al-Mīm wa-l-Wāw wa-l-Nūn*, in *Rasā'il.*

—— *Mishkāt al-anwār*, edited and translated into English by S. Hirtenstein and M. Notcutt as *Divine Sayings*, Oxford, 2004.

—— *Rasā'il Ibn al-'Arabī*, edited by 'Abd al-'Azīz al-Manṣūb, Cairo, 2017.

—— *al-Tanazzulāt al-Mawṣiliyya* (under the title of *Laṭā'if al-asrār*), Cairo, 1961.

—— *Tarjumān al-ashwāq*, edited and translated by Reynold A. Nicholson as *The Tarjumān al-ashwāq*, London, reprinted 1978.

Knysh, Alexander, *Ibn 'Arabi in the Later Islamic Tradition*, Albany, NY, 1999.

Lings, Martin, *Muhammad*, London, 1983/1986.

Qushayrī, *Naḥw al-qulūb al-kabīr*, Cairo, 1994.

Rašić, Dunja, *The Written World of God: the Cosmic Script and the Art of Ibn 'Arabī*, Oxford, 2021.

Schimmel, Anne-Marie, *And Muhammad is His Messenger*, Chapel Hill, NC, 1985.

Sezgin, Fuad, *Geschichte des arabischen Schrifttums*, Leiden, 1967–84.

Wensinck, A. J., *et al.*, *Concordance et indices de la tradition musulmane*, Leiden, 1936–69.

Yahia, Osman, *Histoire et Classification de l'Oeuvre d'Ibn 'Arabī*, Damascus, 1964.

THE PRAYERS

TRANSLITERATION

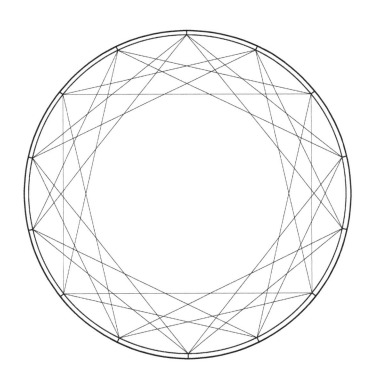

Notes on transliteration

For those that do not know any Arabic, we recommend listening to the recording of the prayers while following the transliteration. If you wish to consult a technical description of the special Arabic letter-sounds that do not have an immediate English equivalent, we suggest the explanatory notes in a grammar such as *A New Arabic Grammar* by Haywood and Nahmad.

Hyphen
A hyphen indicates a written connection between two words or between the definite article and the noun, which should be read together (e.g. *al-qalb*; *wa-qalb* instead of *wa qalb*; or *fa-inna* instead of *fa inna*).

Elision
Sometimes there is an unbreakable phonic connection between two words, which causes the initial vowel of the second word to disappear in pronunciation (e.g. *bismi Llāh* instead of *bismi Allāh*; *li-Llāh* instead of *li Allāh*; *ilayhi l-abṣār* instead of *ilayhi al-abṣār*).

In addition, if the final vowel of the first word is long in writing, it becomes short in pronunciation (e.g. *illa nqalaba* instead of *illā inqalaba*, *fi l-qalb* instead *fī al-qalb*).

Assimilation
The definite article *al-* ('the') is sometimes written with a different letter before certain words (e.g. *ash-shamsu*, not *al-shamsu*). This 'regressive' assimilation, which works backwards, is applied to the 14 so-called 'sun-letters' (*al-ḥurūf ash-shamsiyya*) [t, th, d, dh, r, z, s, sh, ṣ, ḍ, ṭ, ẓ, l, n]. The remaining 14, which are known as 'moon letters' (*al-ḥurūf al-qamariyya*), do not change their sound. This assimilation also happens with certain letter combinations (e.g. *min mā* becomes *mimmā*): we have kept these to a minimum in the transliteration, but they may occur to you naturally (e.g. *hudan li-l-muttaqīn* becomes *hudal li-l-muttaqīn*).

Pausal forms
There are various rules in Arabic for how to pronounce words at the end of a sentence or unit of meaning. Each phrase ends on either a consonant or a long vowel. In the *Muqaddima* (Preface) there are also brackets to indicate that a long ending vowel can be used if preferred (e.g. *tawfīqih[ī]* may be read as *tawfīqih* or *tawfīqihī*).

Some manuscripts indicate where pauses in the prayers should be, and these have been followed in the English transliteration, with commas, semi-colons or full-stops.

Italics
Italics indicate Quranic quotations.

The Preface Prayer

BISMI LLĀHI R-RAḤMĀNI R-RAḤĪM

Al-ḥamdu li-Llāhi ʿalā ḥusni tawfīqih(ī), wa-asʾaluhu l-hidāyata ilā sulūki ṭarīqih(ī), wa-ilhāman ʿalā taḥqīqih(ī), wa-qalban mūqinan ilā taṣdīqih(ī), wa-ʿaqlan nūrāniyyan bi-ʿināyati tasbīqih(ī), wa-rūḥan rūḥāniyyan ilā tashwīqih(ī), wa-*nafsan muṭmaʾinnatan* mina l-jahli wa-taṭbīqih(ī), wa-fahman ʿāliman bi-almāʿi l-fikri wa-barīqih(ī), wa-sirran zāhiran bi-*salsabīl*i l-fatḥi wa-*raḥīq*ih(ī), wa-lisānan mabsūṭan bi-bisāṭi l-basṭi wa-tarwīqih(ī), wa-fikran sāmiyan ʿan zukhrufi l-fānī wa-tazwīqih(ī), wa-baṣīratan tushāhidu sirra l-wujūdi fī taghrībi l-kawni wa-tashrīqih(ī), wa-ḥawāssan sālimatan bi-majāri l-rawḥi wa-taṭrīqih(ī), wa-fiṭratan ṭāhiratan min zukāmi n-naqṣi wa-taṭbīqih(ī), wa-qarīḥatan munqādatan bi-zimāmi sh-sharʿi wa-tawthīqih(ī), wa-waqtan musāʿidan li-jamʿihi wa-tafrīqih(ī), wa-ṣalātan wa-salāman ʿalā Muhammadin wa-ālihi wa-farīqih(ī), wa-l-khulafāʾi min baʿdihi wa-t-tābiʿīna sulūka ṭarīqih(ī), wa-sallama taslīmā.

Ammā baʿdu fa-inna l-murāda huwa Llāhu fi l-wujūdi wa-sh-shuhūd, wa-huwa l-maqṣūd wa-lā inkāra wa-lā juḥūd. *Wa-huwa ḥasbī wa-niʿma l-wakīl.*

Sunday Eve

BISMI LLĀHI R-RAḤMĀNI R-RAḤĪM

Ilāhī, anta l-muḥīṭu bi-ghaybi kulli shāhid, wa-l-mustawlī ʿalā bāṭini kulli ẓāhir. As'aluka bi-wajhika lladhī sajadat lahu l-jibāh, wa-*ʿanat lahu l-wujūh*, wa-bi-nūrika lladhī *shakhaṣat ilayhi l-abṣār*, an tahdiyanī ilā ṣirāṭika l-khāṣṣi hidāyatan taṣrifu bihā wajhī ilayka ʿamman siwāk.

Yā man huwa l-huwa l-muṭlaq, wa-ana l-huwa l-muqayyad. Lā huwa illā hū.

Ilāhī, sha'nuka qahru l-aʿdā'i wa-qamʿu l-jabbārīn, as'aluka madadan min ʿizzatika tamnaʿunī min kulli man arādanī bi-sū', ḥattā akuffa bihi akuffa l-bāghīn, wa-*aqṭaʿa bihi dābira ẓ-ẓālimīn.* Wa-mallikni nafsī mulkan yuqaddisunī ʿan kulli khuluqin sayyi'. Wa-hdinī ilayka yā hādī, ilayka marjiʿu kulli shay'. Wa-anta *bi-kulli shay'in muḥīṭ.*

Wa-huwa l-qāhiru fawqa ʿibādihi, wa-huwa l-ḥakīmu l-khabīr.

Ilāhī, anta *l-qā'imu ʿalā kulli nafs*, wa-l-qayyūmu ʿalā kulli maʿnan wa-ḥiss. Qadarta fa-qaharta, wa-ʿalimta fa-qaddarta, fa-laka l-qudratu wa-l-qahru, wa-bi-yadika l-khalqu wa-l-amr. Wa-anta maʿa kulli shay'in qurba l-qurbi wa-mawlāh. Wa-bi-l-iḥāṭati mudabbiruhu wa-hudāh.

Ilāhī, innī as'aluka madadan min asmā'ika l-qahriyyā, tuqawwī bihā quwāya l-qalbiyyati wa-l-qālibiyyā, ḥattā lā yalqānī ṣāḥibu qalbin illa *nqalaba ʿalā ʿaqibayhi* maqhūrā. Wa-as'aluka ilāhī lisānan nāṭiqā, wa-qawlan ṣādiqā; wa-fahman lā'iqā, wa-sirran dhā'iqā; wa-qalban qābilā, wa-ʿaqlan ʿāqilā; wa-fikran mushriqā, wa-shawqan muqliqā; wa-ṭarfan muṭriqā, wa-tawqan muḥriqā; wa-habnī yadan qādiratā, wa-quwwatan qāhiratā; wa-*nafsan muṭma'innatā*, wa-jawāriḥa li-ṭāʿatika layyinatā. Wa-qaddisnī li-l-qudūmi ʿalayk, wa-rzuqni t-taqadduma ilayk.

Ilāhī, hab lī qalban uqbilu bihi ʿalayka bi-faqri l-fuqarā', yaqūduhu sh-shawqu wa-yasūquhu t-tawq, zāduhu l-khawfu wa-rafīquhu l-qalaq, wa-qaṣduhu l-qurbu wa-l-qabūl. Wa-ʿindaka zulfa l-qāṣidīn, wa-muntahā raghbati ṭ-ṭālibīn.

Ilāhī, alqi ʿalayya s-sakīnata wa-l-waqār, wa-jannibni l-ʿaẓamata wa-l-istikbār. Wa-aqimnī fī maqāmi l-qabūli bi-l-inābah, wa-qābil qawlī bi-l-ijābah.

Rabbī, qarribnī ilayka qurba l-ʿārifīn. Wa-qaddisnī ʿan ʿalā'iqi ṭ-ṭabʿ, wa-azil minnī ʿalaqa dami dh-dhamm, li-akūna mina l-muṭahharīn. Wa-ṣalla Llāhu ʿalā sayyidinā Muḥammadin wa-ʿalā ālihi wa-ṣaḥbihi ajmaʿīn. *Wa-l-ḥamdu li-Llāhi rabbi l-ʿālamīn.*

Sunday Morning

BISMI LLĀHI R-RAḤMĀNI R-RAḤĪM

Bismi Llāh fātiḥi l-wujūd. Wa-*l-ḥamdu li-Llāh* muẓhiri kulli mawjūd. Wa-*lā ilāha illa-Llāh* tawḥīdan muṭlaqan ʿan kashfin wa-shuhūd. Wa-*Llāhu akbaru* minhu bada'a l-amru wa-ilayhi yaʿūd. Wa-*subḥāna-Llāh* mā thamma siwāhu fa-yushhadu, wa-lā maʿahu ghayruhu maʿbūd. Wāḥidun aḥadun ʿalā mā kāna ʿalayhi qabla ḥurūfi l-ḥudūd. Lahu fī kulli shay'in āyatun tadullu ʿalā annahu wāḥidun mawjūd. Sirruhu sitruhu ʿani l-idrāki wa-n-nufūd. Wa-*lā ḥawla wa-lā quwwata illā bi-Llāhi l-ʿaliyyi l-ʿaẓīm*, kanzun ikhtaṣṣanā bihi min khazā'ini l-ghaybi wa-l-jūd: astanzilu bihi kulla khayr, wa-adfaʿu bihi kulla sharrin wa-ḍayr, wa-aftuqu bihi kulla ratqin masdūd. Wa-*innā li-Llāhi wa-innā ilayhi rājiʿūn*, fī kulli amrin nazala aw huwa nāzil, wa-fī kulli ḥālin wa-maqāmin, wa-khāṭirin wa-wāridin, wa-maṣdarin wa-wurūd. Wa-Llāhu huwa l-marjuwwu li-kulli shay', wa-fī kulli shay'in huwa l-ma'mūlu wa-l-maqṣūd. Wa-l-ilhāmu minhū, wa-l-fahmu ʿanhū, wa-l-mawjūdu huwa, wa-lā inkāra wa-lā juḥūd. Idhā kashafa fa-lā ghayr, wa-idhā satara fa-kullun ghayr, wa-kullun maḥjūbun mabʿūd. Bāṭinun bi-l-aḥadiyya, ẓāhirun bi-l-wāḥidiyya. Wa-ʿanhu wa-bihi kāna kawnu kulli shay'in, fa-lā shay'. Idhi sh-shay'u fi l-ḥaqīqati maʿdūmun mafqūd. Fa-*huwa l-awwalu wa-l-ākhir, wa-ẓ-ẓāhiru wa-l-bāṭin, wa-huwa bi-kulli shay'in ʿalīm*, qabla kawni sh-shay'i wa-baʿda l-wujūd. Lahu l-iḥāṭatu l-wāsiʿa, wa-l-ḥaqīqatu l-jāmiʿa; wa-s-sirru l-qā'im, wa-l-mulku d-dā'im, wa-l-ḥukmu l-lāzim. Ahlu th-thanā'i wa-l-majd, huwa ka-mā athnā ʿalā nafsih, fa-huwa l-ḥāmidu wa-l-maḥmūd.

Aḥadiyyu dh-dhāt, wāḥidiyyu l-asmā'i wa-ṣ-ṣifāt. 'Alīmun bi-l-kulliyyāti wa-l-juz'iyyāt, muḥīṭun bi-l-fawqiyyāti wa-t-taḥtiyyāt. Wa-lahu *'anati l-wujūhu* min kulli l-jihāt.

Allāhumma, yā man huwa l-muḥīṭu l-jāmi', wa-yā man lā yamna'uhu mina l-'aṭā'i māni'; yā man lā yanfadu mā 'indahū, wa-'amma jamī'a l-khalā'iqi jūduhu wa-rifduhū.

Allāhumma ftaḥ lī aghlāqa hādhihi l-kunūz, wa-kshif lī ḥaqā'iqa hādhihi r-rumūz; wa-kun anta muwājihī wa-wijhatī, wa-ḥjubnī bi-ru'yatika 'an ru'yatī, wa-mḥu bi-ẓuhūri tajallīka jamī'a ṣifatī, ḥattā lā yakūna lī wijhatun illā ilayk, wa-lā yaqa'u minnī naẓarun illā 'alayk.

Wa-nẓur Allāhumma ilayya bi-'ayni r-raḥmati wa-l-'ināya, wa-l-ḥifẓi wa-r-ri'āya, wa-l-ikhtiṣāṣi wa-l-wilāya, fī kulli shay', ḥattā lā yaḥjubunī 'an ru'yatī laka shay', wa-akūna nāẓiran ilayka bi-mā amdadtanī bihi min naẓarika fī kulli shay'. Wa-j'alnī khāḍi'an li-tajallīk, ahlan li-khtiṣāṣika wa-tawallīk; maḥalla naẓarika min khalqik, wa-mufīḍan 'alayhim min 'aṭā'ika wa-faḍlik.

Yā man lahu l-ghinā'u l-muṭlaq, wa-li-'abdihi l-faqru l-muḥaqqaq. Yā ghaniyyan 'an kulli shay', wa-kullu shay'in muftaqirun ilayh. Wa-yā man bi-yadihi amru kulli shay', wa-amru kulli shay'in rāji'un ilayh. Wa-yā man lahu l-wujūdu l-muṭlaq, fa-lā ya'lamu mā huwa illā hū, wa-lā yustadallu 'alayhi illā bih. Wa-yā musakhkhira l-a'māli ṣ-ṣāliḥati li-l-'abd, li-ya'ūda naf'uhā 'alayh. Lā maqṣada lī ghayruk, wa-lā yasa'unī illā jūduka wa-khayruk.

Yā jawād fawqa l-murād. Yā mu'ṭiya n-nawāl qabla s-su'āl. Yā man waqafa dūnahu qadamu kulli ṭālib. Yā man huwa 'alā amrihi qādirun wa-ghālib. Yā man huwa li-kulli shay'in wāhib, wa-idhā shā'a sālib. Ahimmu ilayka bi-s-su'āl, fa-ajidunī 'abdan laka 'alā kulli ḥāl. Fa-tawallanī yā mawlāy, fa-anta awlā bihi minnī.

Kayfa aqṣiduka wa-anta warā'a l-qaṣd, am kayfa aṭlubuka wa-ṭ-ṭalabu 'aynu l-bu'd. A-yuṭlabu man huwa qarībun ḥāḍir, am yuqṣadu mani l-qāṣidu fīhi tā'ihun ḥā'ir. Aṭ-ṭalabu lā yaṣilu ilayk, wa-l-qaṣdu lā yaṣduru ʿalayk.

Tajalliyātu ẓāhirik, lā tulḥaqu wa-lā tudrak; wa-rumūzu asrārik, lā tanḥallu wa-lā tanfakk. A-yaʿlamu l-mawjūdu kunha man awjadah, am yablughu l-ʿabdu ḥaqīqata mani staʿbadah. Aṭ-ṭalabu wa-l-qaṣdu wa-l-qurbu wa-l-buʿdu ṣifātu l-ʿabd, fa-mādhā yablughu l-ʿabdu bi-ṣifātih, mimman huwa munazzahun mutaʿālin fī dhātih. Wa-kullu makhlūqin maḥalluhu l-ʿajz, fī mawqifi dh-dhulli ʿalā bābi l-ʿizz, ʿan nayli idrāki hādha l-kanz.

Kayfa aʿrifuk, wa-anta l-bāṭinu lladhī lā tuʿraf. Wa-kayfa lā aʿrifuk, wa-anta ẓ-ẓāhiru lladhī ilayya fī kulli shay'in tataʿarraf. Kayfa uwaḥḥiduk, wa-lā wujūda lī fī ʿayni l-aḥadiyya. Wa-kayfa lā uwaḥḥiduk, wa-t-tawḥīdu sirru l-ʿubūdiyya.

Subḥānaka lā ilāha illā anta, mā waḥḥadaka min aḥad, idh anta ka-mā anta, fī sābiqi l-azal wa-lāḥiqi l-abad. Fa-ʿala t-taḥqīqi mā waḥḥadaka aḥadun siwāk, wa-fi l-jumlati mā ʿarafaka illā iyyāk. Baṭanta wa-ẓahart, fa-lā ʿanka baṭanta wa-lā li-ghayrika ẓahart, fa-anta anta lā ilāha illā anta. Fa-kayfa bi-hādha sh-shakli yanḥall, wa l-awwalu ākhiru wa-l-ākhiru awwal. Fa-yā man abhama l-amr, wa-abṭana s-sirr, wa-awqaʿa fi l-ḥayrah, wa-lā ghayrah.

As'aluka Llāhumma kashfa sirri l-aḥadiyya, wa-taḥqīqa l-ʿubūdiyya, wa-l-qiyāma bi-r-rubūbiyya, bi-mā yalīqu bi-ḥaḍratiha l-ʿaliyya. Fa-ana mawjūdun bika ḥādithun maʿdūm, wa-anta mawjūdun bāqin ḥayyun qayyūm, qadīmun azaliyyun ʿālimun maʿlūm. Fa-yā man lā yaʿlamu mā huwa illā hū.

As'aluka Llāhumma l-haraba minnī ilayk, wa-l-jamʿa bi-jamīʿi majmūʿī ʿalayk, ḥattā lā yakūna wujūdī hijābī ʿan shuhūdī. Yā maqṣūdī, yā maʿbūdī, mā fātanī shay'un idhā ana wajadtuk, wa-lā jahiltu shay'an idhā ana ʿalimtuk, wa-lā faqadtu shay'an idhā ana shahidtuk. Fanā'ī fīk, wa-baqā'ī bik, wa-mashhūdī anta, lā ilāha illā anta, anta ka-mā shahidtu wa-ka-mā umirtu. Fa-shuhūdī ʿaynu wujūdī. Fa-mā shahidtu siwāʾī, fī fanāʾī wa-baqāʾī. Wa-l-ishāratu ilayya, wa-l-ḥukmu lī wa-ʿalayya. Wa-n-nisabu nisabī, wa-kullu dhālika rutabī. Wa-sh-shaʾnu shaʾnī, fī ẓ-ẓuhūri wa-l-buṭūn, wa-sarayāni s-sirri l-maṣūn.

Huwiyyatun sāriyah, maẓāhirun bādiyah, wujūdun wa-ʿadam, nūrun wa-ẓulam, lawḥun wa-qalam, samʿun wa-ṣamam, jahlun wa-ʿilm, ḥarbun wa-silm, ṣamtun wa-nuṭq, ratqun wa-fatq, ḥaqīqatun wa-ḥaqq, ghaybūbiyyatu azal, daymūmiyyatu abad. *Qul: huwa Llāhu aḥad, Allāhu ṣ-ṣamad, lam yalid wa-lam yūlad, wa-lam yaku(l) lahu kufuwan aḥad.*

Wa-ṣalla Llāhu ʿala l-awwali fī l-ījādi wa-l-wujūd; al-fātiḥi li-kulli shāhidin ḥaḍratayi sh-shāhidi wa-l-mashhūd; as-sirri l-bāṭini, wa-n-nūri ẓ-ẓāhiri, ʿayni l-maqṣūd; mumayyizi qabḍatayi s-sabqi, fī ʿālami l-khalqi, mina l-makhṣūṣi wa-l-mabʿūd; ar-rūḥi l-aqdasi l-ʿalī, wa-n-nūri l-akmali l-bahī; al-qāʾimi bi-kamāli l-ʿubūdiyyati fī ḥaḍrati l-maʿbūd; alladhī ufīḍa ʿalā rūḥihi min ḥaḍrati rūḥāniyyatih, wa-ttaṣalat bi-mishkāti qalbihi ashiʿʿatu nūrāniyyatih. Fa-huwa r-rasūlu l-aʿẓam, wa-n-nabiyyu l-mukarram, wa-l-waliyyu l-muqarrabu l-masʿūd. Wa-ʿalā ālihi wa-aṣḥābih, khazāʾini asrārih, wa-maʿādini anwārih, wa-maṭāliʿi aqmārih; kunūzi l-ḥaqāʾiq, hudāti l-khalāʾiq; nujūmi l-hudā li-man iqtadā. Wa-sallama taslīman kathīran ilā yawmi d-dīn. *Wa-subḥāna Llāhi wa-mā ana mina l-mushrikīn. Wa-ḥasbuna Llāhu wa-niʿma l-wakīl. Wa-lā ḥawla wa-lā quwwata illā bi-Llāhi l-ʿaliyyi l-ʿaẓīm. Wa-l-ḥamdu li-Llāhi rabbi l-ʿālamīn.*

Monday Eve

BISMI LLĀHI R-RAḤMĀNI R-RAḤĪM

Ilāhī, wasi'a 'ilmuka kulla ma'lūm, wa-aḥāṭat khubratuka bāṭina kulli mafhūm, wa-taqaddasta fī 'ulāka 'an kulli madhmūm. Tasāmat ilayka l-himam, wa-ṣa'ida ilayka l-kalim. Anta l-muta'ālī fī sumuwwik, fa-aqrabu ma'ārijinā ilayka t-tanazzul. Wa-anta l-muta'azzizu fī 'uluwwik, fa-ashrafu akhlāqinā ilayka t-tadhallul. Ẓaharta fī kulli bāṭinin wa-ẓāhir, wa-dumta ba'da kulli awwalin wa-ākhir. Subḥānaka lā ilāha illā anta, sajadat li-'aẓamatika l-jibāh, wa-tana''amat bi-dhikrika sh-shifāh. As'aluka bi-smika l-'aẓīmi lladhī ilayhi sumuwwu kulli mutaraqqin, wa-minhu qabūlu kulli mutalaqqin, sirran taṭlubunī fīhi l-himamu l-'aliyyah, wa-tanqādu ilayya fīhi n-nufūsu l-abiyyah.

Wa-as'aluka rabbī an taj'ala sullamī ilayka t-tanazzul, wa-mi'rājī ilayka t-tawāḍu'a wa-t-tadhallul. Wa-knufnī bi-ghāshiyatin min nūrika takshifu lī bihā kulla mastūr. Wa-taḥjubnī 'an kulli ḥāsidin wa-maghrūr. Wa-hab lī khuluqan asa'u bihi kulla khalq, wa-aqḍī bihi kulla ḥaqq, ka-mā *wasi'ta kulla shay'in raḥmatan wa-'ilmā.*

Lā ilāha illā anta, *yā ḥayyu yā qayyūm.*

Rabbī, rabbinī bi-laṭīfi rubūbiyyatik, tarbiyata muftaqirin ilayka lā yastaghnī 'anka abadā. Wa-rāqibnī bi-'ayni 'ināyatik, bi-murāqabatin taḥfaẓunī 'an kulli ṭāriqin yaṭruqunī bi-amrin yasū'unī fī nafsī, aw yukaddiru 'alayya waqtī wa-ḥissī. Aw yaktubu fī lawḥi irādatī khaṭṭan mina l-khuṭūṭ. Wa-rzuqnī rāḥata l-unsi bik, wa-raqqinī ilā maqāmi l-qurbi mink. Wa-rawwiḥ rūḥī bi-dhikrik, wa-raddidnī bayna raghabin fīka wa-rahabin mink. Wa-raddinī bi-riḍā'i r-riḍwān, wa-awridnī mawārida l-qabūl. Wa-hab lī raḥmatan minka talummu bihā sha'athī, wa-tukammilu bihā naqṣī, wa-tuqawwimu 'iwajī, wa-taruddu shāridī, wa-tahdī ḥā'irī, fa-innaka rabbu kulli shay'in wa-murabbih. Raḥimta dh-dhawāt, wa-rafa'ta d-darajāt. Qurbaka rawḥu l-arwāḥ, wa-rayḥānu l-afrāḥ, wa-'unwānu l-falāḥ, wa-rāḥatu kulli murtāḥ. Tabārakta rabba l-arbāb, wa-mu'tiqa r-riqāb, wa-kāshifa l-'adhāb. Wasi'ta kulla shay'in raḥmatan wa-'ilmā, wa-ghafarta dh-dhunūba ḥanānan wa-ḥilmā. Wa-anta l-ghafūru r-raḥīm, al-ḥalīmu l-'alīm, al-'aliyyu l-'aẓīm. Wa-ṣalla Llāhu 'alā sayyidinā Muḥammadin wa-'alā ālihi wa-ṣaḥbihi ajma'īn. *Wa-l-ḥamdu li-Llāhi rabbi l-'ālamīn.*

Monday Morning

BISMI LLĀHI R-RAḤMĀNI R-RAḤĪM

Allāhumma, innī as'aluka *n-nūra wa-l-hudā*, wa-l-adaba fī l-iqtidā'. Wa-a'ūdhu bika min sharri nafsī, wa-min sharri kulli qāṭi'in yaqṭa'unī 'ank. Lā ilāha illā anta, qaddis nafsī mina sh-shubuhāti wa-l-akhlāqi s-sayyi'āt, wa-l-ḥuẓūẓi wa-l-ghafalāt. Wa-j'alnī 'abdan muṭī'an laka fī jamī'i l-ḥālāt.

Yā 'alīmu, 'allimnī min 'ilmik. Yā ḥakīmu, ayyidnī bi-ḥukmik. Yā samī'u, asmi'nī mink. Yā baṣīru, baṣṣirnī fī ālā'ik. Yā khabīru, fahhimnī 'ank. Yā ḥayyu, aḥyinī bi-dhikrik. Yā murīdu, khalliṣ irādatī bi-qudratika wa-'aẓamatik. *Innaka 'alā kulli shay'in qadīr.*

Allāhumma, innī as'aluka bi-l-lāhūti dhi t-tadbīr, wa-n-nāsūti dhi t-taskhīr, wa-l-'aqli dhi t-ta'thīr, al-muḥīṭi bi-l-kulli wa-l-jumlati, wa-t-tafṣīli fī t-taṣwīri wa-t-taqdīr.

Ilāhī, as'aluka bi-dhātika llatī lā tudrak, wa-lā tutrak; wa-bi-aḥadiyyatika llatī man tawahhama fīha l-ma'iyyata fa-qad ashrak; wa-bi-iḥāṭatika llatī man ẓanna fī azaliyyatihā ghayran fa-qad afak; wa-min niẓāmi l-ikhlāṣ fa-qadi nfakk.

Yā man suliba 'anhu tanzīhan mā lam yakun fī qidamih. Yā man qadara 'alā kulli shay'in bi-iḥāṭatihi wa-'aẓamatih. Yā man abraza nūra wujūdihi min ẓulmati 'adamih. Yā man ṣawwara ashkhāṣa l-aflāki bi-mā awda'ahu min 'ilmihi fī qalamih. Yā man ṣarrafa aḥkāmahu bi-asrāri ḥikamih. Unādīka stighāthata ba'īdin li-qarīb, wa-aṭlubuka ṭalaba muḥibbin li-ḥabīb, wa-as'aluka su'āla muḍṭarrin li-mujīb.

As'aluka Llāhumma raf'a ḥijābi l-ghayb, wa-ḥalla 'iqāli r-rayb. Allāhumma, aḥyinī bika ḥayātan wājibā, wa-'allimnī ka-dhālika 'ilman muḥīṭan bi-asrāri l-ma'lūmāt. Wa-ftaḥ lī bi-qudratika kanza l-jannati wa-l-'arshi wa-dh-dhāt. Wa-mḥaqnī taḥta anwāri ṣ-ṣifāt. Wa-khalliṣnī bi-minnatika min jamī'i l-quyūdi l-mu'qidāt.

Subḥānaka, tanzīhan subbūḥun tanazzaha 'an simāti l-ḥudūthi wa-ṣifāti n-naqḍ; quddūsun taṭahhara min ashbāhi dh-dhammi wa-mūjibāti r-rafḍ. Subḥānaka, a'jazta kulla ṭālibin 'ani l-wuṣūli ilayka illā bik. Subḥānaka, lā ya'lamu man anta siwāk. Subḥānaka, mā aqrabaka ma'a taraffu'i 'ulāk.

Allāhumma, albisnī subḥata l-ḥamd, wa-raddinī bi-ridā'i l-'izz, wa-tawwijnī bi-tāji l-jalāli wa-l-majd. Wa-jarridnī 'an ṣifāti dhawāti l-hazli wa-l-jidd. Wa-khalliṣnī min quyūdi l-'addi wa-l-ḥadd, wa-mubāsharati l-khilāfi wa-n-naqīḍi wa-ḍ-ḍidd.

Ilāhī, 'adamī bika 'aynu l-wujūd, wa-baqā'ī ma'aka 'aynu l-'adam. Fa-abdilnī makāna tawahhumi wujūdī ma'aka bi-taḥqīqi 'adamī bik, wa-jma' shamlī bi-stihlākī fīk.

Lā ilāha illā anta, tanazzahta 'ani l-mathīl. Lā ilāha illā anta, ta'ālayta 'ani n-naẓīr. Lā ilāha illā anta, istaghnayta 'ani l-wazīri wa-l-mushīr. Lā ilāha illā anta, yā aḥadu yā ṣamad. Lā ilāha illā anta, bika l-wujūd, wa-laka s-sujūd, wa-anta l-ḥaqqu l-ma'būd. A'ūdhu bika minnī, wa-as'aluka zawālī 'annī. Wa-staghfiruka min baqiyyatin tuba''adu wa-tudannā, wa-tusammā wa-tukannā.

Anta l-wāḍi'u wa-r-rāfi', wa-l-mubdi'u wa-l-qāṭi', wa-l-mufarriqu wa-l-jāmi'. Yā wāḍi'u, yā rāfi'. Yā mubdi'u, yā qāṭi'. Yā mufarriqu, yā jāmi'. Al-'iyādha l-'iyādh, al-ghiyātha l-ghiyāth. Yā 'iyādhī, yā ghiyāthī. An-najāta n-najāt, al-malādha l-malādh. Yā man bihi najātī wa-malādhī.

As'aluka fī-mā sa'altuk, wa-atawassalu ilayk, bi-muqaddimati l-wujūdi l-awwal, wa-nūri l-'ilmi l-akmal, wa-rūḥi l-ḥayāti l-afḍal, wa-bisāṭi r-raḥmati l-azal, wa-samā'i l-khuluqi l-ajall; as-sābiqi bi-r-rūḥi wa-l-faḍl, wa-l-khātami bi-ṣ-ṣūrati wa-l-ba'th; wa-n-nūri bi-l-hidāyati wa-l-bayān, wa-r-raḥmati bi-l-'ilmi wa-t-tamkīni wa-l-amān, Muḥammadini l-muṣṭafā, wa-r-rasūli l-mujtabā. Ṣalla Llāhu 'alayhi wa-'alā ālihi wa-ṣaḥbihi, wa-sallama taslīman kathīran ilā yawmi d-dīn. *Wa-l-ḥamdu li-Llāhi rabbi l-'ālamīn.*

Tuesday Eve

BISMI LLĀHI R-RAḤMĀNI R-RAḤĪM

Ilāhī, anta sh-shadīdu l-baṭsh, al-alīmu l-akhdh, al-ʿaẓīmu l-qahr, al-mutaʿālī ʿani l-aḍdādi wa-l-andād, wa-l-munazzahu ʿani *ṣ-ṣāḥibati wa-l-awlād*. Shaʾnuka qahru l-aʿdāʾ, wa-qamʿu l-jabbārīn; tamkuru bi-man tashāʾu, wa-*anta khayru l-mākirīn*.

Asʾaluka bi-smika lladhī akhadhta bihi n-nawāṣī, wa-anzalta bihi *mina ṣ-ṣayāṣī, wa-qadhafta bihi r-ruʿba fī qulūbi* l-aʿdāʾ, wa-ashqayta bihi ahla sh-shaqāʾ, an tumiddanī bi-raqīqatin min raqāʾiqi smika sh-shadīd, tasrī fī quwāya l-kulliyyati wa-l-juzʾiyyati, ḥattā atamakkana min fiʿli mā urid. Fa-lā yaṣilu ilayya ẓulmu ẓālimin bi-sūʾ, wa-lā yasṭū ʿalayya mutakabbirun bi-jawr. Wa-jʿal ghaḍabī laka wa-fik, maqrūnan bi-ghaḍabika li-nafsik. Wa-*ṭmis* ʿalā wujūhi aʿdāʾī, wa-*msakhhum ʿalā makānatihim*, *wa-shdud ʿalā qulūbihim, wa-ḍrib* baynī wa-*baynahum bi-sūrin lahu bāb, bāṭinuhu fīhi r-raḥmatu wa-ẓāhiruhu min qibalihi l-ʿadhāb*. Innaka shadīdu l-baṭsh, alīmu l-akhdh, ʿaẓīmu l-ʿiqāb.

Wa-ka-dhālika akhdhu rabbika, idhā akhadha l-qurā wa-hiya ẓālimatun. Inna akhdhahu alīmun shadīd.

Rabbī, aghninī bika ʿamman siwāk, ghināʾan yughnīnī ghāyata l-ghināʾ, ʿan kulli ḥaẓẓin yadʿūnī ilā ẓāhiri khalq, aw bāṭini amr. Wa-ballighnī ghāyata taysīrī, wa-rfaʿnī ilā sidrati muntahāy. Wa-ashhidnī l-wujūda dawriyyā, wa-s-sayra kawriyyā, li-uʿāyina sirra t-tanzīli ila n-nihāyāt, wa-l-ʿawda ila l-bidāyāt, ḥattā yanqaṭiʿa l-kalām, wa-taskuna ḥarakatu l-lām, wa-tumḥā ʿannī nuqṭatu l-ghayn, wa-yaʿūda l-wāḥidu ila l-ithnayn.

Ilāhī, yassir ʿalayya bi-s-sirri lladhī yassartahu ʿalā kathīrin min awliyāʾik, taysīran yuʿjimu ʿannī ghayma ghināʾī, wa-ayyidnī fī dhālika kullihi bi-nūrin shaʿshaʿānī, *yakhṭafu baṣara* kulli ḥāsidin *mina l-jinni wa-l-ins.* Wa-habnī malakata l-ghalabati li-kulli maqām. Wa-aghninī bika ʿamman siwāk, ghināʾan yuthbitu faqrī ilayk. Innaka *l-ghaniyyu l-ḥamīd*, al-waliyyu l-majīd, al-karīmu r-rashīd. Wa-ṣalla Llāhu ʿalā sayyidinā Muḥammadin wa-ālihi wa-ṣaḥbihi ajmaʿīn, wa-sallama taslīman ilā yawmi d-dīn. *Wa-l-ḥamdu li-Llāhi rabbi l-ʿālamīn.*

Tuesday Morning

BISMI LLĀHI R-RAḤMĀNI R-RAḤĪM

Rabbī, adkhilnī fī *lujjati baḥri* aḥadiyyatik, wa-ṭamṭāmi *yammi* wāḥidiyyatik. Wa-qawwinī bi-quwwati saṭwati *sulṭāni* fardiyyatik, ḥattā akhruja ilā faḍā'i si'ati raḥmatik, wa-fī wajhī lama'ānu barqi l-qurbi min āthāri raḥmatik, mahīban bi-haybatik, 'azīzan bi-'ināyatik, mubajjalan mukarraman bi-ta'līmika wa-tazkiyatik. Wa-albisnī khila'a l-'izzati wa-l-qabūl. Wa-sahhil lī manāhija l-wuṣlati wa-l-wuṣūl. Wa-tawwijnī bi-tāji l-karāmati wa-l-waqār. Wa-allif baynī wa-bayna aḥbābika fī dāri d-dunyā wa-dāri l-qarār. Wa-rzuqnī min nūri smika, bi-nūri smika, saṭwatan wa-haybā, ḥattā tanqāda ilayya l-qulūbu wa-l-arwāḥ, wa-takhḍa'a ladayya n-nufūsu wa-l-ashbāḥ.

Yā man dhallat lahu riqābu l-jabābira, wa-khaḍa'at ladayhi a'nāqu l-akāsira. Yā mālika d-dunyā wa-l-ākhira. *Lā malja'a* wa-lā manja'a *minka illā ilayk*, wa-lā i'ānata illā mink, wa-lā ttikāla illā 'alayk. Idfa' 'annī kayda l-ḥāsidīn, wa-ẓulumāti sharri l-mu'ānidīn. Wa-ḥminī taḥta surādiqāti 'izzatik, yā akrama l-akramīn.

Ilāhī, ayyid ẓāhirī fī taḥṣīli marāḍīk. Wa-nawwir qalbī wa-sirrī li-l-iṭṭilā'i 'alā manāhiji masā'īk.

Ilāhī, kayfa aṣduru 'an bābika bi-khaybatin mink, wa-qad waradtuhu 'alā thiqatin bik. Wa-kayfa tu'ayyisunī min 'aṭā'ik, wa-qad amartanī bi-du'ā'ik. Wa-hā ana muqbilun 'alayk, multaji'un ilayk.

Ilāhī, bāʿid baynī wa-bayna aʿdāʾī, ka-mā bāʿadta bayna l-mashriqi wa-l-maghrib. Wa-*khṭif abṣārahum* wa-zalzil aqdāmahum, wa-dfaʿ ʿannī sharrahum wa-ḍarrahum bi-nūri qudsika wa-jalāli majdik. Fa-innaka anta Llāhu l-muʿṭī jalāʾila n-niʿam, al-mubajjalu l-mukarram, li-man nājāka bi-laṭāʾifi r-raʾfati wa-r-raḥma. Yā ḥayyu yā qayyūm. Yā kāshifa asrāri l-maʿārifi wa-l-ʿulūm. Wa-ṣalla Llāhu ʿalā sayyidinā Muḥammadin wa-ʿalā ālihi wa-ṣaḥbihi ajmaʿīn. *Subḥāna rabbika rabbi l-ʿizzati ʿammā yaṣifūn. Wa-salāmun ʿala l-mursalīn, wa-l-ḥamdu li-Llāhi rabbi l-ʿālamīn.*

Wednesday Eve

BISMI LLĀHI R-RAḤMĀNI R-RAḤĪM

Ilāhī, ismuka sayyidu l-asmā', wa-bi-yadika malakūtu l-arḍi wa-s-samā'. Anta *l-qā'imu* bi-kulli shay', wa-*'alā kulli shay'*. Thabata laka l-ghinā', wa-ftaqara ilā fayḍi jūdika l-aqdasi kullu mā siwāka l-huwa wa-l-anā. As'aluka bi-smika lladhī jama'ta bihi bayna l-mutaqābilāti wa-mutafarriqāti l-khalqi wa-l-amr. Wa-aqamta bihi ghayba kulli ẓāhir, wa-aẓharta bihi shahādata kulli ghā'ib, an tahaba lī ṣamadāniyyatan usakkinu bihā mutaḥarrika qudratik, ḥattā yataḥarraka fiyya kullu sākin, wa-yusakkana fiyya kullu mutaḥarrik. Fa-ajidanī qiblata kulli mutawajjih, wa-jāmi'a shatāti kulli mutafarriq, min ḥaythu smuka lladhī tawajjahat ilayhi wijhatī, wa-ḍmaḥallat 'indahu irādatī wa-kalimatī. Fa-yaqtabisa kullun minnī jadhwata hudan tāmmin tūḍiḥu lahu mā amma imāmatu Muḥammadini l-muṣṭafā, al-fardi lladhī lawlāhu lam tathbut anāniyyatu l-muqtabisi li-Mūsā. Yā man huwa huwa wa-lā anā.

As'aluka bi-kulli-smin istamadda min alifi l-ghaybi l-muḥīṭi bi-ḥaqīqati kulli mashhūd, an tushhidanī waḥdata kulli mutakaththir, fī bāṭini kulli ḥaqq, wa-kathrata kulli muwaḥḥid, fī ẓāhiri kulli ḥaqīqa; thumma waḥdata ẓ-ẓāhiri wa-l-bāṭin, ḥattā lā yakhfā 'alayya ghaybun ẓāhir, wa-lā yaghību 'annī khafiyyun bāṭin, wa-an tushhidani l-kulla fī l-kull, yā *man bi-yadihi malakūtu kulli shay'*. Innaka anta anta.

Quli Llāh, thumma dharhum fī khawḍihim yal'abūn.

Alif lām mīm. Allāhu lā ilāha illā huwa l-ḥayyu l-qayyūm.

Sayyidī, *salāmun ʿalayya* mink. Anta sanadī, sawāʾun ʿindaka sirrī wa-jahrī. Tasmaʿu nidāʾī, wa-tujību duʿāʾī. Maḥawta bi-nūrika ẓulmatī, wa-aḥyayta bi-rūḥika maytatī. Fa-anta rabbī, wa-bi-yadika samʿī wa-baṣarī wa-qalbī. Malakta jamīʿī, wa-sharrafta waḍīʿī. Wa-aʿlayta qadrī, wa-rafaʿta dhikrī. Tabārakta nūra l-anwār, wa-kāshifa l-asrār, wa-wāhiba l-aʿmār, wa-musbila l-astār. Tanazzahta fī sumuwwi jalālika ʿan simāti l-muḥdathāt. Wa-ʿalat rutbatu kamālika ʿan taṭarruqi l-muyūli ilayhā bi-sh-shahawāt, wa-n-naqāʾiṣi wa-l-āfāt. Wa-anārat bi-shuhūdi dhātika l-araḍūna wa-s-samāwāt. Laka l-majdu l-arfaʿ, wa-l-janābu l-awsaʿ, wa-l-ʿizzu l-amnaʿ.

Subbūḥun quddūsun rabbunā wa-rabbu l-malāʾikati wa-r-rūḥ. Munawwiru ṣ-ṣayāṣi l-muẓlimati, wa-l-jawāhiri l-mudlahimmati, wa-munqidhu l-gharqā, min baḥri l-hayūlā. *Aʿūdhu bika min ghāsiqin idhā waqab*, *wa-ḥāsidin* idha rtaqab.

Malīkī, unādīka wa-unājīk, munājāta ʿabdin kasīrin yaʿlamu annaka tasmaʿ, wa-yaʿtaqidu annaka tujīb, wāqifun bi-bābika waqfata *muḍṭarrin* lā yajidu *min dūnika wakīlā*.

Asʾaluka ilāhī bi-smika lladhī afaḍta bihi l-khayrāt, wa-anzalta bihi l-barakāt, wa-manaḥta bihi ahla sh-shukri z-ziyādāt, wa-akhrajta bihi mina ẓ-ẓulumāt, wa-nasakhta bihi ahla sh-shirki wa-d-danāʾāt, an tufīḍa ʿalayya min malābisi anwārika mā turaddu bihi ʿannī abṣāra l-aʿādī ḥāsiratan, wa-aydīhim khāsiratan. Wa-jʿal ḥaẓẓī minka ishrāqan yajlū lī kulla amrin khafī, wa-yakshifu lī ʿan kulli sirrin ʿalī, wa-yaḥriqu kulla shayṭānin ghawī.

Yā nūra n-nūr. Yā kāshifa kulli mastūr. Ilayka turjaʿu l-umūr, wa-bika tudfaʿu sh-shurūr. Yā rabbī, yā raḥīmu, yā ghafūr.

Wa-ṣalla Llāhu ʿalā sayyidinā Muḥammadin wa-ʿalā ālihi wa-ṣaḥbihi ajmaʿīn. *Wa-salāmun ʿala l-mursalīn, wa-l-ḥamdu li-Llāhi rabbi l-ʿālamīn.*

Wednesday Morning

BISMI LLĀHI R-RAḤMĀNI R-RAḤĪM

Rabbī, akrimnī bi-shuhūdi anwāri qudsik, wa-ayyidnī bi-ẓuhūri saṭwati sulṭāni unsik, ḥattā ataqallaba fī subuḥāti maʿārifi asmāʾik, taqalluban yuṭliʿunī ʿalā asrāri dharrāti wujūdī, fī ʿawālimi shuhūdī, li-ushāhida bihā mā awdaʿtahu fī ʿawālimi l-mulki wa-l-malakūt, wa-uʿāyina sarayāna sirri qudratika fī shawāhidi l-lāhūti wa-n-nāsūt.

Wa-ʿarrifnī maʿrifatan tāmmā, wa-ḥikmatan ʿāmmā, ḥattā lā yabqā maʿlūmun illā wa-aṭṭaliʿu ʿalā raqāʾiqi daqāʾiqihi l-munbasiṭati fi l-mawjūdāt. Wa-adfaʿu bihā ẓulmata l-ikrāhi l-māniʿati ʿan idrāki ḥaqāʾiqi l-āyāt. Wa-ataṣarrafu bihā fi l-qulūbi wa-l-arwāḥ, bi-muhayyijāti l-maḥabbati wa-l-widād, wa-r-rushdi wa-r-rashād.

Innaka anta l-muḥibbu l-maḥbūb, wa-ṭ-ṭālibu l-maṭlūb. Yā muqalliba l-qulūb. Wa-yā kāshifa l-kurūb. Wa-anta ʿallāmu l-ghuyūb, sattāru l-ʿuyūb, ghaffāru dh-dhunūb. Yā man lam yazal ghaffārā. Wa-yā man lam yazal sattārā. Yā ghaffāru, yā sattāru, yā ḥafīẓu, yā wāqī, yā dāfiʿu, yā muḥsinu, yā ʿaṭūfu, yā raʾūfu, yā laṭīfu, yā ʿazīzu, yā salām. Ighfir lī wa-sturnī wa-ḥfaẓnī. Wa-qinī wa-dfaʿ ʿannī. Wa-aḥsin ilayya wa-taʿaṭṭaf ʿalayya. Wa-rʾaf bī wa-lṭuf bī. Wa-aʿizzanī wa-sallimnī. Wa-lā tuʾākhidhnī bi-qabīḥi fiʿālī, wa-*lā tujāzīnī* bi-sūʾi aʿmālī. Wa-tadāraknī ʿājilan bi-luṭfika t-tāmm, wa-khāliṣi raḥmatika l-ʿāmm. Wa-lā tuḥwijnī ilā aḥadin siwāk. Wa-ʿāfinī wa-ʿfu ʿannī, wa-aṣliḥ lī shaʾnī kullah.

Lā ilāha illā anta, subḥānaka innī kuntu mina ẓ-ẓālimīn. Wa-anta arḥamu r-rāḥimīn. Wa-ṣalla Llāhu ʿalā sayyidinā Muḥammadin wa-ʿalā ālihi wa-ṣaḥbihi ajmaʿīn. *Wa-salāmun ʿala l-mursalīn, wa-l-ḥamdu li-Llāhi rabbi l-ʿālamīn.*

Thursday Eve

BISMI LLĀHI R-RAḤMĀNI R-RAḤĪM

Sayyidī, anta musabbibu l-asbābi wa-murattibuhā, wa-muṣarrifu l-qulūbi wa-muqallibuhā. As'aluka bi-l-ḥikmati llati qtaḍat tartība l-asbābi l-uwal, wa-ta'thīra l-a'lā fī l-asfal, an tushhidanī tartība l-asbābi ṣu'ūdan wa-nuzūlā, ḥattā ashhada l-bāṭina minhā bi-shuhūdi ẓ-ẓāhir, wa-l-awwala fī 'ayni l-ākhir, wa-alḥaẓa ḥikmata t-tartībi bi-shuhūdi l-murattib, wa-musabbaba l-asbābi masbūqan bi-l-musabbib, fa-lā aḥjuba 'ani l-'ayni bi-l-ghayn.

Ilāhī, alqi ilayya miftāḥa l-udhuni lladhī huwa *kahfu* l-ma'ārif, ḥattā anṭiqa fī kulli bidāyatin bi-smika l-badī'i lladhi ftataḥta bihi kulla *raqīmin masṭūr*. Yā man li-sumuwwi asmā'ihi yankhafiḍu kullu muta'ālī. Wa-kullun bik, wa-anta bi-lā naḥn. Anta mubdi'u kulli shay'in wa-bāri'uh. Fa-laka l-ḥamdu, yā bāri', 'alā kulli bidāyah. Wa-laka sh-shukru, yā bāqī, 'alā kulli nihāyah. Anta l-bā'ithu 'alā kulli khayr, bāṭinu l-bawāṭin, bālighu ghāyāti l-umūr, bāsiṭu r-rizqi li-l-'ālamīn. Bāriki Llāhumma lī wa-'alayya fī l-ākhirīn, ka-mā bārakta 'alā Muḥammadin wa-Ibrāhīm. *Innahu minka wa-ilayka, wa-innahu Bismi Llāhi r-raḥmāni r-raḥīm, badī'u s-samāwāti wa-l-arḍ, wa-idhā qaḍā amrā, fa-innamā yaqūlu lahu kun fa-yakūn.*

Ilāhī, anta th-thābitu qabla kulli thābit, wa-l-bāqī ba'da kulli nāṭiqin wa-ṣāmit. Lā ilāha illā anta, wa-lā mawjūda siwāk. Laka l-kibriyā'u wa-l-jabarūt, wa-l-'aẓamatu wa-l-malakūt. Taqharu l-jabbārīn, wa-tubīdu kayda ẓ-ẓālimīn; wa-tubaddidu shamla l-mulḥidīn, wa-tudhillu riqāba l-mutakabbirīn.

As'aluka yā ghāliba kulli ghālib, wa-yā mudrika kulli hārib, raddinī bi-ridā'i kibriyā'ik, wa-izāri ʿaẓamatik, wa-surādiqāti haybatik, wa-bi-mā warā'a dhālika kullihi mimmā lā yaʿlamuhu illā ant, an taksuwanī haybatan min haybatik, tajillu laha l-qulūbu wa-*takhshaʿu laha l-abṣār.* Wa-malliknī nāṣiyata *kulli jabbārin ʿanīd, wa-shayṭānin marīd*, nāṣiyatuhu bi-yadik. Wa-abqi ʿalayya dhulla l-ʿubūdiyyati fī dhālika kullih. Wa-aʿṣimnī mina z-zayghi wa-z-zalal, wa-ayyidnī fi l-qawli wa-l-ʿamal. Anta muthabbitu l-qulūb wa-kāshifu l-kurūb. Lā ilāha illā anta. Wa-ṣalla Llāhu ʿalā sayyidinā Muḥammadin wa-ʿalā ālihi wa-ṣaḥbihi ajmaʿīn. *Wa-l-ḥamdu li-Llāhi rabbi l-ʿālamīn.*

Thursday Morning

BISMI LLĀHI R-RAḤMĀNI R-RAḤĪM

Ilāhī, anta l-qā'imu bi-dhātik, wa-l-mutajallī bi-ṣifātik, wa-l-muḥīṭu bi-asmā'ik, wa-ẓ-ẓāhiru bi-afʿālik, wa-l-bāṭinu bi-mā lā yaʿlamuhu illā anta. Tawaḥḥadta fī jalālik, fa-anta l-wāḥidu l-aḥad, wa-tafarradta bi-l-baqā'i fi l-azali wa-l-abad. Anta, anta Llāhu l-munfaridu bi-l-waḥdāniyyati fī *iyyāk*, lā maʿaka ghayruka wa-lā fīka siwāk.

As'aluka Llāhumma l-fanā'a fī baqā'ik, wa-l-baqā'a bika lā maʿak. Lā ilāha illā anta. Ilāhī, ghayyibnī fī ḥuḍūrik, wa-afninī fī wujūdik, wa-stahliknī fī shuhūdik. Wa-qṭaʿ baynī wa-bayna l-qawāṭiʿi llatī taqṭaʿu baynī wa-baynak, wa-shghalnī bi-sh-shughli bika ʿan kulli shāghilin yashghalunī ʿank.

Lā ilāha illā anta. Ilāhī, anta l-mawjūdu l-ḥaqq, wa-ana l-maʿdūmu l-aṣl. Baqā'uka bi-dh-dhāt, wa-baqā'ī bi-l-ʿaraḍ. Ilāhī, fa-jud bi-wujūdika l-ḥaqqi ʿalā ʿadamiya l-aṣl, ḥattā akūna ka-mā kuntu ḥaythu lam akun, wa-anta ka-mā anta ḥaythu lam tazal.

Lā ilāha illā anta. Ilāhī, anta *l-faʿʿālu li-mā turīd*. Wa-ana ʿabdun laka *min baʿḍi l-ʿabīd*. Ilāhī, aradtanī wa-aradta minnī, fa-ana l-murādu wa-anta l-murīd. Fa-kun anta murādaka minnī, ḥattā takūnu anta l-murāda wa-ana l-murīd.

Lā ilāha illā anta. Ilāhī, anta l-bāṭinu fī kulli ghayb, wa-ẓ-ẓāhiru fī kulli ʿayn, wa-l-masmūʿu fī kulli khabarin sidqin wa-mayn, wa-l-maʿlūmu fī martabati l-wāḥidi wa-l-ithnayn. Tasammayta bi-asmā'i n-nuzūl. Fa-ḥtajabta ʿan lawāḥiẓi l-ʿuyūn, wa-khtafayta ʿan madāriki l-ʿuqūl.

Ilāhī, tajallayta bi-khaṣā'iṣi tajalliyāti ṣ-ṣifāt, fa-tanawwa'at marātibu l-mawjūdāt. Wa-tasammayta fī kulli martabatin bi-ḥaqā'iqi l-musammayāt. Wa-naṣabta shawāhida l-'uqūli 'alā daqā'iqi ḥaqā'iqi ghuyūbi l-ma'lūmāt. Wa-aṭlaqta sawābiqa l-arwāḥi fī mayādīni l-ma'ārifi l-ilāhiyya, fa-ḥārat thumma tāhat fī ishārāti laṭā'ifiha s-suryāniyya; fa-lammā ghayyabtahā 'ani l-kulliyyati wa-l-juz'iyya; wa-naqaltahā 'ani l-aniyyati wa-l-ayniyya; wa-salabtahā 'ani l-kammiyyati wa-l-māhiyya; wa-ta'arrafta lahā fī ma'ārifi t-tankīri bi-l-ma'ārifi dh-dhātiyya; wa-ḥarrartahā bi-muṭāla'āti r-rubūbiyyati fi l-mawāqifi l-ilāhiyya. Wa-asqaṭta 'anha l-bayn, 'inda raf'i ḥijābi-l-ghayn; fa-ntaẓamat bi-n-niẓāmi l-qadīm, fī silki *bismi Llāhi r-raḥmāni r-raḥīm.*

Ilāhī, kam unādīka fi n-nādī, wa-anta l-munādī li-n-nādī; wa-kam unājīka bi-munājāti l-munājī, wa-anta l-munājī li-n-nājī.

Ilāhī, idhā kāna l-waṣlu 'ayna l-qaṭ', wa-l-qurbu nafsa l-bu'd, wa-l-'ilmu mawḍi'a l-jahl, wa-l-ma'rifatu mustaqarra t-tankīr, fa-kayfa l-qaṣdu wa-min ayna s-sabīl.

Ilāhī, anta l-maṭlūbu warā'a kulli qāṣid, wa-l-iqrāru fī 'ayni l-jāḥid, wa-qurbu l-qurbi fi l-farqi l-mutabā'id. Wa-qad istawla l-wahmu 'ala l-fahm, fa-mani l-mub'adu wa-mani l-mutabā'id, wa-mani l-mus'adu wa-mani l-musā'id. Al-ḥusnu yaqūlu *iyyāka* aṭlaqah, wa-l-qubḥu yunādī *alladhī aḥsana kulla shay'in khalaqah.* Fa-l-awwalu ghāyatun yaqifu 'indaha s-sayr, wa-th-thānī ḥijābun bi-ḥukmi tawahhumi l-ghayr.

Ilāhī, matā yatakhallaṣu l-'aqlu min 'iqāli l-'awā'iq, wa-talḥaẓu lawāḥiẓu l-fikri maḥāsina l-ḥusnā min a'yuni l-ḥaqā'iq; wa-yanfakku l-fahmu 'an aṣli l-ifk, wa-yataḥallalu l-wahmu min awḥāli ḥibāli ishrāki sh-shirk; wa-yanjū t-taṣawwuru min farqi firaqi l-farq; wa-tatajarradu n-nafsu n-nafīsatu min khuluqi akhlāqi takhalluqāti l-khalq.

Ilāhī, anta lā tanfaʿuka ṭ-ṭāʿātu wa-lā taḍurruka l-maʿāṣī. Wa-bi-yadi qahri sulṭānika malakūtu l-qulūbi wa-n-nawāṣī. *Wa-ilayka yurjaʿu l-amru kulluh*, fa-lā nisbata li-ṭ-ṭāʾiʿi wa-l-ʿāṣī.

Ilāhī, anta lā yashghaluka shaʾnun ʿan shaʾn.

Ilāhī, anta lā yaḥṣuruka l-wujūbu wa-lā yaḥudduka l-imkān; wa-lā yaḥjubuka l-ibhāmu wa-lā yūḍiḥuka l-bayān.

Ilāhī, anta lā yurajjiḥuka d-dalīlu wa-lā yuḥaqqiquka l-burhān.

Ilāhī, anta l-abadu wa-l-azalu fī ḥaqqika siyyān.

Ilāhī, mā anta wa-mā ana, wa-mā huwa wa-mā hiya.

Ilāhī, a-fi l-kathrati aṭlubuk, am fi l-waḥda; wa-bi-l-amadi antaẓiru farajak, am bi-l-mudda; wa-lā ʿuddata li-ʿabdin dūnak, wa-lā ʿumda.

Ilāhī, baqāʾī bika, fī fanāʾī ʿannī, am fīka am bika, wa-fanāʾī ka-dhālika muḥaqqaqun bika, am mutawahhamun bī am bi-l-ʿaks, am huwa amrun mushtarak, wa-ka-dhālika baqāʾī fik.

Ilāhī, sukūtī kharasun yūjibu ṣ-ṣamam, wa-kalāmī ṣamamun yūjibu l-bakam; wa-l-ḥayratu fī kullin wa-lā ḥayra.

Bismi Llāh *ḥasbiya Llāh*; bismi Llāh *tawakkaltu ʿala Llāh*; bismi Llāh *saʾaltu mina Llāh*; bismi Llāh wa-*lā ḥawla wa-lā quwwata illā bi-Llāhi l-ʿaliyyi l-ʿaẓīm*.

Rabbanā, ʿalayka tawakkalnā, wa-ilayka anabnā, wa-ilayka l-maṣīr.

Allāhumma, innī asʾaluka bi-sirri amrik, wa-ʿaẓīmi qadrik, wa-iḥāṭati ʿilmik, wa-khaṣāʾiṣi irādatik, wa-taʾthīri qudratik, wa-nufūdhi samʿika wa-baṣarik, wa-qayyūmiyyati ḥayātik, wa-wujūbi dhātika wa-ṣifātik. Ya Allāh, ya Allāh, ya Allāh. Yā awwalu yā ākhir; yā ẓāhiru, yā bāṭin; yā nūru yā ḥaqqu yā mubīn.

Allāhumma, khaṣṣiṣ sirrī bi-asrāri waḥdāniyyatik, wa-qaddis rūḥī bi-qudsiyyati tajalliyāti ṣifātik, wa-ṭahhir qalbī bi-ṭahārati maʿārifi ilāhiyyatik.

Allāhumma, wa-ʿallim ʿaqlī min ʿulūmi ladunniyyatik; wa-khalliq nafsī bi-akhlāqi rubūbiyyatik; wa-ayyid ḥissī bi-madadi anwāri ḥaḍarāti nūrāniyyatik; wa-khalliṣ khulāṣata jawāhiri jismāniyyatī min quyūdi ṭ-ṭabʿi, wa-kathāfati l-ḥissi, wa-ḥaṣri l-makāni wa-l-kawn.

Allāhumma, wa-nqulnī min darakāti khalqī wa-khuluqī ilā darajāti ḥaqqika wa-ḥaqīqatik. Anta waliyyi wa-mawlāy, wa-bika mamātī wa-maḥyāy. *Iyyāka naʿbudu wa-iyyāka nastaʿīn.* Unẓuri Llāhumma ilayya naẓratan tanẓimu bihā jamīʿa aṭwārī; wa-tuṭahhiru bihā sarīrata asrārī. Wa-tarfaʿu bihā fi l-malaʾi l-aʿlā arwāḥa adhkārī; wa-tuqawwī bihā midāda anwārī.

Allāhumma, ghayyibnī ʿan jamīʿi khalqik, wa-jmaʿnī ʿalayka bi-ḥaqqik. Wa-ḥfaẓnī bi-shuhūdi taṣarrufāti amrika fī ʿawālimi farqik.

Allāhumma, bika tawassaltu, wa-ilayka tawajjahtu, wa-minka saʾaltu, wa-fīka lā fī shayʾin siwāka raghibtu. Lā asʾalu minka siwāk, wa-lā aṭlubu minka illā iyyāk.

Allāhumma, wa-atawassalu ilayka fī qabūli dhālika bi-l-wasīlati l-ʿuẓmā, wa-l-faḍīlati l-kubrā, wa-l-ḥabībi l-adnā, wa-l-waliyyi l-mawlā, Muḥammadini l-muṣṭafā, wa-ṣ-ṣafiyyi l-murtaḍā, wa-n-nabiyyi l-mujtabā. Wa-bihi asʾaluka an tuṣalliya ʿalayhi ṣalātan abadiyyatan daymūmiyyatan qayyūmiyyatan ilāhiyyatan rabbāniyyā, bi-ḥaythu tushhidunī fī dhālika ʿayna kamālih, wa-tastahlikunī fī shuhūdi maʿārifi dhātih. Wa-ʿalā ālihi wa-ṣaḥbihi ka-dhālik, fa-anta waliyyu dhālik. Wa-*lā ḥawla wa-lā quwwata illā bi-Llāhi l-ʿaliyyi l-ʿaẓīm. Wa-l-ḥamdu li-Llāhi rabbi l-ʿālamīn.*

Friday Eve

BISMI LLĀHI R-RAḤMĀNI R-RAḤĪM

Ilāhī, kullu l-ābā'i l-'ulwiyyati 'abīduk, wa-anta r-rabbu 'ala l-iṭlāq. Jama'ta bayna l-mutaqābilāt, fa-anta l-jalīla l-jamīl. Lā ghāyata li-btihājika bi-dhātik, idh lā ghāyata li-shuhūdika mink. Anta ajallu min shuhūdinā wa-akmal, wa-a'lā mimmā naṣifuka bihi wa-ajmal. Ta'ālayta fī jalālika 'an simāti l-muḥdathāt, wa-taqaddasa jamāluka l-'aliyyu 'an muwāqa'ati l-muyūli ilayhi bi-sh-shahawāt.

As'aluka bi-s-sirri lladhī jama'ta bihi bayna l-mutaqābilāt, an tajma'a 'alayya mutafarriqa amrī, jam'an yushhidunī waḥdata wujūdī. Wa-ksinī ḥullata jamālik, wa-tawwijnī bi-tāji jalālik, ḥattā takhḍa'a liya n-nufūsu l-bashariyya, wa-tanqāda ilayya l-qulūbu l-abiyya, wa-tanbasiṭa ilayya l-asrāru l-aqdasiyya. Wa-a'li qadrī 'indaka 'uluwwan yankhafiḍu lī bihi kullu muta'āl, wa-yadhillu lī bihi kullu 'azīz. Wa-khudh bi-nāṣiyatī ilayk, wa-mallikni nāṣiyata kulli dhī rūḥin nāṣiyatuhu bi-yadik.

Wa-j'al lī lisāna ṣidqin fī khalqika wa-amrik. Wa-mla'nī minka, wa-ḥfaẓnī *fī barrika wa-baḥrik. Wa-akhrijnī min qaryati* ṭ-ṭab'i *ẓ-ẓālimi ahluhā*, wa-a'tiqnī min riqqi l-akwān. Wa-j'al lī minka burhānan yūrithu amānā, wa-lā taj'al li-ghayrika 'alayya sulṭānā. Wa-j'al ghinā'ī fi l-faqri ilayka 'an kulli maṭlūb, wa-ṣḥabnī bi-'ināyatika 'an kulli marghūb. Anta wijhatī wa-jāhī, wa-ilayka l-marji'u wa-t-tanāhī. Tajburu l-kasīra wa-taksiru l-jabbārīn; wa-tujīru l-khā'ifīn wa-tukhīfu ẓ-ẓālimīn. Laka l-majdu l-arfa', wa-t-tajalli l-ajma', wa-l-ḥijābu l-amna'. Subḥānaka lā ilāha illā anta, anta *ḥasbī wa-ni'ma l-wakīl.*

Wa-ka-dhālika akhdhu rabbika idhā akhadha l-qurā wa-hiya ẓālimatun, inna akhdhahu alīmun shadīd. Fa-ntaqamnā mina lladhīna ajramū wa-kāna ḥaqqan ʿalaynā naṣru l-muʾminīn.

Allāhumma, yā khāliqa l-mahklūqāt, wa-muḥyi l-amwāt, wa-jāmiʿa sh-shitāt, wa-mufīḍa l-anwāri ʿala dh-dhawāt. Laka l-mulku l-awsaʿ, wa-l-janābu l-arfaʿ. Al-arbābu ʿabīduk, wa-l-mulūku khadamatuk, wa-l-aghniyāʾu fuqarāʾuk. Wa-anta l-ghaniyyu bi-dhātika ʿamman siwāk.

Asʾaluka bi-smika lladhī *khalaqta bihi kulla shayʾin fa-qaddartahu taqdīrā*, wa-manaḥta bihi man shiʾta *jannatan wa-ḥarīrā*, wa-khilāfatan *wa-mulkan kabīrā*, an tudhhiba ḥirṣī, wa-tukmila naqṣī; wa-an tufīḍa ʿalayya min malābisi naʿmāʾik, wa-an tuʿallimanī min asmāʾik, mā yaṣluḥu li-l-idhni wa-l-ilqāʾ. Wa-mlaʾ bāṭinī khashyatan wa-raḥmā, wa-ẓāhirī haybatan wa-ʿaẓamā, ḥattā takhāfanī qulūbu l-aʿdāʾ, wa-tartāḥu ilayya arwāḥu l-awliyāʾ, *yakhāfūna rabbahum min fawqihim, wa-yafʿalūna mā yuʾmarūn.*

Rabbī, hab lī istiʿdādan kāmilan li-qabūli fayḍika l-aqdas, li-akhlafaka fī bilādik, wa-adfaʿa bihi sakhaṭaka ʿan ʿibādik. Fa-innaka tastakhlifu man tashāʾ, wa-anta *ʿalā kulli shayʾin qadīr*. Wa-anta *l-khabīru l-baṣīr*. Wa-ṣalla Llāhu ʿalā sayyidinā Muḥammadin wa-ʿalā ālihi wa-ṣaḥbihi wa-sallam. *Wa-huwa ḥasbī wa-niʿma l-wakīl.*

Friday Morning

BISMI LLĀHI R-RAḤMĀNI R-RAḤĪM

Rabbī, raqqinī fī madāriji l-maʿārif; wa-qallibnī fī aṭwāri asrāri l-ḥaqāʾiq; wa-ḥjubnī fī surādiqāti ḥifẓik, wa-maknūni sirri sitrik, ʿan wurūdi l-khawāṭiri llatī lā talīqu bi-subuḥāti jalālik.

Rabbī, aqimnī bika fī kulli shaʾn, wa-ashhidnī luṭfaka fī kulli qāṣin wa-dān. Wa-ftaḥ ʿayna baṣīratī fī qaḍāʾi sāḥati t-tawḥīd, li-ashhada qiyāma l-kulli bika shuhūdan yaqṭaʿu naẓarī ʿan kulli mawjūd. Yā dha l-faḍli wa-l-jūd.

Rabbī, afiḍ ʿalayya min biḥāri tajrīdi alifi dh-dhāti l-aqdas, mā yaqṭaʿu ʿannī kulla ʿalāqatin tuʿjimu idrākī, wa-tughliqu dūnī bāba maṭlabī. Wa-asbigh ʿalayya min hayūlā nuqṭatiha l-kulliyya, al-bārizati min malakūti ghaybi dhātik, mā amuddu bihi ḥurūfa l-akwān, maḥfūẓan fī dhālika mina n-naqṣi wa-sh-shayn. *Yā man wasiʿa kulla shayʾin raḥmatan wa-ʿilmā, yā rabba l-ʿālamīn.*

Rabbī, ṭahhirnī ẓāhiran wa-bāṭinan min lawthi l-aghyār, wa-l-wuqūfi ʿala l-aṭwār, bi-fayḍin min ṭuhūri qudsik. Wa-ghayyibnī ʿanhum bi-shuhūdi bawāriqi unsik. Wa-ṭṭaliʿnī ʿalā ḥaqāʾiqi l-ashyāʾ, wa-daqāʾiqi l-ashkāl. Wa-asmiʿnī nuṭqa l-akwāni bi-ṣarīḥi tawḥīdika fi l-ʿawālimi kulliha. Wa-qābil mirʾātī bi-tajallin tammin min jawāhiri asmāʾi jalālika wa-qahrik. Fa-lā yaqaʿu ʿalayya baṣaru jabbārin mina l-insi wa-l-jinn, illa nʿakasa ʿalayhi min shuʿāʿi dhālika l-jawhari mā yuḥriqu *nafsahu l-ammārata bi-s-sūʾ*; wa-tarudduhu dhalīlā, *wa-yanqalibu ʿannī baṣarahu khāsiʾan kalīlā*. Yā man *ʿanat lahu l-wujūhu* wa-khaḍaʿat lahu r-riqāb, yā rabba l-arbāb.

Rabbī, wa-ab'idnī 'ani l-qawāṭi'i llatī taqṭa'unī 'an ḥaḍarāti qurbik. Wa-slubnī mā lā yalīqu min ṣifātī bi-ghalabati anwāri ṣifātik. Wa-aziḥ ẓulma ṭab'ī wa-bashariyyatī bi-tajallī bāriqatin min bawāriqi nūri dhātik. Wa-mdudnī bi-quwwatin malakiyya, aqharu bihā ma stawlā 'alayya min aṭ-ṭabā'i'i d-daniyya, wa-l-akhlāqi r-radiyya. Wa-mḥu min lawḥi fikrī ashkāla l-akwān. Wa-athbit fīhi bi-yadi 'inayatik, sirra ḥirzi qurbik, as-sābiqi l-maknūn, bayna l-kāfi wa-n-nūn. Yā nūra n-nūr, yā mufīḍa l-kulli min fayḍihi l-midrār. Yā quddūs, yā ṣamad, yā ḥafīẓ, yā laṭīf, yā rabba l-'ālamīn.

Wa-ṣalla Llāhu 'alā sayyidinā Muḥammadin wa-'alā ālihi wa-ṣaḥbihi ajma'īn. *Wa-l-ḥamdu li-Llāhi rabbi l-'ālamīn.*

Saturday Eve

BISMI LLĀHI R-RAḤMĀNI R-RAḤĪM

Sayyidī, dāma baqā'uk, wa-nafadha fī l-khalqi qaḍā'uk. Wa-taqaddasta fī 'ulāk, wa-ta'ālayta fī qudsik. *Lā ya'uduka ḥifẓu* kawn, wa-lā yakhfā 'anka kashfu 'ayn. Tad'ū man tashā'u ilayk, wa-tadullu bika 'alayk. Fa-laka l-ḥamdu d-dā'im, wa-d-dawāmu l-amjad. As'aluka waqtan ṣāfiyan bi-mā turīd, bi-mu'āmalatin lā'iqatin takūnu ghāyatuhā qurbak, min natā'iji l-a'māli mawqūfatan 'alā riḍwānik. Wa-hab lī sirran ẓāhiran, yakshifu lī 'an ḥaqā'iqi l-a'māl. Wa-khṣuṣnī bi-ḥikmatin ma'ahā ḥukm, wa-ishāratin yaṣḥabuhā fahm. Innaka waliyyu man tawallāk, wa-mujību man da'āk.

Ilāhī, dāma baqā'u na'mā'ika 'alayya, fa-adim mushāhadatik. Wa-ashhidnī dhātī min ḥaythu anta, lā min ḥaythu ana, ḥattā akūna bika wa-lā ana. Wa-hab lī min ladunka 'ilman tanqādu ilayya fīhi kullu rūḥin 'ālima. Innaka anta l-'alīmu l-'allām, *tabāraka smu rabbika dhu l-jalāli wa-l-ikrām.*

Wa-'indahu mafātiḥu l-ghayb, lā ya'lamuhā illā anta.

Rabbī, afiḍ 'alayya shu'ā'an min nūrika yakshifu lī 'an kulli mastūrin fiyya, ḥattā ushāhida wujūdī kāmilan min ḥaythu anta, lā min ḥaythu ana. Fa-ataqarrabu ilayka bi-maḥwi ṣifatī minnī, ka-mā taqarrabta ilayya, bi-ifāḍati nūrika 'alayya.

Rabbī, al-imkānu ṣifatī, wa-l-'adamu māddatī; wa-l-faqru muqawwimī, wa-wujūduka 'illatī; wa-qudratuka fā'ilī, wa-anta ghāyatī. Ḥasbī minka 'ilmuka bi-jahlī. Anta ka-mā a'lam, wa-fawqa mā a'lam. Wa-anta ma'a kulli shay', wa-laysa ma'aka shay'.

Qaddarta l-manāzila li-s-sayr; wa-rattabta l-marātiba li-n-naf'i wa-ḍ-ḍayr; wa-athbatta minhāja l-khayr. Fa-naḥnu fī dhālika kullihi bik, wa-anta bi-lā naḥn. Fa-anta l-khayru l-maḥḍ, wa-l-jūdu ṣ-ṣirf, wa-l-kamālu l-muṭlaq.

As'aluka bi-smika lladhī afaḍta bihi n-nūra 'ala l-qawābil, wa-maḥawta bihi min ẓulmati l-ghawāsiq, an tamla'a wujūdī nūran min nūrik, alladhī huwa māddatu kulli nūr, wa-ghāyatu kulli maṭlūb, ḥattā lā yakhfā 'alayya shay'un mimmā awda'tahu fī dhāti wujūdī. Wa-hab lī lisāna ṣidq, mu'abbiran 'an shuhūdi ḥaqq. Wa-khṣuṣnī min *jawāmi'i l-kalim*, bi-mā taḥṣulu bihi l-ibānatu wa-l-balāgh. Wa-'ṣimnī fī kulli kalimatin min da'wā mā laysa lī bi-ḥaqq. *Wa-j'alnī 'alā baṣīratin* minka, *ana wa-man ittaba'anī.*

Allāhumma, innī a'ūdhu bika min qawlin yūjibu ḥayrā, aw yu'qibu fitnā, aw yūhimu shubhā. Minka tutalaqqa l-kalim, wa-'anka tu'khadhu l-ḥikam. Anta mumsiku s-samā', wa-mu'allimu l-asmā'. Lā ilāha illā anta, al-wāḥidu l-*aḥad*, al-fardu *ṣ-ṣamad*, alladhī *lam yalid wa-lam yūlad, wa-lam yaku(l) lahu kufuwan aḥad.* Wa-ṣalla Llāhu 'alā sayyidinā Muḥammadin wa-'alā ālihi wa-ṣaḥbihi 'ajma'īn. *Wa-l-ḥamdu li-Llāhi rabbi l-'ālamīn.*

Saturday Morning

BISMI LLĀHI R-RAḤMĀNI R-RAḤĪM

Wa-man yaʿtaṣimu bi-Llāhi fa-qad hudiya ilā ṣirāṭin mustaqīm.

Al-ḥamdu li-Llāhi lladhī aḥallanī ḥimā luṭfi Llāh. Al-ḥamdu li-Llāhi lladhī anzalanī jannata raḥmati Llāh. Al-ḥamdu li-Llāhi lladhī ajlasanī fī maqāmi maḥabbati Llāh. Al-ḥamdu li-Llāhi lladhī adhāqanī min mawāʾidi madadi Llāh. Al-ḥamdu li-Llāhi lladhī wahaba lī biṭāqata l-iḍāfati li-ṣṭifāʾi Llāh. Al-ḥamdu li-Llāhi lladhī saqānī min mawāridi wāridi wafāʾi Llāh. Al-ḥamdu li-Llāhi lladhī kasānī ḥulala ṣidqi l-ʿubūdiyyati li-Llāh. Kullu dhālika ʿalā *mā farraṭtu fī janbi Llāh*, wa-ḍayyaʿtu min ḥuqūqi Llāh, fa-*dhālika l-faḍlu mina Llāh, wa-man yaghfiru dh-dhunūba illa Llāh.*

Ilāhī, inʿāmuka ʿalayya bi-l-ījād, min ghayri jihādin wa-la-jtihād. Wa-jarraʾta maṭāmiʿī min karamika ʿalā bulūghi l-murād, min ghayri stiḥqāqin lī wa-la stiʿdād. Fa-asʾaluka bi-wāḥidi l-āḥād, wa-mashhūdi l-ashhād, salāmata minḥati l-widād, min miḥnati l-biʿād; wa-maḥwa ẓulmati l-ʿinād, bi-nūri shamsi r-rashād; wa-fatḥa abwābi s-sadād, bi-aydī madadi *inna Llāha laṭīfun bi-l-ʿibād.*

Rabbī, asʾaluka fanāʾa aniyyati wujūdī, wa-baqāʾa amniyyati shuhūdī, wa-firāqa bayniyyati shāhidī wa-mashhūdī, bi-jamʿi ʿayniyyati mawjūdī li-wujūdī.

Sayyidī, sallim ʿubūdiyyatī bi-ḥaqqika min ʿamāʾi wahmi ruʾyati l-aghyār. Wa-alḥiq bī kalimataka s-sābiqata li-l-muṣṭafayna l-akhyār. Wa-ghlib ʿalā amrī bi-khtiyārika fi l-awṭāri wa-l-aṭwār. Wa-nṣurnī bi-t-tawḥīdi wa-l-istiwāʾi fi l-ḥarakati wa-l-istiqrār.

Ḥabībī, as'aluka sarī'a l-wiṣāl, wa-badī'a l-jamāl, wa-manī'a l-jalāl, wa-rafī'a l-kamāl, fī kulli ḥālin wa-ma'āl.

Yā man huwa huwa hū; yā hū, wa-yā man laysa illā hū. As'aluka l-ghayba l-aṭlas, bi-l-'ayni l-aqdas, wa-r-rūḥa l-anfas, *fī l-layli idhā 'as'as, wa-s-subḥi idhā tanaffas. Innahu la-qawlu rasūlin karīm, dhī quwwatin 'inda dhi l-'arshi makīn, muṭā'in thamma amīn, bi-lisānin 'arabiyyin mubīn. Wa-innahu la-tanzīlu rabbi l-'ālamīn*, ḥukmun muḥkamu l-amri bi-rūḥihi l-mutalawwini fī ṣiyaghi t-tabyīn, bi-ṣibghi t-tamkīn.

Wa-as'aluka Llāhumma ḥamla dhālika li-dhātī, 'alā yadi nasīmi ḥayātī, bi-arwāḥi taḥiyyātī, fī ṣalawātika ṭ-ṭayyibāt, wa-taslīmātika d-dā'imāt, 'alā wasīlati ḥuṣūli l-maṭālib, wa-wuṣlati wuṣūli l-ḥabā'ib, wa-'alā kulli mansūbin ilayhi fī kulli l-marātib. Innāhu *'alā l-ḥaqqi l-mubīn*, wa-j'alnā min khawaṣṣihim, āmīn.

Wa-ṣalla Llāhu 'alā sayyidinā Muḥammadin wa-ālihi wa-ṣaḥbihi ajma'īn. *Subḥāna rabbika rabbi l-'izzati 'ammā yaṣifūn, wa-salāmun 'ala l-mursalīn, wa-l-ḥamdu li-Llāhi rabbi l-'ālamīn.*

THE PRAYERS

ARABIC TEXT

أَوْرَادُ ٱلأُسْبُوعِ
لِلشَّيْخِ ٱلْأَكْبَرِ مُحْيِي ٱلدِّينِ

مُحَمَّدِ بْنِ عَلِيٍّ بْنِ مُحَمَّدٍ بْنِ ٱلْعَرَبِيِّ ٱلطَّائِيِّ ٱلْحَاتِمِي

Arabic text edited by

Stephen Hirtenstein and Pablo Beneito

أَوْرَادُ ٱلأُسْبُوعِ

هٰذِهِ أَوْرَادُ ٱللَّيَالِي ٱلسَّبْعَةِ وَٱلْأَيَّامِ ٱلسَّبْعَةِ عَلَى ٱلتَّرْتِيبِ تَأْلِيفُ سَيِّدِي ٱلشَّيْخِ ٱلْأَكْبَرِ وَٱلْكِبْرِيتِ ٱلأَحْمَرِ ٱلْقُطْبِ ٱلْكَبِيرِ وَٱلْوَلِيِّ ٱلشَّهِيرِ ٱلشَّيْخِ مُحَمَّدٍ مُحْيِي ٱلدِّينِ بْنِ ٱلْعَرَبِيِّ – قَدَّسَ ٱللّٰهُ رُوحَهُ وَنوَّرَ ضَرِيحَهُ – آمِين.

ٱلْمُقَدِّمَة

بِسْمِ ٱللّٰهِ ٱلرَّحْمٰنِ ٱلرَّحِيمِ. ٱلْحَمْدُ لِلّٰهِ عَلَى حُسْنِ تَوْفِيقِهِ * وأَسأَلُهُ ٱلْهِدَايَةَ إِلَى سُلُوكِ[١] طَرِيقِهِ * وَإِلْهَامًا عَلَى تَحْقِيقِهِ * وَقَلْبًا مُوقِنًا إِلَى تَصْدِيقِهِ * وَعَقْلاً نُورَانِيًّا بِعِنَايَةِ تَسْبِيقِهِ * وَرُوحًا رُوحَانِيًّا إِلَى تَشْوِيقِهِ[٢] * وَ﴿نَفْسًا مُطْمَئِنَّةً﴾ مِنَ ٱلْجَهْلِ وَتَطْبِيقِهِ * وَفَهْمًا عَالِمًا[٣] بِأَلْمَاعِ ٱلْفِكْرِ وَبَرِيقِهِ * وَسِرًّا زَاهِرًا بِسَلْسَبِيلِ ٱلْفَتْحِ وَرَحِيقِهِ * وَلِسَانًا مَبْسُوطًا بِبِسَاطِ ٱلْبَسْطِ وَتَرْوِيقِهِ * وَفِكْرًا سَامِيًا عَنْ زُخْرُفِ ٱلْفَانِي وَتَزْوِيقِهِ * وَبَصِيرَةً تُشَاهِدُ سِرَّ ٱلْوُجُودِ فِي تَغْرِيبِ ٱلْكَوْنِ وَتَشْرِيقِهِ * وَحَوَاسًّا سَالِمَةً بِمَجَارِي ٱلرَّوْحِ وَتَطْرِيقِهِ[٤] * وَفِطْرَةً طَاهِرَةً مِنْ زُكَامِ ٱلنَّقْصِ وَتَطْبِيقِهِ * وَقَرِيحَةً مُنْقَادَةً بِزِمَامِ ٱلشَّرْعِ وَتَوْثِيقِهِ * وَوَقْتًا مُسَاعِدًا لِجَمْعِهِ وَتَفْرِيقِهِ * وَصَلَاةً وَسَلَامًا عَلَى مُحَمَّدٍ وَآلِهِ وَفَرِيقِهِ * وَٱلْخُلَفَاءِ مِنْ بَعْدِهِ وَٱلتَّابِعِينَ سُلُوكَ طَرِيقِهِ * وَسَلَّمَ تَسْلِيمًا. أَمَّا بَعْدُ فَإِنَّ ٱلْمُرَادَ هُوَ ٱللّٰهُ فِي ٱلْوُجُودِ وَٱلشُّهُودِ * وَهُوَ ٱلْمَقْصُودُ * وَلَا إِنْكَارَ وَلَا جُحُودَ * وَ﴿هُوَ حَسْبِيَ وَنِعْمَ ٱلْوَكِيلُ﴾.[٥]

١. N - سُلُوكِ .
٢. R1 = بِتَشْوِيقِه ; N = تَشْرِيقِه .
٣. P, N = لَامِعًا .
٤. R1 = وَطَرِيقِه .
٥. *Muqaddima* included in P, N, R1 (margin); missing in all other mss.

وِرْدُ لَيْلَةِ ٱلْأَحَدِ

بِسْمِ ٱللّٰهِ ٱلرَّحْمٰنِ ٱلرَّحِيمِ. إِلٰهِي أَنْتَ ٱلْمُحِيطُ بِغَيْبِ كُلِّ شاهِدٍ٭ وَٱلْمُسْتَوْلِي عَلَى بَاطِنِ كُلِّ ظَاهِرٍ٭ أَسْأَلُكَ بِوَجْهِكَ[6] ٱلَّذِي سَجَدَتْ لَهُ ٱلْجِبَاهُ٭ وَ﴿عَنَتْ لَهُ ٱلْوُجُوهُ﴾٭ وَبِنُورِكَ ٱلَّذِي ﴿شَخَصَتْ إِلَيْهِ ٱلْأَبْصَارُ﴾٭ أَنْ تَهْدِيَنِي إِلَى صِرَاطِكَ ٱلْخَاصِّ٭ هِدَايَةً تَصْرِفُ بِهَا وَجْهِي إِلَيْكَ عَمَّنْ سِوَاكَ٭ يَا مَنْ هُوَ ٱلْهُوَ ٱلْمُطْلَقُ٭ وأَنَا ٱلْهُوَ ٱلْمُقَيَّدُ٭[7] لَا هُوَ إِلَّا هُو. إِلٰهِي شَأْنُكَ قَهْرُ ٱلْأَعْدَاءِ وَقَمْعُ ٱلْجَبَّارِينَ٭ أَسْأَلُكَ مَدَداً مِنْ عِزَّتِكَ[8] تَمْنَعُنِي مِنْ كُلِّ مَنْ أَرَادَنِي بِسُوءٍ٭ حَتَّى أَكُفَّ بِهِ أَكُفَّ ٱلْبَاغِينَ٭ وَ﴿أَقْطَعَ بِهِ دَابِرَ ٱلظَّالِمِينَ﴾٭ وَمَلِّكْنِي نَفْسِي مُلْكًا يُقَدِّسُنِي عَنْ كُلِّ خُلُقٍ سَيِّءٍ٭ وَٱهْدِنِي إِلَيْكَ يَا هَادِي٭ إِلَيْكَ مَرْجِعُ كُلِّ شَيْءٍ٭ وَأَنْتَ ﴿بِكُلِّ شَيْءٍ مُحِيطٌ﴾. ﴿وَهُوَ ٱلْقَاهِرُ فَوْقَ عِبَادِهِ وَهُوَ ٱلْحَكِيمُ[9] ٱلْخَبِيرُ﴾. إِلٰهِي أَنْتَ ﴿ٱلْقَائِمُ عَلَى كُلِّ نَفْسٍ﴾٭ وَٱلْقَيُّومُ عَلَى كُلِّ مَعْنًى وَحِسٍّ٭ قَدَرْتَ فَقَهَرْتَ٭ وَعَلِمْتَ فَقَدَّرْتَ٭ فَلَكَ ٱلْقُدْرَةُ وَٱلْقَهْرُ٭ وَبِيَدِكَ ٱلْخَلْقُ وَٱلْأَمْرُ٭ وَأَنْتَ مَعَ كُلِّ شَيْءٍ

٦. P = بِنُورِ وَجْهِكَ ; P1 + ٱلْكَرِيمِ .

٧. P, P1 + يَا مَن .

٨. G = مِنْ عِنْدَكَ ; R1 = مِنْ عَزْمِكَ .

٩. I, P, W = ٱللَّطِيفُ .

قُرْبَ ٱلْقُرْبِ[١٠] وَمَوْلَاهُ* وَبِٱلْإِحَاطَةِ مُدَبِّرُهُ وَهُدَاهُ. **إِلٰهِي** إِنِّي أَسْأَلُكَ مَدَدًا مِنْ أَسْمَائِكَ ٱلْقَهْرِيَّةِ* تُقَوِّي بِهَا قُوَايَ ٱلْقَلْبِيَّةِ وَٱلْقَالِبِيَّةِ* حَتَّى لَا يَلْقَانِي صَاحِبُ قَلْبٍ إِلَّا ﴿ٱنْقَلَبَ عَلَى عَقِبَيْهِ﴾ مَقْهُورًا. وَأَسْأَلُكَ **إِلٰهِي** لِسَانًا نَاطِقًا* وَقَوْلًا صَادِقًا* وَفَهْمًا لَائِقًا* وَسِرًّا ذَائِقًا[١١]* وَقَلْبًا قَابِلًا* وَعَقْلًا عَاقِلًا* وَفِكْرًا مُشْرِقًا* وَشَوْقًا مُقْلِقًا* وَطَرْفًا مُطْرِقًا* وَتَوْقًا[١٢] مُحْرِقًا[١٣]* وَهَبْ لِي يَدًا قَادِرَةً[١٤]* وَقُوَّةً قَاهِرَةً* وَ﴿نَفْسًا مُطْمَئِنَّةً﴾* وَجَوَارِحَ لِطَاعَتِكَ لَيِّنَةً* وَقَدِّسْنِي لِلْقُدُومِ عَلَيْكَ* وَٱرْزُقْنِي ٱلتَّقَدُّمَ إِلَيْكَ. **إِلٰهِي** هَبْ لِي قَلْبًا أُقْبِلُ بِهِ عَلَيْكَ[١٥] بِفَقْرِ ٱلْفُقَرَاءِ* يَقُودُهُ ٱلشَّوْقُ* وَيَسُوقُهُ ٱلتَّوْقُ* زَادُهُ ٱلْخَوْفُ وَرَفِيقُهُ ٱلْقَلَقُ* وَقَصْدُهُ ٱلْقُرْبُ وَٱلْقَبُولُ[١٦]* وَعِنْدَكَ زُلْفَى ٱلْقَاصِدِينَ* وَمُنْتَهَى رَغْبَةِ ٱلطَّالِبِينَ[١٧]. **إِلٰهِي** أَلْقِ عَلَيَّ ٱلسَّكِينَةَ وَٱلْوَقَارَ* وَجَنِّبْنِي ٱلْعَظَمَةَ وَٱلْإِسْتِكْبَارَ* وَأَقِمْنِي فِي مَقَامِ ٱلْقَبُولِ بِٱلْإِنَابَةِ* وَقَابِلْ قَوْلِي بِٱلْإِجَابَةِ. **رَبِّ** قَرِّبْنِي إِلَيْكَ قُرْبَ ٱلْعَارِفِينَ[١٨]* وَقَدِّسْنِي عَنْ[١٩] عَلَائِقِ ٱلطَّبْعِ وَأَزِلْ مِنِّي عَلَقَ دَمِ ٱلذَّمِّ

١٠. V = قَرِيبَ ٱلْمُتَقَرِّب ; R1 = بِٱلْقُرْبِ وَوَرَاه .
١١. G, V – وَسِرًّا ذَائِقًا .
١٢. G = تَوَقّيً ; R = نُورًا .
١٣. R1, V, W (note) + وَوَجْداً مُذْلِقًّا .
١٤. G, R, R1, W + هَامِيَةً .
١٥. R, R1, V, W = إِلٰهِي قَلْبٌ أُقْبِلُ عَلَيْكَ ; missing in G .
١٦. I, R, G – ٱلْقُرْب .
١٧. G, R, R1, V – وَمُنْتَهَى رَغْبَةِ ٱلطَّالِبِينَ .
١٨. G, R, R1, W = الْعَالِمِين .
١٩. R = مِنْ .

لِأَكُونَ مِنَ ٱلْمُطَهَّرِينَ.[٢٠] وَصَلَّى ٱللّٰهُ عَلَى[٢١] سَيِّدِنَا مُحَمَّدٍ وَعَلَى آلِهِ وَصَحْبِهِ[٢٢] أَجْمَعِينَ ۞ ﴿وَٱلْحَمْدُ لِلّٰهِ رَبِّ ٱلْعَالَمِينَ﴾.

وِرْدُ يَوْمِ ٱلْأَحَدِ[٢٣]

بِسْمِ ٱللّٰهِ ٱلرَّحْمٰنِ ٱلرَّحِيمِ. ﴿بِسْمِ ٱللّٰهِ﴾ فَاتِحِ ٱلْوُجُودِ ۞ وَ﴿ٱلْحَمْدُ لِلّٰهِ﴾ مُظْهِرِ كُلِّ مَوْجُودٍ ۞ وَ﴿لَا إِلٰهَ إِلَّا ٱللّٰهُ﴾ تَوْحِيدًا مُطْلَقًا عَنْ كَشْفٍ وَشُهُودٍ ۞ وَ﴿ٱللّٰهُ أَكْبَرُ﴾ مِنْهُ بَدَأَ ٱلْأَمْرُ وَإِلَيْهِ يَعُودُ ۞ وَ﴿سُبْحَانَ ٱللّٰهِ﴾ مَا ثَمَّ سِوَاهُ فَيُشْهَدُ وَلَا مَعَهُ غَيْرُهُ مَعْبُودٌ ۞ وَاحِدٌ أَحَدٌ عَلَى مَا كَانَ عَلَيْهِ قَبْلَ حُرُوفِ ٱلْحُدُودِ ۞ لَهُ فِي كُلِّ شَيْءٍ آيَةٌ تَدُلُّ عَلَى أَنَّهُ وَاحِدٌ مَوْجُودٌ[٢٤] ۞ سِرُّهُ سِتْرُهُ[٢٥] عَنِ ٱلْإِدْرَاكِ وَٱلنُّفُودِ[٢٦] ۞ وَ﴿لَا حَوْلَ وَلَا قُوَّةَ إِلَّا بِٱللّٰهِ ٱلْعَلِيِّ ٱلْعَظِيمِ﴾ كَنْزٌ اخْتَصَّنَا بِهِ مِنْ خَزَائِنِ ٱلْغَيْبِ وَ ٱلْجُودِ ۞ أَسْتَنْزِلُ بِهِ كُلَّ خَيْرٍ ۞ وَأَدْفَعُ بِهِ كُلَّ شَرٍّ وَضَيْرٍ[٢٧] ۞ وَأَفْتُقُ بِهِ كُلَّ رَتْقٍ مَسْدُودٍ ۞ وَ﴿إِنَّا لِلّٰهِ وَإِنَّا إِلَيْهِ رَاجِعُونَ﴾ فِي كُلِّ أَمْرٍ نَزَلَ أَوْ هُوَ نَازِلٌ ۞ وَفِي كُلِّ حَالٍ وَمَقَامٍ ۞ وَخَاطِرٍ وَوَارِدٍ ۞ وَمَصْدَرٍ وَوُرُودٍ ۞

٢٠. P1, R1, W + يَا رَبِّ ٱلْعَالَمِين .

٢١. G + السَّيِّدِ ٱلْفَاتِحِ ٱلْخَاتَمِ نُورِ انْوَارِ ٱلْمَعَارِفِ صَفْوَتِكَ مِنْ خَلْقِكَ وَزَيْنِ عِبَادِكَ .

٢٢. G + وَوَارِثِيهِ وَحِزْبِهِ ; R, G + وَسَلَّمَ تَسْلِيمًا إِلَى يَوْمِ ٱلدِّين .

٢٣. B + وِرْد ٱلْأَحَدِيَّة .

٢٤. U - مَوْجُودٌ .

٢٥. G = سُتِرَ (margin) ; B, P1 = سَتَرَهُ .

٢٦. B, V = ٱلنُّفُوذ ; H, R1 = ٱلنُّقُود .

٢٧. B, G, K, P1, V - وَضَيْر .

وَٱللّٰهُ هُوَ ٱلْمَرْجُوُّ لِكُلِّ شَيْءٍ * وَفِي كُلِّ شَيْءٍ هُوَ ٱلْمَأْمُولُ وَٱلْمَقْصُودُ * وَٱلْإِلْهَامُ مِنْهُ وَٱلْفَهْمُ عَنْهُ وَٱلْمَوْجُودُ[٢٨] هُوَ وَلَا إِنْكَارَ وَلَا جُحُودَ * إِذَا كَشَفَ فَلَا غَيْرَ * وَإِذَا سَتَرَ فَكُلٌّ غَيْرٌ * وَكُلٌّ مَحْجُوبٌ مَبْعُودٌ[٢٩] * بَاطِنٌ بِٱلْأَحَدِيَّةِ * ظَاهِرٌ بِٱلْوَاحِدِيَّةِ * وَعَنْهُ وَبِهِ كَانَ كَوْنُ كُلِّ شَيْءٍ فَلَا شَيْءَ * إِذَ ٱلشَّيْءُ فِي ٱلْحَقِيقَةِ مَعْدُومٌ مَفْقُودٌ * ﴿فَهُوَ ٱلْأَوَّلُ وَٱلْآخِرُ * وَٱلظَّاهِرُ وَٱلْبَاطِنُ * وَهُوَ بِكُلِّ شَيْءٍ عَلِيمٌ﴾ قَبْلَ كَوْنِ ٱلشَّيْءِ وَبَعْدَ ٱلْوُجُودِ * لَهُ ٱلْإِحَاطَةُ ٱلْوَاسِعَةُ * وَٱلْحَقِيقَةُ ٱلْجَامِعَةُ * وَٱلسِّرُّ ٱلْقَائِمُ * وَٱلْمُلْكُ ٱلدَّائِمُ * وَٱلْحُكْمُ ٱللَّازِمُ * أَهْلُ ٱلثَّنَاءِ وَٱلْمَجْدِ * هُوَ ﴿كَمَا أَثْنَى عَلَى نَفْسِهِ﴾ فَهُوَ ٱلْحَامِدُ وَٱلْمَحْمُودُ * أَحَدِيُّ ٱلذَّاتِ * وَاحِدِيُّ ٱلْأَسْمَاءِ وَٱلصِّفَاتِ * عَلِيمٌ بِٱلْكُلِّيَّاتِ وَٱلْجُزْئِيَّاتِ * مُحِيطٌ بِٱلْفَوْقِيَّاتِ وَٱلتَّحْتِيَّاتِ * وَلَهُ ﴿عَنَتِ ٱلْوُجُوهُ﴾ مِنْ كُلِّ ٱلْجِهَاتِ.

اَللّٰهُمَّ يَا مَنْ هُوَ ٱلْمُحِيطُ ٱلْجَامِعُ * وَيَا مَنْ لَا يَمْنَعُهُ مِنَ ٱلْعَطَاءِ مَانِعٌ * يَا مَنْ لَا يَنْفَدُ[٣٠] مَا عِنْدَهُ * وَعَمَّ جَمِيعَ ٱلْخَلَائِقِ[٣١] جُودُهُ وَرِفْدُهُ. **اَللّٰهُمَّ** افْتَحْ لِي أَغْلَاقَ هٰذِهِ ٱلْكُنُوزِ * وَٱكْشِفْ لِي حَقَائِقَ هٰذِهِ ٱلرُّمُوزِ * وَكُنْ أَنْتَ مُوَاجِهِي وَوِجْهَتِي * وَٱحْجُبْنِي بِرُؤْيَتِكَ عَنْ رُؤْيَتِي * وَٱمْحُ بِظُهُورِ تَجَلِّيكَ جَمِيعَ صِفَتِي * حَتَّى لَا يَكُونَ لِي

٢٨. RI = ٱلْمُوجِدُ ٱلْمَوْجُودُ.
٢٩. I, P1, V, Y = مَعْبُودٌ.
٣٠. B, U = يَنْفُذُ.
٣١. K = الْبَرَايَا.

وِجْهَةٌ إِلَّا إِلَيْكَ * وَلَا يَقَعُ مِنِّي نَظَرٌ إِلَّا عَلَيْكَ. وَٱنْظُرِ ٱللّٰهُمَّ إِلَيَّ بِعَيْنِ ٱلرَّحْمَةِ وَٱلْعِنَايَةِ * وَٱلْحِفْظِ وَٱلرِّعَايَةِ * وَٱلْاِخْتِصَاصِ وَٱلْوِلَايَةِ * فِي كُلِّ شَيْءٍ * حَتَّى لَا يَحْجُبُنِي عَن رُؤْيَتِي لَكَ شَيْءٌ * وَأَكُونَ نَاظِرًا إِلَيكَ بِمَا أَمْدَدْتَنِي بِهِ مِن نَظَرِكَ فِي كُلِّ شَيْءٍ * وَٱجْعَلْنِي خَاضِعًا لِتَجَلِّيكَ * أَهْلًا لِاخْتِصَاصِكَ وَتَوَلِّيكَ * مَحَلَّ نَظَرِكَ مِنْ خَلْقِكَ * وَمُفِيضًا عَلَيْهِمْ مِنْ عَطَائِكَ وَفَضْلِكَ * يَا مَنْ لَهُ ٱلْغِنَاءُ ٱلْمُطْلَقُ * وَلِعَبْدِهِ ٱلْفَقْرُ ٱلْمُحَقَّقُ * يَا غَنِيًّا عَنْ كُلِّ شَيْءٍ * وَكُلُّ شَيْءٍ مُفْتَقِرٌ إِلَيْهِ * وَيَا مَنْ بِيَدِهِ أَمْرُ كُلِّ شَيْءٍ * وَأَمْرُ[٣٢] كُلِّ شَيْءٍ رَاجِعٌ إِلَيْهِ * وَيَا مَنْ لَهُ ٱلْوُجُودُ ٱلْمُطْلَقُ *[٣٣] فَلَا يَعْلَمُ مَا هُوَ إِلَّا هُوَ وَلَا يُسْتَدَلُّ عَلَيْهِ إِلَّا بِهِ * وَيا مُسَخِّرَ ٱلْأَعْمَالِ ٱلصَّالِحَةِ لِلْعَبْدِ لِيَعُودَ نَفْعُهَا عَلَيْهِ * لَا مَقْصَدَ لِي غَيْرُكَ * وَلَا يَسَعُنِي إِلَّا جُودُكَ وَخَيْرُكَ * يَا جَوَادُ * فَوْقَ ٱلْمُرَادِ[٣٤] * يَا مُعْطِيَ ٱلنَّوَالِ * قَبْلَ ٱلسُّؤَالِ * يَا مَنْ وَقَفَ دُونَهُ قَدَمُ[٣٥] كُلِّ طَالِبٍ * يَا مَنْ هُوَ عَلَى أَمْرِهِ قَادِرٌ وَغَالِبٌ * يَا مَنْ هُوَ لِكُلِّ شَيْءٍ وَاهِبٌ * وَإِذَا شَاءَ سَالِبٌ * أَهِمُّ إِلَيْكَ بِٱلسُّؤَالِ * فَأَجِدْنِي عَبْدًا لَكَ عَلَى كُلِّ حَالٍ * فَتَوَلَّنِي يَا مَوْلَايَ * فَأَنْتَ أَوْلَى بِهِ مِنِّي * كَيْفَ أَقْصِدُكَ وَأَنْتَ وَرَاءَ ٱلْقَصْدِ * أَمْ كَيْفَ أَطْلُبُكَ وَٱلطَّلَبُ عَيْنُ ٱلْبُعْدِ * أَيُطْلَبُ مَنْ هُوَ قَرِيبٌ

٣٢. G, V – أَمْرُ.

٣٣. B + وَلِعَبْدِهِ ٱلْفَقْرُ ٱلْمُحَقَّقُ.

٣٤. H = ٱلْأَمَالِ.

٣٥. B, B2, G, K, I, P (margin), P1, R, R1, W + عَقْلِ.

حَاضِرٌ* أَمْ يُقْصَدُ مَنِ ٱلْقَاصِدُ[٣٦] فِيهِ تَائِهٌ حَائِرٌ* اَلطَّلَبُ لَا يَصِلُ[٣٧] إِلَيْكَ* وَٱلْقَصْدُ لَا يَصْدُرُ عَلَيْكَ[٣٨]* تَجَلِّيَاتُ ظَاهِرِكَ* لَا تُلْحَقُ وَلَا تُدْرَكُ* وَرُمُوزُ أَسْرَارِكَ* لَا تَنحَلُّ وَلَا تَنْفَكُّ* أَيَعْلَمُ ٱلْمَوْجُودُ كُنْهَ مَنْ أَوْجَدَهُ* أَمْ يَبْلُغُ ٱلْعَبْدُ حَقِيقَةَ مَنِ ٱسْتَعْبَدَهُ* اَلطَّلَبُ وَٱلْقَصْدُ وَٱلْقُرْبُ وَٱلْبُعْدُ[٣٩] صِفَاتُ ٱلْعَبْدِ* فَمَاذَا يَبْلُغُ[٤٠] ٱلْعَبْدُ بِصِفَاتِهِ* مِمَّنْ هُوَ مُنَزَّهٌ مُتَعَالٍ فِي ذَاتِهِ* وَكُلُّ مَخْلُوقٍ مَحَلُّهُ ٱلْعَجْزُ* فِي مَوْقِفِ ٱلذُّلِّ عَلَى بَابِ ٱلْعِزِّ[٤١]* عَنْ نَيْلِ إِدْرَاكِ[٤٢] هٰذَا ٱلْكَنْزِ* كَيْفَ أَعْرِفُكَ* وَأَنْتَ ٱلْبَاطِنُ ٱلَّذِي لَا تُعْرَفُ* وَكَيْفَ لَا أَعْرِفُكَ* وَأَنْتَ ٱلظَّاهِرُ ٱلَّذِي إِلَيَّ فِي كُلِّ شَيْءٍ تَتَعَرَّفُ* كَيْفَ أُوَحِّدُكَ* وَلَا وُجُودَ لِي فِي عَيْنِ ٱلْأَحَدِيَّةِ* وَكَيْفَ لَا أُوَحِّدُكَ* وَٱلتَّوْحِيدُ سِرُّ ٱلْعُبُودِيَّةِ* سُبْحَانَكَ لَا إِلٰهَ إِلَّا أَنْتَ* مَا وَحَّدَكَ مِنْ أَحَدٍ* إِذْ أَنْتَ كَمَا أَنْتَ* فِي سَابِقِ ٱلْأَزَلِ وَلَاحِقِ ٱلْأَبَدِ* فَعَلَى ٱلتَّحْقِيقِ مَا وَحَّدَكَ أَحَدٌ[٤٣] سِوَاكَ* وَفِي ٱلْجُمْلَةِ مَا عَرَفَكَ إِلَّا ﴿إِيَّاكَ﴾* بَطَنْتَ وَظَهَرْتَ* فَلَا عَنْكَ بَطَنْتَ وَلَا لِغَيْرِكَ ظَهَرْتَ* فَأَنْتَ أَنْتَ[٤٤] لَا إِلٰهَ إِلَّا أَنْتَ* فَكَيْفَ بِهٰذَا

٣٦. G, R1, V = ٱلْقَصْدُ .
٣٧. H, R = يُوصِلُ ; R1, W = يُوصَلُ .
٣٨. B2, R = عَنْكَ .
٣٩. G, P1 + مِنْ .
٤٠. B, B2, G, H, K, P1, U, V = يُدْرِكُ .
٤١. K = فِي مَوْقِفِ ٱلْعِزِّ .
٤٢. B2 = عَنْ إِدْرَاكِ نَيْلِ .
٤٣. G, H, K, I – أَحَدٌ; R, R1, W = مِنْ احدٍ .
٤٤. G + اللّٰه ٱلَّذِي ; R1, V, W + اللّٰه .

ٱلشَّكْلِ يَنْحَلُّ* وَٱلْأَوَّلُ آخِرُ وَٱلْآخِرُ أَوَّلُ* فَيَا مَنْ أَبْهَمَ ٱلْأَمْرَ* وَأَبْطَنَ ٱلسِّرَّ* وَأَوْقَعَ فِي ٱلْحَيْرَةِ وَلَا غَيْرَهُ. أَسْأَلُكَ ٱللّٰهُمَّ كَشْفَ سِرِّ ٱلْأَحَدِيَّةِ* وَتَحْقِيقَ ٱلْعُبُودِيَّةِ* وَٱلْقِيَامَ بِٱلرُّبُوبِيَّةِ* بِمَا يَلِيقُ بِحَضْرَتِهَا ٱلْعَلِيَّةِ* فَأَنَا مَوْجُودٌ بِكَ حَادِثٌ مَعْدُومٌ* وَأَنْتَ مَوْجُودٌ[٤٥] بَاقٍ حَيٌّ قَيُّومٌ* قَدِيمٌ أَزَلِيٌّ عَالِمٌ مَعْلُومٌ* فَيَا مَنْ لَا يَعْلَمُ مَا هُوَ إِلَّا هُوَ[٤٦]. أَسْأَلُكَ ٱللّٰهُمَّ ٱلْهَرَبَ مِنِّي إِلَيْكَ* وَٱلْجَمْعَ بِجَمِيعِ مَجْمُوعِي عَلَيْكَ* حَتَّى لَا يَكُونَ وُجُودِي حِجَابِي[٤٧] عَنْ شُهُودِي* يَا مَقْصُودِي* يَا مَعْبُودِي* مَا فَاتَنِي شَيْءٌ إِذَا أَنَا وَجَدْتُكَ* وَلَا جَهِلْتُ شَيْئًا إِذَا أَنَا عَلِمْتُكَ* وَلَا فَقَدْتُ شَيْئًا إِذَا أَنَا شَهِدْتُكَ[٤٨]* فَنَائِي فِيكَ* وَبَقَائِي بِكَ* وَمَشْهُودِي أَنْتَ* لَا إِلٰهَ إِلَّا أَنْتَ* أَنْتَ كَمَا شَهِدْتُ وَكَمَا أُمِرْتُ[٤٩]* فَشُهُودِي عَيْنُ وُجُودِي* فَمَا شَهِدْتُ سِوَائِي فِي فَنَائِي وَبَقَائِي* وَٱلْإِشَارَةُ إِلَيَّ* وَٱلْحُكْمُ لِي وَعَلَيَّ* وَٱلنِّسَبُ نِسَبِي* وَكُلُّ ذٰلِكَ رُتَبِي[٥٠]* وَٱلشَّأْنُ شَأْنِي[٥١] فِي ٱلظُّهُورِ وَٱلْبُطُونِ* وَسَرَيَانِ ٱلسِّرِّ ٱلْمَصُونِ* هُوِيَّةٌ سَارِيَةٌ* مَظَاهِرُ بَادِيَةٌ* وُجُودٌ وَعَدَمٌ* نُورٌ وَظُلَمٌ* لَوْحٌ وَقَلَمٌ* سَمْعٌ وَصَمَمٌ* جَهْلٌ وَعِلْمٌ* حَرْبٌ وَسِلْمٌ* صَمْتٌ وَنُطْقٌ* رَتْقٌ

٤٥. G, V - مَوْجُودٌ.
٤٦. R1 + يَا هُو.
٤٧. G = حِجَابًا.
٤٨. G, U, V - عَلِمْتُكَ وَلَا فَقَدْتُ شَيْئًا إِذَا أَنَا.
٤٩. B, B2, K, P1 = كَمَا شَهِدْتَ وَكَمَا أَمَرْتَ.
٥٠. B2 = رَاتِبِي ; P, P1 = النِسْبَةُ نِسْبَتِي وكل ذلك رُتْبَتِي.
٥١. H, U - شَأْنِي.

وَفَتْقٌ * حَقِيقَةٌ وَحَقٌّ * غَيْبُوبِيَّةٌ أَزَلٍ * دَيْمُومِيَّةُ أَبَدٍ * ﴿قُلْ هُوَ ٱللَّٰهُ أَحَدٌ * ٱللَّٰهُ ٱلصَّمَدُ * لَمْ يَلِدْ وَلَمْ يُولَدْ * وَلَمْ يَكُن لَّهُۥ كُفُوًا أَحَدٌ﴾. وَصَلَّى ٱللَّٰهُ عَلَى ٱلْأَوَّلِ فِي ٱلْإِيجَادِ[٥٢] وَٱلْوُجُودِ * ٱلْفَاتِحِ لِكُلِّ شَاهِدٍ حَضْرَتَي ﴿ٱلشَّاهِدِ وَٱلْمَشْهُودِ﴾ * ٱلسِّرِّ ٱلْبَاطِنِ وَٱلنُّورِ ٱلظَّاهِرِ عَيْنِ ٱلْمَقْصُودِ[٥٣] * مُمَيِّزِ قَبْضَتَيِ[٥٤] ٱلسَّبْقِ فِي عَالَمِ ٱلْخَلْقِ مِنَ[٥٥] ٱلْمَخْصُوصِ[٥٦] وَٱلْمَبْعُودِ[٥٧] * ٱلرُّوحِ ٱلْأَقْدَسِ ٱلْعَلِيِّ * وَٱلنُّورِ ٱلْأَكْمَلِ ٱلْبَهِيِّ * ٱلْقَائِمِ بِكَمَالِ ٱلْعُبُودِيَّةِ فِي حَضْرَةِ ٱلْمَعْبُودِ * ٱلَّذِي أُفِيضَ عَلَى رُوحِهِ مِنْ حَضْرَةِ رُوحَانِيَّتِهِ * وَٱتَّصَلَتْ بِمِشْكَاةِ قَلْبِهِ أَشِعَّةُ نُورَانِيَّتِهِ * فَهُوَ ٱلرَّسُولُ ٱلْأَعْظَمُ * وَٱلنَّبِيُّ ٱلْمُكَرَّمُ *[٥٨] وَٱلْوَلِيُّ[٥٩] ٱلْمُقَرَّبُ ٱلْمَسْعُودُ[٦٠] * وَعَلَى آلِهِ وَأَصْحَابِهِ خَزَائِنِ أَسْرَارِهِ * وَمَعَادِنِ أَنْوَارِهِ * وَمَطَالِعِ أَقْمَارِهِ[٦١] * كُنُوزِ ٱلْحَقَائِقِ * هُدَاةِ[٦٢] ٱلْخَلَائِقِ * نُجُومِ ٱلْهُدَى[٦٣] لِمَنِ ٱقْتَدَى * وَسَلَّمَ تَسْلِيمًا كَثِيرًا إِلَى يَوْمِ ٱلدِّينِ[٦٤] * وَ﴿سُبْحَانَ ٱللَّٰهِ وَمَا أَنَا مِنَ ٱلْمُشْرِكِينَ﴾ *

٥٢. R + وَٱلْجُودِ.
٥٣. B - عَيْنِ ٱلْمَقْصُو.
٥٤. P, P1 = ٱلْمُمَيِّزِ قَصَبِ.
٥٥. B, G, U, V = فِي ; K - مِنْ.
٥٦. G = ٱلْمَقْصُودِ.
٥٧. B2, H, K, R = بِٱلْعُبُودِيَةِ ; P, P1, R1, V, W = ٱلْمَعْبُود ; B = ٱلْمَعْسُود.
٥٨. I, R1 = ٱلْأَكْرَم ; U, V, W - ٱلرَّسُولُ ٱلْأعظَمُ وٱلنَّبِيّ ٱلْمُكَرَّمُ وَ.
٥٩. G = وَهُوَ ٱلْوَلِيُ وَٱلْمَوْلَى.
٦٠. B2, K + بِالْأَحَدِيَّةِ.
٦١. G, K, P1, I, U, V = خَزائِنَ اسْرَارِهِ ومَطْلَع انْوَارِهِ ; B, H, R1 (margin) = خَزانَة اسْرَارِهِ ومَطْلَع انْوَارِهِ.
٦٢. R + ٱلطَّرِيقِ اِلَى.
٦٣. B = ٱلْإِهْتِدَاء.
٦٤. G, V - اِلَى يَوْمِ ٱلدِّين.

وَ﴿حَسْبُنَا ٱللّٰهُ وَنِعْمَ ٱلْوَكِيلُ﴾ * وَ﴿لَا حَوْلَ وَلَا قُوَّةَ إِلَّا بِٱللّٰهِ ٱلْعَلِيِّ ٱلْعَظِيمِ﴾ * وَ﴿ٱلْحَمْدُ لِلّٰهِ رَبِّ ٱلْعَالَمِينَ﴾.

وِرْدُ لَيْلَةِ ٱلِاثْنَيْنِ

بِسْمِ ٱللّٰهِ ٱلرَّحْمٰنِ ٱلرَّحِيمِ. **إِلٰهِي** وَسِعَ عِلْمُكَ كُلَّ مَعْلُومٍ * وَأَحَاطَتْ خُبْرَتُكَ بَاطِنَ كُلِّ مَفْهُومٍ * وَتَقَدَّسْتَ فِي عُلَاكَ عَنْ كُلِّ مَذْمُومٍ * تَسَامَتْ إِلَيْكَ ٱلْهِمَمُ * وَصَعِدَ إِلَيْكَ ٱلْكَلِمُ * أَنْتَ ٱلْمُتَعَالِي فِي سُمُوِّكَ * فَأَقْرَبُ مَعَارِجِنَا إِلَيْكَ ٱلتَّنَزُّلُ * وَأَنْتَ[٦٥] ٱلْمُتَعَزِّزُ فِي عُلُوِّكَ * فَأَشْرَفُ أَخْلَاقِنَا إِلَيْكَ ٱلتَّذَلُّلُ * ظَهَرْتَ فِي كُلِّ بَاطِنٍ وَظَاهِرٍ * وَدُمْتَ بَعْدَ كُلِّ أَوَّلٍ وَآخِرٍ * سُبْحَانَكَ لَا إِلٰهَ إِلَّا أَنْتَ * سَجَدَتْ لِعَظَمَتِكَ ٱلْجِبَاهُ * وَتَنَعَّمَتْ بِذِكْرِكَ ٱلشِّفَاهُ. أَسْأَلُكَ بِٱسْمِكَ ٱلْعَظِيمِ ٱلَّذِي إِلَيْهِ سُمُوُّ كُلِّ مُتَرَقٍّ * وَمِنْهُ قَبُولُ كُلِّ مُتَلَقٍّ[٦٦] * سِرًّا تَطْلُبُنِي[٦٧] فِيهِ ٱلْهِمَمُ ٱلْعَلِيَّةُ * وَتَنْقَادُ إِلَيَّ فِيهِ ٱلنُّفُوسُ[٦٨] ٱلْأَبِيَّةُ. وَأَسْأَلُكَ **رَبِّ**[٦٩] أَنْ تَجْعَلَ سُلَّمِي إِلَيْكَ ٱلتَّنَزُّلَ * وَمِعْرَاجِي إِلَيْكَ ٱلتَّوَاضُعَ[٧٠] وَٱلتَّذَلُّلَ * وَٱكْنُفْنِي بِغَاشِيَةٍ مِنْ نُورِكَ تَكْشِفُ لِي بِهَا كُلَّ مَسْتُورٍ * وَتَحْجُبْنِي عَنْ كُلِّ

٦٥. G, R - انْتَ.
٦٦. V + بِرَعْفَةٍ تَضْمَحِلُّ مَعَهَا عُلو ٱلْعَالِين وتُقِيضُ عنْها غُلو ٱلْغَالِين حَتَّى ارْقِي بِكَ وَإِلَيْكَ مُرَقِّي.
٦٧. G = يُطَالِبُنِي.
٦٨. R1 = ٱلْأَرْوَاحُ.
٦٩. G = رَبِّ أَسْأَلُكَ ; V = سَيِّدِي.
٧٠. G, I, P1, R = ٱلتَّخَضُّعَ.

حَاسِدٍ وَمَغْرُورٍ* وَهَبْ لِي[٧١] خُلُقًا أَسَعُ بِهِ كُلَّ خَلْقٍ* وَأَقْضِي بِهِ كُلَّ حَقٍّ* كَمَا ﴿وَسِعْتَ كُلَّ شَيْءٍ رَحْمَةً وَعِلْمًا﴾.[٧٢] ﴿لَا إِلٰهَ إِلَّا﴾ أَنْتَ ﴿يَا حَيُّ يَا قَيُّومُ﴾[٧٣]. رَبِّ رَبِّنِي بِلَطِيفِ رُبُوبِيَّتِكَ تَرْبِيَةَ مُفْتَقِرٍ إِلَيْكَ لَا يَسْتَغْنِي عَنْكَ أَبَدًا* وَرَاقِبْنِي بِعَيْنِ عِنَايَتِكَ[٧٤] بِمُرَاقَبَةٍ تَحْفَظُنِي عَنْ كُلِّ طَارِقٍ يَطْرُقُنِي بِأَمْرٍ يَسُوؤُنِي فِي نَفْسِي* أَوْ يُكَدِّرُ عَلَيَّ وَقْتِي وَحِسِّي[٧٥]* أَوْ يَكْتُبُ[٧٦] فِي لَوْحِ إِرَادَتِي[٧٧] خَطًّا مِنَ ٱلْخُطُوطِ[٧٨]* وَٱرْزُقْنِي رَاحَةَ ٱلْأُنْسِ بِكَ* وَرَقِّنِي إِلَى مَقَامِ ٱلْقُرْبِ مِنْكَ* وَرَوِّحْ رُوحِي بِذِكْرِكَ* وَرَدِّدْنِي بَيْنَ رَغَبٍ فِيكَ وَرَهَبٍ مِنْكَ[٧٩]* وَرَدِّنِي بِرِدَاءِ ٱلرِّضْوَانِ* وَأَوْرِدْنِي مَوَارِدَ ٱلْقَبُولِ* وَهَبْ لِي[٨٠] رَحْمَةً مِنْكَ تَلُمُّ بِهَا شَعَثِي* وَتُكَمِّلُ بِهَا نَقْصِي* وَتُقَوِّمُ عِوَجِي* وَتَرُدُّ شَارِدِي[٨١]* وَتَهْدِي حَائِرِي* فَإِنَّكَ ﴿رَبُّ كُلِّ شَيْءٍ﴾ وَمُرَبِّيهِ*

٧١. G, R, V = وَهَبْنِي.

٧٢. I, P1 + يَا رَحْمن يَا رَحِيم.

٧٣. G, I, P1, R, W + ٱللّٰه لَا اله الا هو; V + ٱللّٰه لَا اله الا هو ٱلحي ٱلْقيوم لَا تاخذه سنة ... وهو ٱلعلي ٱلعظيم.

٧٤. G, P1, R, W - عنايتك ...تَرْبِيَةَ مفتقر.

٧٥. G, R, V - وَحِسّي.

٧٦. G, I, P1, R, V = وَيُثْبِتُ.

٧٧. G, R = لَوْحي.

٧٨. G, W = خَطًّا مِنْ حُظوظ حُظوظي; V = خَطًّا مِنَ ٱلْخُطوط; R = حَظًّا مِنَ ٱلْحُظوظ; I, P1 = خَطّ حَظٍّ يوصلنِي إِلَيْك وَٱسْعَدْنِي بِجدٍّ سَعِيدٍ يسعدنِي لَدَيْك.

٧٩. G, P1 - ورددنِي....

٨٠. G, V, W = وَهَبْنِي.

٨١. G = تَزْدَرُ سَادِي.

[٨٢] رَحِمْتَ ٱلذَّوَاتِ * وَرَفَعْتَ ٱلدَّرَجَاتِ * قُرْبُكَ[٨٣] رَوْحُ[٨٤] ٱلْأَرْوَاحِ * وَرَيْحَانُ ٱلْأَفْرَاحِ[٨٥] * وَعُنْوَانُ ٱلْفَلَاحِ[٨٦] * وَرَاحَةُ كُلِّ مُرْتَاحٍ * تبارَكْتَ رَبَّ ٱلْأَرْبَابِ * وَمُعْتِقَ ٱلرِّقَابِ * وَكَاشِفَ ٱلْعَذَابِ * ﴿وَسِعْتَ كُلَّ شَيْءٍ رَحْمَةً وَعِلْمًا﴾ * وَغَفَرْتَ ٱلذُّنُوبَ حَنَانًا وَحِلْمًا * وَأَنْتَ ٱلْغَفُورُ ٱلرَّحِيمُ * ٱلْحَلِيمُ ٱلْعَلِيمُ * ٱلْعَلِيُّ ٱلْعَظِيمُ. وَصَلَّى ٱللّٰهُ عَلَى سَيِّدِنَا مُحَمَّدٍ وَعَلَى آلِهِ وَصَحْبِهِ أَجْمَعِينَ * ﴿وَٱلْحَمْدُ لِلّٰهِ رَبِّ ٱلْعَالَمِينَ﴾.

وِرْدُ يَوْمِ ٱلِاثْنَيْنِ[٨٧]

بِسْمِ ٱللّٰهِ ٱلرَّحْمٰنِ ٱلرَّحِيمِ. **ٱللّٰهُمَّ** إِنِّي أَسْأَلُكَ ﴿ٱلنُّورَ وَٱلْهُدَى﴾ * وَٱلْأَدَبَ فِي ٱلِاقْتِدَاءِ * وَأَعُوذُ بِكَ مِنْ شَرِّ نَفْسِي * وَمِنْ شَرِّ كُلِّ قَاطِعٍ يَقْطَعُنِي عَنْكَ * لَا إِلٰهَ إِلَّا أَنْتَ * قَدِّسْ نَفْسِي مِنَ ٱلشُّبُهَاتِ * وَٱلْأَخْلَاقِ ٱلسَّيِّئَاتِ * وَٱلْحُظُوظِ وَٱلْغَفَلَاتِ * وَٱجْعَلْنِي عَبْدًا مُطِيعًا لَكَ فِي جَمِيعِ ٱلْحَالَاتِ * يَا عَلِيمُ عَلِّمْنِي مِنْ عِلْمِكَ * يَا حَكِيمُ أَيِّدْنِي بِحُكْمِكَ * يَا سَمِيعُ أَسْمِعْنِي مِنْكَ * يَا بَصِيرُ بَصِّرْنِي فِي آلَائِكَ * يَا خَبِيرُ فَهِّمْنِي عَنْكَ * يَا حَيُّ أَحْيِنِي بِذِكْرِكَ * يَا مُرِيدُ

٨٢. P1 + أَنْتَ.
٨٣. R1 = فَإِنَّكَ.
٨٤. P, P1, R = رُوحُ.
٨٥. I + ٱلْإِرْتِيَاح.
٨٦. G = ٱلصَّلَاحِ.
٨٧. B + وِرْدُ ٱلنُّور.

خَلِّصْ إِرَادَتِي بِقُدْرَتِكَ وَعَظَمَتِكَ * ﴿إِنَّكَ عَلَى كُلِّ شَيْءٍ قَدِيرٌ﴾. اَللّٰهُمَّ إِنِّي أَسْأَلُكَ بِٱللَّاهُوتِ ذِي ٱلتَّدْبِيرِ * وَٱلنَّاسُوتِ ذِي ٱلتَّسْخِيرِ * وَٱلْعَقْلِ ذِي ٱلتَّأْثِيرِ * ٱلْمُحِيطِ بِٱلْكُلِّ وَٱلْجُمْلَةِ وَٱلتَّفْصِيلِ فِي ٱلتَّصْوِيرِ وَٱلتَّقْدِيرِ. إِلٰهِي أَسْأَلُكَ بِذَاتِكَ ٱلَّتِي لَا تُدرَكُ وَلَا تُتْرَكُ * وَبِأَحَدِيَّتِكَ ٱلَّتِي مَنْ تَوَهَّمَ فِيهَا ٱلْمَعِيَّةَ فَقَدْ أَشْرَكَ * وَبِإِحَاطَتِكَ ٱلَّتِي مَنْ ظَنَّ فِي أَزَلِيَّتِهَا غَيْرًا فَقَدْ أَفَكَ[٨٨] * وَمِنْ نِظَامِ ٱلْإِخْلَاصِ فَقَدِ انْفَكَّ * يَا مَنْ سُلِبَ عَنْهُ تَنْزِيهًا مَا لَمْ يَكُنْ فِي قِدَمِهِ * يَا مَنْ قَدَرَ[٨٩] عَلَى كُلِّ شَيْءٍ بِإِحَاطَتِهِ وَعَظَمَتِهِ * يَا مَنْ أَبْرَزَ نُورَ وُجُودِهِ[٩٠] مِنْ ظُلْمَةِ عَدَمِهِ * يَا مَنْ صَوَّرَ أَشْخَاصَ ٱلْأَفْلَاكِ[٩١] بِمَا أَوْدَعَهُ مِنْ عِلْمِهِ فِي قَلَمِهِ * يَا مَنْ صَرَّفَ أَحْكَامَهُ بِأَسْرَارِ حِكَمِهِ[٩٢] * أُنَادِيكَ ٱسْتِغَاثَةَ بَعِيدٍ لِقَرِيبٍ * وَأَطْلُبُكَ طَلَبَ مُحِبٍّ لِحَبِيبٍ * وَأَسْأَلُكَ سُؤَالَ مُضْطَرٍّ لِمُجِيبٍ. أَسْأَلُكَ ٱللّٰهُمَّ رَفْعَ حِجَابِ ٱلْغَيْبِ * وَحَلَّ عِقَالِ ٱلرَّيْبِ. اَللّٰهُمَّ أَحْيِنِي بِكَ حَيَاةً وَاجِبَةً[٩٣] * وَعَلِّمْنِي كَذٰلِكَ[٩٤] عِلْمًا مُحِيطًا بِأَسْرَارِ ٱلْمَعْلُومَاتِ * وَٱفْتَحْ لِي بِقُدْرَتِكَ كَنْزَ ٱلْجَنَّةِ وَٱلْعَرْشِ وَٱلذَّاتِ * وَٱمْحَقْنِي تَحْتَ أَنْوَارِ ٱلصِّفَاتِ * وَخَلِّصْنِي بِمِنَّتِكَ مِنْ جَمِيعِ ٱلْقُيُودِ

٨٨. K = أَفِكَ.
٨٩. B1, P1 = قَدَّرَ ; P = قَدَّرَ عَن.
٩٠. B = كُلِّ مَوْجُودٍ.
٩١. G = ٱلْأَفْلَاكَ ٱلْأَشْخاصَ.
٩٢. G, H, L = حِكْمَتِه ; K, R1 = حُكْمِهِ.
٩٣. G = نَاجِيًا ; R, R1 = طَيِّبَةً.
٩٤. R1, H, L = مِن لَدُنْكَ.

ٱلْمُعْقِدَاتِ٭ سُبْحَانَكَ تَنْزِيهًا سُبُّوحٌ تَنَزَّهَ عَنْ سِمَاتِ ٱلْحُدُوثِ[٩٥] وَصِفَاتِ ٱلنَّقْضِ[٩٦]٭ قُدُّوسٌ تَطَهَّرَ مِنْ أَشْبَاهِ ٱلذَّمِّ وَمُوجِبَاتِ ٱلرَّفْضِ[٩٧]٭ سُبْحَانَكَ أَعْجَزْتَ كُلَّ طَالِبٍ عَنِ ٱلْوُصُولِ إِلَيْكَ إِلَّا بِكَ٭ سُبْحَانَكَ لَا يَعْلَمُ مَنْ أَنْتَ سِوَاكَ٭ سُبْحَانَكَ مَا أَقْرَبَكَ مَعَ تَرَفُّعِ عُلَاكَ. **اَللّٰهُمَّ** أَلْبِسْنِي سُبْحَةَ ٱلْحَمْدِ٭ وَرَدِّنِي بِرِدَاءِ ٱلْعِزِّ٭ وَتَوِّجْنِي بِتَاجِ ٱلْجَلَالِ وَٱلْمَجْدِ٭ وَجَرِّدْنِي عَنْ صِفَاتِ ذَوَاتِ ٱلْهَزْلِ وَٱلْجِدِّ٭ وَخَلِّصْنِي مِنْ قُيُودِ ٱلْعَدِّ وَٱلْحَدِّ٭ وَمُبَاشَرَةِ ٱلْخِلَافِ وَٱلنَّقِيضِ[٩٨] وَٱلضِّدِّ. **إِلٰهِي** عَدَمِي بِكَ عَيْنُ ٱلْوُجُودِ٭ وَبَقَائِي مَعَكَ عَيْنُ ٱلْعَدَمِ٭ فَأَبْدِلْنِي مَكَانَ تَوَهُّمِ وُجُودِي مَعَكَ بِتَحْقِيقِ عَدَمِي بِكَ٭ وَٱجْمَعْ شَمْلِي بِٱسْتِهْلَاكِي فِيكَ٭ لَا إِلٰهَ إِلَّا أَنْتَ٭ تَنَزَّهْتَ عَنِ ٱلْمَثِيلِ٭ لَا إِلٰهَ إِلَّا أَنْتَ٭ تَعَالَيْتَ عَنِ ٱلنَّظِيرِ٭ لَا إِلٰهَ إِلَّا أَنْتَ٭ اِسْتَغْنَيْتَ عَنِ ٱلْوَزِيرِ وَٱلْمُشِيرِ٭ لَا إِلٰهَ إِلَّا أَنْتَ٭ يَا أَحَدُ يَا صَمَدُ٭ لَا إِلٰهَ إِلَّا أَنْتَ٭ بِكَ ٱلْوُجُودُ٭ وَلَكَ ٱلسُّجُودُ٭ وَأَنْتَ ٱلْحَقُّ ٱلْمَعْبُودُ٭ أَعُوذُ بِكَ مِنِّي٭ وَأَسْأَلُكَ زَوَالِي عَنِّي٭ وَأَسْتَغْفِرُكَ مِنْ بَقِيَّةٍ تُبَعِّدُ وَتُدَنِّي٭ وَتُسَمِّي وَتُكَنِّي[٩٩]٭ أَنْتَ ٱلْوَاضِعُ وَٱلرَّافِعُ٭ وَٱلْمُبْدِعُ وَٱلْقَاطِعُ٭ وَٱلْمُفَرِّقُ[١٠٠]

٩٥. B, G, U, V, W = ٱلْحُدُودِ.
٩٦. B1, B2, H, I, L, P, P1, U, V, W = ٱلنَّقْصِ.
٩٧. B = سُبُوحٌ تَطَهَّرَ مِنْ أَشْبَاهِ ٱلذَّمِّ وَمُوجِبَاتِ ٱلرَّفْضِ قُدُّوسٌ تَنَزَّهَ عَنْ سِمَاتِ ٱلْحُدُودِ وَصِفَاتِ ٱلنَّقْضِ.
٩٨. G = مُخَالَفَةِ ٱلنَّقِيضِ ; B1, H, L, U = ٱلنَّقْصِ ; B2 - وَٱلنَّقِيضِ.
٩٩. B = وتُكَنّى وتُسَمّى تُبْعِدُ وتُدْنَى.
١٠٠. V - وَٱلْمُفَرِّق.

وَٱلْجَامِعُ * يَا وَاضِعُ يَا رَافِعُ * يَا مُبْدِعُ يَا قَاطِعُ * يَا مُفَرِّقُ يَا جَامِعُ * اَلْعِيَاذَ ٱلْعِيَاذَ * اَلْغِيَاثَ ٱلْغِيَاثَ * يَا عِيَاذِي يَا غِيَاثِي * اَلنَّجَاةَ ٱلنَّجَاةَ * اَلْمَلَاذَ ٱلْمَلَاذَ * يَا مَنْ بِهِ نَجَاتِي وَمَلَاذِي. أَسْأَلُكَ فِيمَا سَأَلْتُكَ وَأَتَوَسَّلُ إِلَيْكَ بِمُقَدِّمَةِ ٱلْوُجُودِ ٱلْأَوَّلِ * وَنُورِ ٱلْعِلْمِ ٱلْأَكْمَلِ * وَرُوحِ ٱلْحَيَاةِ ٱلْأَفْضَلِ * وَبِسَاطِ ٱلرَّحْمَةِ[١٠١] ٱلْأَزَلِ * وَسَمَاءِ ٱلْخُلُقِ ٱلْأَجَلِّ * اَلسَّابِقِ بِٱلرُّوحِ وَٱلْفَضْلِ * وَٱلْخَاتَمِ بِٱلصُّورَةِ وَٱلْبَعْثِ * وَٱلنُّورِ بِٱلْهِدَايَةِ وَٱلْبَيَانِ * وَٱلرَّحْمَةِ بِٱلْعِلْمِ وَٱلتَّمْكِينِ وَٱلْأَمَانِ * مُحَمَّدٍ ٱلْمُصْطَفَى * وَٱلرَّسُولِ ٱلْمُجْتَبَى[١٠٢] * صَلَّى ٱللّٰهُ عَلَيْهِ وَعَلَى آلِهِ وَصَحْبِهِ وَسَلَّمَ تَسْلِيمًا كَثِيرًا إِلَى يَوْمِ ٱلدِّينِ * ﴿وَٱلْحَمْدُ لِلّٰهِ رَبِّ ٱلْعَالَمِينَ﴾.

وِرْدُ لَيلَةِ ٱلثُّلَاثاءِ

بِسْمِ ٱللّٰهِ ٱلرَّحْمٰنِ ٱلرَّحِيمِ. إِلٰهِي أَنْتَ ٱلشَّدِيدُ ٱلْبَطْشِ * ٱلْأَلِيمُ ٱلْأَخْذِ * ٱلْعَظِيمُ ٱلْقَهْرِ * ٱلْمُتَعَالِي عَنِ ٱلْأَضْدَادِ وَٱلْأَنْدَادِ * وَٱلْمُنَزَّهُ عَنِ ﴿ٱلصَّاحِبَةِ وَٱلْأَوْلَادِ﴾ * شَأْنُكَ قَهْرُ ٱلْأَعْدَاءِ وَقَمْعُ ٱلْجَبَّارِينَ[١٠٣] * تَمْكُرُ بِمَنْ تَشَاءُ ﴿وَأَنْتَ خَيْرُ ٱلْمَاكِرِينَ﴾. أَسْأَلُكَ بِٱسْمِكَ ٱلَّذِي أَخَذْتَ بِهِ ٱلنَّوَاصِي * وَأَنْزَلْتَ[١٠٤] بِهِ ﴿مِنَ ٱلصَّيَاصِي﴾ * وَقَذَفْتَ بِهِ

١٠١. G, I, R1 = رَحْمَةِ .

١٠٢. R1 = + وَٱلنَّبِيِّ ٱلْمُقْتَدَى .

١٠٣. R = ٱلْجَبَابِرَةِ .

١٠٤. G, R, W = وَأَخْرَجْتَ .

ٱلرُّعْبَ فِي قُلُوبِ﴾ ٱلْأَعْدَاءِ * وَأَشْقَيْتَ بِهِ أَهْلَ ٱلشَّقَاءِ * أَنْ تُمِدَّنِي بِرَقِيقَةٍ مِنْ رَقَائِقِ ٱسْمِكَ ٱلشَّدِيدِ[١٠٥] * تَسْرِي فِي قُوَايَ ٱلْكُلِّيَّةِ وَٱلْجُزْئِيَّةِ حَتَّى أَتَمَكَّنَ مِنْ فِعْلِ مَا أُرِيدُ * فَلَا يَصِلُ إِلَيَّ ظُلْمُ ظَالِمٍ بِسُوءٍ * وَلَا يَسْطُو عَلَيَّ مُتَكَبِّرٌ بِجَوْرٍ * وَٱجْعَلْ غَضَبِي لَكَ وَفِيكَ * مَقْرُونًا بِغَضَبِكَ لِنَفْسِكَ * وَ﴿ٱطْمِسْ﴾ عَلَى وُجُوهِ أَعْدَائِي ﴿وَٱمْسَخْهُمْ عَلَى مَكَانَتِهِمْ * وَٱشْدُدْ عَلَى قُلُوبِهِمْ﴾ * وَ﴿ٱضْرِبْ﴾ بَيْنِي وَ﴿بَيْنَهُمْ بِسُورٍ لَهُ بَابٌ * بَاطِنُهُ فِيهِ ٱلرَّحْمَةُ وَظَاهِرُهُ مِنْ قِبَلِهِ ٱلْعَذَابُ﴾ * إِنَّكَ شَدِيدُ ٱلْبَطْشِ * أَلِيمُ ٱلْأَخْذِ * عَظِيمُ ٱلْعِقَابِ[١٠٦] . ﴿وَكَذَٰلِكَ أَخْذُ رَبِّكَ إِذَا أَخَذَ ٱلْقُرَىٰ وَهِيَ ظَالِمَةٌ إِنَّ أَخْذَهُۥٓ أَلِيمٌ شَدِيدٌ﴾. **رَبِّ** أَغْنِنِي بِكَ عَمَّنْ سِوَاكَ * غِنَاءً يُغْنِينِي غَايَةَ ٱلْغِنَاءِ * عَنْ كُلِّ حَظٍّ يَدْعُونِي إِلَى[١٠٧] ظَاهِرِ خَلْقٍ * أَوْ بَاطِنِ أَمْرٍ * وَبَلِّغْنِي غَايَةَ تَيْسِيرِي * وَٱرْفَعْنِي إِلَى سِدْرَةِ مُنْتَهَايَ * وَأَشْهِدْنِي ٱلْوُجُودَ دَوْرِيًّا * وَٱلسَّيْرَ كَوْرِيًّا * لِأُعَايِنَ سِرَّ ٱلتَّنْزِيلِ إِلَى ٱلنِّهَايَاتِ * وَٱلْعَوْدَ إِلَى ٱلْبِدَايَاتِ * حَتَّى يَنْقَطِعَ ٱلْكَلَامُ * وَتَسْكُنَ حَرَكَةُ ٱللَّامِ * وَتُمْحَى نُقْطَةُ ٱلْغَيْنِ * وَيَعُودَ ٱلْوَاحِدُ إِلَى ٱلِاثْنَيْنِ[١٠٨] . **إِلٰهِي** يَسِّرْ عَلَيَّ بِٱلسِّرِّ ٱلَّذِي يَسَّرْتَهُ عَلَى كَثِيرٍ مِنْ أَوْلِيَائِكَ * تَيْسِيرًا يُعْجِمُ عَنِّي غَيْمَ غِنَائِي * وَأَيِّدْنِي فِي ذٰلِكَ كُلِّهِ بِنُورٍ شَعْشَعَانِيٍّ *

١٠٥. G, I, P1, R, R1, V, W = ٱلشَّرِيفِ.

١٠٦. G, I, R, V = أَلِيمُ ٱلْعِقَابِ.

١٠٧. G, I, R = يَدْعُو إِلَيَّ.

١٠٨. R (margin), R1 = وَيَغْلِبُ ٱلْوَاحِدُ عَلَى ٱلِاثْنَيْنِ.

﴿يَخْطَفُ[١٠٩] بَصَرَ﴾ كُلِّ حَاسِدٍ ﴿مِنَ ٱلْجِنِّ وَٱلْإِنْسِ﴾ * وَهَبْنِي[١١٠] مَلَكَةَ ٱلْغَلَبَةِ لِكُلِّ مَقَامٍ * وَٱغْنِنِي بِكَ عَمَّنْ سِوَاكَ * غِنَاءً يُثْبِتُ فَقْرِي إِلَيْكَ * إِنَّكَ ﴿ٱلْغَنِيُّ ٱلْحَمِيدُ﴾ * ٱلْوَلِيُّ ٱلْمَجِيدُ * ٱلْكَرِيمُ ٱلرَّشِيدُ[١١١]. وَصَلَّى ٱللّٰهُ عَلَى[١١٢] سَيِّدِنَا مُحَمَّدٍ وَآلِهِ وَصَحْبِهِ[١١٣] أَجْمَعِينَ * وَسَلَّمَ تَسْلِيمًا إِلَى يَوْمِ ٱلدِّينِ * ﴿وَٱلْحَمْدُ لِلّٰهِ رَبِّ ٱلْعَالَمِينَ﴾.

وِرْدُ يَوْمِ ٱلثُّلَاثَاءِ[١١٤]

بِسْمِ ٱللّٰهِ ٱلرَّحْمٰنِ ٱلرَّحِيمِ. رَبِّ أَدْخِلْنِي فِي ﴿لُجَّةِ بَحْرِ﴾ أَحَدِيَّتِكَ * وَطَمْطَامِ ﴿يَمِّ﴾ وَاحِدِيَّتِكَ * وَقَوِّنِي بِقُوَّةِ سَطْوَةِ ﴿سُلْطَانِ﴾ فَرْدِيَّتِكَ[١١٥] * حَتَّى أَخْرُجَ إِلَى فَضَاءِ سِعَةِ رَحْمَتِكَ * وَفِي وَجْهِي لَمَعَانُ بَرْقِ ٱلْقُرْبِ مِنْ آثَارِ رَحْمَتِكَ * مَهِيبًا بِهَيْبَتِكَ[١١٦] * عَزِيزًا بِعِنَايَتِكَ * مُبَجَّلًا مُكَرَّمًا بِتَعْلِيمِكَ[١١٧] وَتَزْكِيَتِكَ * وَأَلْبِسْنِي خِلَعَ ٱلْعِزَّةِ وَٱلْقَبُولِ * وَسَهِّلْ لِي

١٠٩. R + عَنِّي ; W + بِهِ .
١١٠. I, P, P1 = هَبْ لِي .
١١١. R = ٱلْغَنِيُّ ٱلْحَمِيدُ ٱلْمَجِيدُ ٱلرَّشِيدُ ; I = ٱلْغَنِيُّ ٱلْحَمِيدُ ٱلْمَجِيدُ ٱلْكَرِيمُ ٱلرَّشِيدُ ;
P1, V = ٱلْغَنِيُّ ٱلْمَجِيدُ وَٱلْوَلِيُّ ٱلْحَمِيدُ .
١١٢. G + جِيمِ جِلَاءِ ٱلْقُلوبِ وَمَفَاتِيحِ ٱلْغُيوبِ مَعْدِنِ ٱلْحِكَمِ ٱلرَّسُولِ ٱلْمُكَرَّمِ .
١١٣. R = وَسَلَّمَ تَسْلِيمًا إِلَى يَوْمِ ٱلدِّينِ وَٱلْحَمْدُ لِلّٰهِ رَبِّ ٱلْعَالَمِين .
١١٤. B + وِرْد ٱلسَّطْوَة ; V + دُعا ٱلْكَشْف .
C, K, P + فِي ٱلْخَلْوَةِ قَالَ ٱلشَّيْخُ ٱلْعَارِفُ بِاللّٰهِ تَعَالَى ٱلشَّيْخُ مُحِي ٱلدِّينِ بِنْ ٱلْعَرَبِي رَضِيَ ٱللّٰهُ عَنْهُ: ظَهَرَ عَلَيَّ شَيْخَانِ مَهِيْبَانِ فِي جَبَل ٱلْفَتْحِ سَنَةَ عَشَرَ وَسِتَّ مِائَةً فَقَال أَحَدُهُمَا: أَرْوِ عَنِّي إِلَى كُلِّ طَالِبٍ صَادِقٍ وَإِلَى كُلِّ مُرِيدٍ مُوَافِقٍ
R1 + وقال ٱلشيخ محيي ٱلدين ٱلعربي قدّس ٱللّٰه سرّه ٱلقرير ونوّر صريحه: طَلَعَ عَلَيَّ فِي ٱلْخَلْوَةِ رَجُلَانُ مَهِيبَانُ عَلَيْهُمَا ثِيَابٌ بَيْضٌ فَقَالَا لِي: ادع بِهذا ٱلدُّعَاءِ وَٱسْمُهُ دُعَاءَ ٱلْكَشْفِ
١١٥. L, P, P1 = فَرْدِانِيَتِك .
١١٦. H (note),K + قَوِيًّا بِقُوَّتِكَ .
١١٧. B, G, R, R1, V + وَتَرْبِيَتِكَ ; P1 = بِتَعْلِيمِكَ وَتَرْبِيَتِكَ ; C = بِتَكْرِيمِك ; I, K = وبِتَكْرِيمِكَ وَتَرْبِيَتِكَ .

مَنَاهِجَ ٱلْوُصْلَةِ وَٱلْوُصُولِ٭ وَتَوِّجْنِي بِتَاجِ ٱلْكَرَامَةِ وَٱلْوَقَارِ٭ وَأَلِّفْ بَيْنِي وَبَيْنَ أَحْبَابِكَ فِي دَارِ ٱلدُّنْيَا وَدَارِ ٱلْقَرَارِ٭ وَٱرْزُقْنِي مِنْ نُورِ ٱسْمِكَ[١١٨]٭ بِنُورِ ٱسْمِكَ[١١٩]٭ سَطْوَةً وَهَيْبَةً٭ حَتَّى تَنْقَادَ إِلَيَّ ٱلْقُلُوبُ وَٱلْأَرْوَاحُ٭ وَتَخْضَعَ لَدَيَّ ٱلنُّفُوسُ وَٱلْأَشْبَاحُ٭ يَا مَنْ ذَلَّتْ لَهُ رِقَابُ ٱلْجَبَابِرَةِ٭ وَخَضَعَتْ لَدَيْهِ أَعْنَاقُ ٱلْأَكَاسِرَةِ٭ يَا مَالِكَ ٱلدُّنْيَا وَٱلْآخِرَةِ[١٢٠]٭ ﴿لَا مَلْجَأَ﴾ وَلَا مَنْجَأَ ﴿مِنْكَ إِلَّا إِلَيْكَ﴾٭ وَلَا إِعَانَةَ إِلَّا مِنْكَ[١٢١]٭ وَلَا ٱتِّكَالَ إِلَّا عَلَيْكَ٭ ٱدْفَعْ عَنِّي كَيْدَ ٱلْحَاسِدِينَ٭ وَظُلُمَاتِ شَرِّ ٱلْمُعَانِدِينَ٭ وَٱحْمِنِي[١٢٢] تَحْتَ سُرَادِقَاتِ عِزَّتِكَ[١٢٣]٭ يَا أَكْرَمَ ٱلْأَكْرَمِينَ[١٢٤]. إِلٰهِي أَيِّدْ ظَاهِرِي[١٢٥] فِي تَحْصِيلِ مَرَاضِيكَ٭ وَنَوِّرْ قَلْبِي وَسِرِّي لِلِاطِّلَاعِ عَلَى مَنَاهِجِ مَسَاعِيكَ. إِلٰهِي كَيْفَ أَصْدُرُ عَنْ بَابِكَ بِخَيْبَةٍ مِنْكَ٭ وَقَدْ وَرَدْتُهُ عَلَى ثِقَةٍ بِكَ٭ وَكَيْفَ تُؤَيِّسُنِي مِنْ عَطَائِكَ٭ وَقَدْ أَمَرْتَنِي بِدُعَائِكَ٭ وَهَا أَنَا مُقْبِلٌ عَلَيْكَ٭ مُلْتَجِئٌ إِلَيْكَ. إِلٰهِي بَاعِدْ بَيْنِي وَبَيْنَ أَعْدَائِي٭ كَمَا بَاعَدْتَ بَيْنَ ٱلْمَشْرِقِ وَٱلْمَغْرِبِ٭ وَ﴿ٱخْطِفْ أَبْصَارَهُمْ﴾٭ وَزَلْزِلْ أَقْدَامَهُمْ٭ وَٱدْفَعْ عَنِّي شَرَّهُمْ وَضَرَّهُمْ٭ بِنُورِ

١١٨. B, P1 = أَسْمَائِكَ .
١١٩. G, I - بِنُورِ اسْمِكَ ; K= بِنُورِ ذَاتِكَ .
١٢٠. B, G, I, L, P1, R - يَا مَالِكَ ٱلدُّنْيَا وَٱلْآخِرَةِ .
١٢١. P1, R1 = بِكَ .
١٢٢. B, B2, P1, U, V = وَٱرْحَمْنِي ; G, I = وَٱدْخِلْنِي ; L = وَٱحْجُبْنِي ; K = وَٱرْحَمْنِي وَٱدْخِلْنِي .
١٢٣. G = عَرْشِكَ .
١٢٤. B, P1, (R+) = يَا أَرْحَمَ ٱلرَّاحِمِينَ .
١٢٥. P1, R (margin) + وَبَاطِنِي .

قُدْسِكَ وَجَلَالِ مَجْدِكَ۞ فَإِنَّكَ أَنْتَ ٱللّٰهُ ٱلْمُعْطِي جَلَائِلَ ٱلنِّعَمِ۞ ٱلْمُبَجَّلُ ٱلْمُكَرَّمُ۞ لِمَنْ نَاجَاكَ بِلَطَائِفِ ٱلرَّأْفَةِ وَٱلرَّحْمَةِ[١٢٦]۞ يَا حَيُّ يَا قَيُّومُ۞ يَا كَاشِفَ أَسْرَارِ ٱلْمَعَارِفِ وَٱلْعُلُومِ[١٢٧]. وَصَلَّى ٱللّٰهُ عَلَى سَيِّدِنَا مُحَمَّدٍ۞ وَعَلَى آلِهِ وَصَحْبِهِ أَجْمَعِينَ۞ ﴿سُبْحَانَ رَبِّكَ رَبِّ ٱلْعِزَّةِ عَمَّا يَصِفُونَ۞ وَسَلَامٌ عَلَى ٱلْمُرْسَلِينَ۞ وَٱلْحَمْدُ لِلّٰهِ رَبِّ ٱلْعَالَمِينَ﴾.

وِرْدُ لَيْلَةِ ٱلْأَرْبِعَاءِ

بِسْمِ ٱللّٰهِ ٱلرَّحْمٰنِ ٱلرَّحِيمِ. **إِلٰهِي** اِسْمُكَ سَيِّدُ ٱلْأَسْمَاءِ۞ وَبِيَدِكَ ﴿مَلَكُوتُ﴾ ٱلْأَرْضِ وَٱلسَّمَاءِ۞ أَنْتَ ﴿ٱلْقَائِمُ﴾ بِكُلِّ شَيْءٍ۞ وَ﴿عَلَى كُلِّ شَيْءٍ﴾[١٢٨]۞ ثَبَتَ لَكَ ٱلْغِنَاءُ۞ وَٱفْتَقَرَ إِلَى فَيْضِ جُودِكَ ٱلْأَقْدَسِ كُلُّ مَا سِوَاكَ ٱلْهُوَ وَٱلْأَنَا[١٢٩]. أَسْأَلُكَ بِٱسْمِكَ[١٣٠] ٱلَّذِي جَمَعْتَ بِهِ بَيْنَ ٱلْمُتَقَابِلَاتِ وَمُتَفَرِّقَاتِ ٱلْخَلْقِ وَٱلْأَمْرِ۞ وَأَقَمْتَ بِهِ غَيْبَ كُلِّ ظَاهِرٍ وَأَظْهَرْتَ بِهِ شَهَادَةَ كُلِّ غَائِبٍ[١٣١]۞ أَنْ تَهَبَ لِي صَمَدَانِيَّةً أُسَكِّنُ بِهَا مُتَحَرِّكَ قُدْرَتِكَ[١٣٢]۞ حَتَّى يَتَحَرَّكَ فِيَّ[١٣٣] كُلُّ سَاكِنٍ۞ وَيُسَكَّنَ فِيَّ

١٢٦. B, B2, G = ٱلرَّحْمَةِ وَٱلرَّأْفَةِ.

١٢٧. B2, G, H, I, K, L, P, P1 + احْفَظْنِي بِجَلَالِ قُدْسِكَ وَمَجْدِكَ لَا شَرِيكَ لَكَ وَأَشْهَدُ انْ مُحَمَّدًا عَبْدُكَ وَرَسُولُكَ وَنَبِيُّكَ وَصَفِيُّكَ.

١٢٨. G – عَلَى كُلِّ شَيْءٍ.

١٢٩. G, R1 = جُودِكَ ٱلْوَرَى ; R = جُودِكَ ٱلْهَوَى ; V = فَيْضِكَ ٱلْأَقْدَسِ ٱلْهَوَى وَٱلْأَنَا ;
I = فَضْلِكَ ٱلْأَقْدَسِ ٱلسِّوَى وَٱلْأَنَا.

١٣٠. I, V, W + ٱلْحَقِّ.

١٣١. G = وأَقَمْتَ بِهِ غَيْبَ كُلِّ غَائِبٍ وَحَاضِرٍ.

١٣٢. R = لِقُدْرَتِكَ ; I = أُسَكِّنُ بِهَا كُلَّ مُتَحَرِّكٍ بِقُدْرَتِكَ ; أُسَكِّنُ كُلَّ مُتَحَرِّكٍ لِقُدْرَتِكَ.

١٣٣. G = لِي ; V = إِلَيَّ ; R = بِي.

كُلُّ مُتَحَرِّكٍ ٭ فَأَجِدَنِي[١٣٤] قِبْلَةَ كُلِّ مُتَوَجِّهٍ ٭ وَجَامِعَ شَتَاتِ كُلِّ مُتَفَرِّقٍ ٭
مِنْ حَيْثُ ٱسْمُكَ ٱلَّذِي تَوَجَّهَتْ إِلَيْهِ وِجْهَتِي ٭ وَٱضْمَحَلَّتْ عِنْدَهُ
إِرَادَتِي وَكَلِمَتِي[١٣٥] ٭ فَيَقْتَبِسَ كُلٌّ مِنِّي جَذْوَةَ هُدًى تَامٍّ تُوضِحُ لَهُ مَا
أَمَّ إِمَامَةُ[١٣٦] مُحَمَّدٍ ٱلْمُصْطَفَى[١٣٧] ٭ ٱلْفَرْدِ[١٣٨] ٱلَّذِي لَوْلَاهُ لَمْ تَثْبُتْ[١٣٩]
أَنَانِيَّةُ ٱلْمُقْتَبِسِ[١٤٠] لِمُوسَى[١٤١] ٭ يَا مَنْ هُوَ هُوَ وَلَا أَنَا. أَسْأَلُكَ بِكُلِّ ٱسْمٍ
ٱسْتَمَدَّ مِنْ أَلِفِ ٱلْغَيْبِ ٱلْمُحِيطِ بِحَقِيقَةِ كُلِّ مَشْهُودٍ ٭ أَنْ تُشْهِدَنِي
وَحْدَةَ كُلِّ مُتَكَثِّرٍ ٭ فِي بَاطِنِ كُلِّ حَقٍّ ٭ وَكَثْرَةَ كُلِّ مُوَحِّدٍ ٭ فِي
ظَاهِرِ كُلِّ حَقِيقَةٍ ٭ ثُمَّ وَحْدَةَ ٱلظَّاهِرِ وَٱلْبَاطِنِ ٭ حَتَّى لَا يَخْفَى عَلَيَّ
غَيْبٌ ظَاهِرٌ ٭ وَلَا يَغِيبُ عَنِّي خَفِيٌّ بَاطِنٌ ٭ وَأَنْ تُشْهِدَنِي ٱلْكُلَّ فِي
ٱلْكُلِّ ٭ يَا ﴿مَنْ بِيَدِهِ مَلَكُوتُ كُلِّ شَيْءٍ﴾ ٭ إِنَّكَ أَنْتَ أَنْتَ[١٤٢]. ﴿قُلِ
ٱللَّهُ ثُمَّ ذَرْهُمْ فِي خَوْضِهِمْ يَلْعَبُونَ﴾. ﴿الم﴾ ﴿ٱللَّهُ لَا إِلَٰهَ إِلَّا هُوَ ٱلْحَيُّ
ٱلْقَيُّومُ﴾. **سَيِّدِي** ﴿سَلَامٌ عَلَيَّ﴾ مِنْكَ[١٤٣] ٭ أَنْتَ سَنَدِي[١٤٤] ٭ سَوَاءٌ
عِنْدَكَ سِرِّي وَجَهْرِي ٭ تَسْمَعُ نِدَائِي ٭ وَتُجِيبُ دُعَائِي ٭ مَحَوْتَ

١٣٤. I = وَٱجعَلْنِي .
١٣٥. G, I, P1, V, W = كَلِمَتِي .
١٣٦. G = مَا أَمَّ أُمَّةُ .
١٣٧. G, P1 + صلى ٱللّٰه عليه وسلم .
١٣٨. G - ٱلْفَرْدُ ; I, V = أمامَهُ ٱلْفَرْد .
١٣٩. G = مَا ثَبَتَتْ ; R = مَا ثَبَتَ .
١٤٠. P1 = إِبَانَةُ ٱلْقَبَسِ ; R1 = ٱلْقَبَسِ .
١٤١. G, P1 + عليه ٱلسلام ; I, V - لِمُوسَى .
١٤٢. G = أنت ٱللّٰه ; V = أنت أنت أنت ; R = أنت أنت لَا إله إلَّا أنت .
١٤٣. G, I, P1 = سَلَامٌ عَلَيْكَ .
١٤٤. R, V = سَيِّدِي .

بِنُورِكَ ظُلْمَتِي * وَأَحْيَيْتَ بِرُوحِكَ مَيْتَتِي * فَأَنْتَ رَبِّي * وَبِيَدِكَ سَمْعِي وَبَصَرِي وَقَلْبِي * مَلَكْتَ جَمِيعِي * وَشَرَّفْتَ وَضِيعِي * وَأَعْلَيْتَ قَدْرِي * وَرَفَعْتَ ذِكْرِي * تَبَارَكْتَ نُورَ ٱلْأَنْوَارِ * وَكَاشِفَ ٱلْأَسْرَارِ * وَوَاهِبَ ٱلْأَعْمَارِ * وَمُسْبِلَ ٱلْأَسْتَارِ * تَنَزَّهْتَ فِي سُمُوِّ جَلَالِكَ * عَنْ سِمَاتِ ٱلْمُحْدَثَاتِ * وَعَلَتْ رُتْبَةُ كَمَالِكَ * عَنِ تَطَرُّقِ ٱلْمُيُولِ إِلَيْهَا بِٱلشَّهَوَاتِ * وَٱلنَّقَائِصِ وَٱلْآفَاتِ[١٤٥] * وَأَنَارَتْ بِشُهُودِ ذَاتِكَ ٱلْأَرَضُونَ وَٱلسَّمٰوَاتُ * لَكَ ٱلْمَجْدُ ٱلْأَرْفَعُ * وَٱلْجَنَابُ ٱلْأَوْسَعُ * وَٱلْعِزُّ ٱلْأَمْنَعُ * سُبُّوحٌ قُدُّوسٌ رَبُّنَا وَرَبُّ ٱلْمَلَائِكَةِ وَٱلرُّوحِ * مُنَوِّرُ ٱلصَّيَاصِي ٱلْمُظْلِمَةِ * وَ[١٤٦] ٱلْجَوَاهِرِ ٱلْمُدْلَهِمَةِ * وَمُنْقِذُ ٱلْغَرْقَى * مِنْ بَحْرِ ٱلْهَيُولَى * ﴿أَعُوذُ بِكَ مِنْ غَاسِقٍ إِذَا وَقَبَ * وَحَاسِدٍ﴾ إِذَا ارْتَقَبَ. **مَلِيكِي** أُنَادِيكَ وَأُنَاجِيكَ * مُنَاجَاةَ عَبْدٍ كَسِيرٍ يَعْلَمُ أَنَّكَ تَسْمَعُ * وَيَعْتَقِدُ أَنَّكَ تُجِيبُ * وَاقِفٌ بِبَابِكَ وَقْفَةَ ﴿مُضْطَرٍّ﴾ لَا يَجِدُ ﴿مِنْ دُونِكَ وَكِيلًا﴾. أَسْأَلُكَ **إِلٰهِي** بِٱسْمِكَ ٱلَّذِي أَفَضْتَ بِهِ ٱلْخَيْرَاتِ * وَأَنْزَلْتَ بِهِ ٱلْبَرَكَاتِ * وَمَنَحْتَ بِهِ أَهْلَ ٱلشُّكْرِ ٱلزِّيَادَاتِ * وَأَخْرَجْتَ بِهِ مِنَ ٱلظُّلُمَاتِ * وَنَسَخْتَ بِهِ أَهْلَ ٱلشِّرْكِ وَٱلدَّنَاءَاتِ[١٤٧] * أَنْ تُفِيضَ عَلَيَّ مِنْ مَلَابِسِ أَنْوَارِكَ مَا تُرَدُّ بِهِ عَنِّي أَبْصَارُ ٱلْأَعَادِي حَاسِرَةً * وَأَيْدِيهِمْ خَاسِرَةً[١٤٨] * وَٱجْعَلْ حَظِّي

١٤٥. V= تَطَرُّقِ ٱلْمُيُولِ بِٱلشَّهَوَاتِ وَٱلنَّقَائِصِ وَٱلْآفَاتِ.

١٤٦. G, P1, R (margin), R1, V + غَوَاسِقِ.

١٤٧. G, P1, R, V – وَنَسَخْتَ بِهِ أَهْلَ ٱلشِّرْكِ وَٱلدَّنَاءَاتِ.

١٤٨. I = وَأَيْدِيهِم خَائِبَةً.

مِنْكَ إِشْرَاقًا يَجْلُو لِي كُلَّ أَمْرٍ خَفِيٍّ * وَيَكْشِفُ لِي عَنْ كُلِّ سِرٍّ عَلِيٍّ * وَيَحْرِقُ كُلَّ شَيْطَانٍ غَوِيٍّ[١٤٩] * يَا نُورَ ٱلنُّورِ * يَا كَاشِفَ كُلِّ مَسْتُورٍ * ﴿إِلَيْكَ تُرْجَعُ ٱلْأُمُورِ﴾ * وَبِكَ[١٥٠] تُدْفَعُ ٱلشُّرُورُ * يَا رَبِّ يَا رَحِيمُ يَا غَفُورُ[١٥١] . وَصَلَّى ٱللّٰهُ عَلَى سَيِّدِنَا مُحَمَّدٍ وعَلَى آلِهِ وَصَحْبِهِ أَجْمَعِينَ * ﴿وَسَلَامٌ عَلَى ٱلْمُرْسَلِينَ * وَٱلْحَمْدُ لِلّٰهِ رَبِّ ٱلْعَالَمِينَ﴾.

وِرْدُ يَوْمِ ٱلْأَرْبِعَاءِ[١٥٢]

بِسْمِ ٱللّٰهِ ٱلرَّحْمٰنِ ٱلرَّحِيمِ. رَبِّ أَكْرِمْنِي بِشُهُودِ أَنْوَارِ قُدْسِكَ * وَأَيِّدْنِي بِظُهُورِ سَطْوَةِ سُلْطَانِ أُنْسِكَ * حَتَّى أَتَقَلَّبَ فِي سُبُحَاتِ مَعَارِفِ أَسْمَائِكَ * تَقَلُّبًا يُطْلِعُنِي عَلَى أَسْرَارِ[١٥٣] ذَرَّاتِ[١٥٤] وُجُودِي * فِي عَوَالِمِ شُهُودِي * لِأُشَاهِدَ بِهَا مَا أَوْدَعْتَهُ فِي عَوَالِمِ ٱلْمُلْكِ وَٱلْمَلَكُوتِ * وَأُعَايِنَ[١٥٥] سَرَيَانَ سِرِّ[١٥٦] قُدْرَتِكَ[١٥٧] فِي شَوَاهِدِ[١٥٨] ٱللَّاهُوتِ وَٱلنَّاسُوتِ * وَعَرِّفْنِي مَعْرِفَةً تَامَّةً * وَحِكْمَةً عَامَّةً * حَتَّى لَا يَبْقَى مَعْلُومٌ إِلَّا وَأَطَّلِعُ

١٤٩. G, R, V - وَيَحْرِقُ كُلَّ شَيْطَانٍ غَوِيٍ.
١٥٠. V = بِيَدِكَ.
١٥١. G, I, R, V - يَا رَبِّ يَا رَحِيمُ يَا غَفُورُ.
١٥٢. U + دُعا ٱلْقُرْبَة ;B + وِرْد ٱلْقُرْبَة.
١٥٣. G - أَسْرَارِ.
١٥٤. B2 = ذَاتِ.
١٥٥. B, C, R, U, V - عَوَالِم....
١٥٦. K, L, R - سِرِّ.
١٥٧. P1 = قُدْسِكَ.
١٥٨. C = فِي مَعالِمِ.

عَلَى رَقَائِقِ دَقَائِقِهِ[١٥٩] ٱلْمُنْبَسِطَةِ فِي ٱلْمَوْجُودَاتِ * وَأَدْفَعُ بِهَا ظُلْمَةَ ٱلْإِكْرَاهِ[١٦٠] ٱلْمَانِعَةِ عَنْ إِدْرَاكِ حَقَائِقِ ٱلْآيَاتِ * وَأَتَصَرَّفُ بِهَا فِي ٱلْقُلُوبِ وَٱلْأَرْوَاحِ بِمُهَيِّجَاتِ ٱلْمَحَبَّةِ وَٱلْوِدَادِ * وَٱلرُّشْدِ وَٱلرَّشَادِ[١٦١] * إِنَّكَ أَنْتَ ٱلْمُحِبُّ ٱلْمَحْبُوبُ * وَٱلطَّالِبُ ٱلْمَطْلُوبُ * يَا مُقَلِّبَ ٱلْقُلُوبِ * وَيَا كَاشِفَ ٱلْكُرُوبِ * وَ﴿أَنْتَ عَلَّامُ ٱلْغُيُوبِ﴾ * سَتَّارُ ٱلْعُيُوبِ * غَفَّارُ ٱلذُّنُوبِ[١٦٢] * يَا مَنْ لَمْ يَزَلْ غَفَّارًا * وَيَا مَنْ لَمْ يَزَلْ سَتَّارًا * يَا غَفَّارُ * يَا سَتَّارُ * يَا حَفِيظُ * يَا وَاقِيُ[١٦٣] * يَا دَافِعُ * يَا مُحْسِنُ * يَا عَطُوفُ * يَا رَؤُوفُ * يَا لَطِيفُ[١٦٤] * يَا عَزِيزُ * يَا سَلَامُ * اِغْفِرْلِي وَٱسْتُرْنِي وَٱحْفَظْنِي * وَقِنِي وَٱدْفَعْ عَنِّي * وَأَحْسِنْ إِلَيَّ وَتَعَطَّفْ عَلَيَّ * وَٱرْأَفْ بِي وَٱلْطُفْ بِي[١٦٥] * وَأَعِزَّنِي وَسَلِّمْنِي * وَلَا تُؤَاخِذْنِي بِقَبِيحِ فِعَالِي * وَ﴿لَا تُجَازِنِي﴾ بِسُوءِ أَعْمَالِي * وَتَدَارَكْنِي عَاجِلًا بِلُطْفِكَ ٱلتَّامِّ * وَخَالِصِ رَحْمَتِكَ ٱلْعَامِّ[١٦٦] * وَلَا تُحْوِجْنِي إِلَى أَحَدٍ سِوَاكَ * وَعَافِنِي وَٱعْفُ عَنِّي * وَأَصْلِحْ لِي شَأْنِي كُلَّهُ * ﴿لَا إِلَٰهَ إِلَّا أَنْتَ * سُبْحَانَكَ إِنِّي كُنْتُ مِنَ ٱلظَّالِمِينَ﴾ * ﴿وَأَنْتَ

١٥٩. I, R1 = رَقَائِقِ دَقَائِقِ حَقَائِقِهِ ; G = دَقَائِقِ غُيُوبِ ٱلْمَعْلُومَاتِ .

١٦٠. R = ٱلْإِكْرَار ; I, P1 = ٱلْأَكْوَانِ .

١٦١. C = ٱلْإِرْشَادِ .

١٦٢. B, G, R, U - غَفّار الذُّنوب .

١٦٣. B2, G, P1, R (note صح) = وَافِي .

١٦٤. B, B2, P1, V - يَا لَطِيفُ .

١٦٥. B, B2, G, K, P1, U, V = وَأرْأَفْ وَأَعْطِف .

١٦٦. B, B2, G, K, P1, U, V - الْعَامّ .

أَرْحَمُ ٱلرَّاحِمِينَ﴾. وَصَلَّى ٱللّٰهُ عَلَى سَيِّدِنَا مُحَمَّدٍ وَعَلَى آلِهِ وَصَحْبِهِ أَجْمَعِينَ * ﴿وَسَلَامٌ عَلَى ٱلْمُرْسَلِينَ * وَٱلْحَمْدُ لِلّٰهِ رَبِّ ٱلْعَالَمِينَ﴾.

وِرْدُ لَيْلَةِ ٱلْخَمِيس

بِسْمِ ٱللّٰهِ ٱلرَّحْمٰنِ ٱلرَّحِيمِ. سَيِّدِي أَنْتَ مُسَبِّبُ ٱلْأَسْبَابِ وَمُرَتِّبُهَا * وَمُصَرِّفُ ٱلْقُلُوبِ وَمُقَلِّبُهَا. أَسْأَلُكَ بِٱلْحِكْمَةِ ٱلَّتِي ٱقْتَضَتْ تَرْتِيبَ ٱلْأَسْبَابِ[١٦٧] ٱلْأُوَلِ * وَتَأْثِيرَ ٱلْأَعْلَى فِي ٱلْأَسْفَلِ * أَنْ تُشْهِدَنِي تَرْتِيبَ ٱلْأَسْبَابِ صُعُودًا وَنُزُولًا * حَتَّى أَشْهَدَ ٱلْبَاطِنَ مِنْهَا بِشُهُودِ ٱلظَّاهِرِ * وَٱلْأَوَّلَ فِي عَيْنِ ٱلْآخِرِ * وَأَلْحَظَ حِكْمَةَ ٱلتَّرْتِيبِ بِشُهُودِ ٱلْمُرَتِّبِ[١٦٨] * وَمُسَبَّبَ[١٦٩] ٱلْأَسْبَابِ مَسْبُوقًا[١٧٠] بِٱلْمُسَبِّبِ * فَلَا أَحْجُبَ عَنِ ٱلْعَيْنِ بِٱلْغَيْنِ. إِلٰهِي أَلْقِ إِلَيَّ مِفْتَاحَ[١٧١] ٱلْأُذُنِ[١٧٢] ٱلَّذِي هُوَ ﴿كٓهيعٓصٓ﴾[١٧٣] ٱلْمَعَارِفِ * حَتَّى أَنْطِقَ فِي كُلِّ بِدَايَةٍ بِٱسْمِكَ ٱلْبَدِيعِ ٱلَّذِي افْتَتَحْتَ بِهِ كُلَّ ﴿رَقِيمٍ﴾ ﴿مَسْطُورٍ﴾ * يَا مَنْ لِسُمُوِّ أَسْمَائِهِ يَنْخَفِضُ كُلُّ مُتَعَالٍ[١٧٤] * وَكُلٌّ بِكَ وَأَنْتَ بِلَا نَحْنُ * أَنْتَ مُبْدِعُ كُلِّ شَيْءٍ وَبَارِئُهُ *

١٦٧. V = ٱلْآخِرِ عَلَى ; I = ٱلْأَسْمَاء.
١٦٨. G, I, P1, R, R1 = ٱلْمَرَاتِبِ.
١٦٩. G, I, R, R1, W = سَبَبَ.
١٧٠. R = مَسْتُورٌ.
١٧١. G = مَفَاتِيحَ.
١٧٢. P, R = ٱلْإِذْنِ.
١٧٣. I, P1, R, R1, W = كَافُ ; V = دكان.
١٧٤. R = يَا مَنْ يَسْمُو سَمَاؤُكَ بِخَفْضِ كُلِّ مُتَعَالٍ.

فَلَكَ ٱلْحَمْدُ يَا بَارِئُ [١٧٥] عَلَى كُلِّ بِدَايَةٍ * وَلَكَ ٱلشُّكْرُ يَا بَاقِي عَلَى كُلِّ نِهَايَةٍ * أَنْتَ ٱلْبَاعِثُ عَلَى كُلِّ خَيْرٍ * بَاطِنُ ٱلْبَوَاطِنِ * بَالِغُ غَايَاتِ ٱلْأُمُورِ * بَاسِطُ ٱلرِّزْقِ لِلْعَالَمِينَ [١٧٦] * بَارِكِ ٱللّٰهُمَّ لِي وَعَلَيَّ فِي ٱلْآخِرِينَ * كَمَا بَارَكْتَ عَلَى مُحَمَّدٍ وَإِبْرَاهِيمَ. إِنَّهُ مِنْكَ وَإِلَيْكَ ﴿وَإِنَّهُ بِسْمِ ٱللّٰهِ ٱلرَّحْمٰنِ ٱلرَّحِيمِ﴾ ﴿بَدِيعُ ٱلسَّمٰوَاتِ وَٱلْأَرْضِ وَإِذَا قَضَى أَمْرًا فَإِنَّمَا يَقُولُ لَهُ كُنْ فَيَكُونُ﴾. **إِلٰهِي** أَنْتَ ٱلثَّابِتُ قَبْلَ كُلِّ ثَابِتٍ * وَٱلْبَاقِي بَعْدَ كُلِّ نَاطِقٍ وَصَامِتٍ * لَا إِلٰهَ إِلَّا أَنْتَ * وَلَا مَوْجُودَ سِوَاكَ * لَكَ ٱلْكِبْرِيَاءُ وَٱلْجَبَرُوتُ * وَٱلْعَظَمَةُ وَٱلْمَلَكُوتُ * تَقْهَرُ ٱلْجَبَّارِينَ * وَتُبِيدُ كَيْدَ [١٧٧] ٱلظَّالِمِينَ * وَتُبَدِّدُ شَمْلَ ٱلْمُلْحِدِينَ * وَتُذِلُّ رِقَابَ ٱلْمُتَكَبِّرِينَ. أَسْأَلُكَ يَا غَالِبَ كُلِّ غَالِبٍ * وَيَا مُدْرِكَ كُلِّ هَارِبٍ * رَدِّنِي بِرِدَاءِ كِبْرِيَائِكَ * وَإِزَارِ عَظَمَتِكَ * وَسُرَادِقَاتِ هَيْبَتِكَ * وَبِمَا وَرَاءَ ذٰلِكَ كُلِّهِ مِمَّا لَا يَعْلَمُهُ إِلَّا أَنْتَ * أَنْ تَكْسُوَنِي [١٧٨] هَيْبَةً مِنْ هَيْبَتِكَ * تَجِلُّ [١٧٩] لَهَا ٱلْقُلُوبُ وَتَخْشَعُ لَهَا ٱلْأَبْصَارُ * وَمَلِّكْنِي نَاصِيَةَ ﴿كُلِّ جَبَّارٍ عَنِيدٍ [١٨٠]﴾ * وَ﴿شَيْطَانٍ مَرِيدٍ [١٨١]﴾ * نَاصِيَتُهُ بِيَدِكَ * وَأَبْقِ

١٧٥. V = بَرّ ; I, P = رَبّ .
١٧٦. V = أَرْزَاقِ ٱلْعَالَمِين .
١٧٧. I – ; G = تُكِيدُ ; R = وَتَكِيدُ كَيْدَ .
١٧٨. R = تُكْسِينِي .
١٧٩. P, P1 = تَخْضَعُ ; I, R1 = تُوجِلّ .
١٨٠. R = كُلِّ آخِذٍ .
١٨١. I, R – وَشَيْطَانٍ مَرِيدٍ .

عَلَيَّ ذُلَّ ٱلْعُبُودِيَّةِ فِي ذٰلِكَ كُلِّهِ۞ وَأَعْصِمْنِي مِنَ ٱلزَّيْغِ[١٨٢] وَٱلزَّلَلِ۞ وَأَيِّدْنِي فِي[١٨٣] ٱلْقَوْلِ وَٱلْعَمَلِ۞ أَنْتَ[١٨٤] مُثَبِّتُ ٱلْقُلُوبِ۞ وَكَاشِفُ ٱلْكُرُوبِ۞ لَا إِلٰهَ إِلَّا أَنْتَ. وَصَلَّى ٱللّٰهُ عَلَى سَيِّدِنَا مُحَمَّدٍ وَعَلَى آلِهِ وَصَحْبِهِ أَجْمَعِينَ۞ ﴿وَٱلْحَمْدُ لِلّٰهِ رَبِّ ٱلْعَالَمِينَ﴾.

وِرْدُ يَوْمِ ٱلْخَمِيسِ[١٨٥]

بِسْمِ ٱللّٰهِ ٱلرَّحْمٰنِ ٱلرَّحِيمِ. **إِلٰهِي** أَنْتَ ٱلْقَائِمُ بِذَاتِكَ۞ وَٱلْمُتَجَلِّي بِصِفَاتِكَ۞ وَٱلْمُحِيطُ بِأَسْمَائِكَ[١٨٦]۞ وَٱلظَّاهِرُ بِأَفْعَالِكَ۞ وَٱلْبَاطِنُ بِمَا لَا يَعْلَمُهُ إِلَّا أَنْتَ تَوَحَّدْتَ فِي جَلَالِكَ۞ فَأَنْتَ ٱلْوَاحِدُ ٱلْأَحَدُ۞ وَتَفَرَّدْتَ بِٱلْبَقَاءِ فِي ٱلْأَزَلِ وَٱلْأَبَدِ۞ أَنْتَ أَنْتَ ٱللّٰهُ ٱلْمُنْفَرِدُ بِٱلْوَحْدَانِيَّةِ فِي ﴿إِيَّاكَ﴾۞ لَا مَعَكَ غَيْرُكَ وَلَا فِيكَ سِوَاكَ. أَسْأَلُكَ **ٱللّٰهُمَّ** ٱلْفَنَاءَ فِي بَقَائِكَ۞ وَٱلْبَقَاءَ بِكَ لَا مَعَكَ۞ لَا إِلٰهَ إِلَّا أَنْتَ. **إِلٰهِي** غَيِّبْنِي فِي حُضُورِكَ۞ وَأَفْنِنِي فِي وُجُودِكَ۞ وَٱسْتَهْلِكْنِي فِي شُهُودِكَ۞ وَٱقْطَعْ بَيْنِي وَبَيْنَ ٱلْقَوَاطِعِ ٱلَّتِي تَقْطَعُ بَيْنِي وَبَيْنَكَ۞ وَٱشْغَلْنِي بِٱلشُّغْلِ بِكَ عَنْ كُلِّ شَاغِلٍ يَشْغَلُنِي[١٨٧] عَنْكَ۞ لَا إِلٰهَ إِلَّا أَنْتَ. **إِلٰهِي** أَنْتَ

١٨٢. R1, V = ٱلْخَطا ; I = ٱلْخَطَايَا ; P = ٱلذَّلَلِ وَٱلْخَطَايَا .
١٨٣. R = مِنَ .
١٨٤. I = إِنَّكَ ; P, P1 + أنت .
١٨٥. B + وِرْد ٱلْقَيُّومِيَّة .
١٨٦. C, P, P1, R1 = وَٱلْمُتَجَلِّي بِأَسْمَائِكَ وَٱلْمُحِيطُ بِصِفَاتِكَ ; R = وَٱلْمُحِيطُ بِصِفَاتِكَ وَٱلْمُتَجَلِّي بِأَسْمَائِكَ .
١٨٧. B = يُشْغِلُنِي .

ٱلْمَوْجُودُ ٱلْحَقُّ وَأَنَا ٱلْمَعْدُومُ ٱلْأَصْلُ * بَقَاؤُكَ بِٱلذَّاتِ وَبَقَائِي بِٱلْعَرَضِ * إِلٰهِي فَجُدْ بِوُجُودِكَ[١٨٨] ٱلْحَقِّ عَلَى عَدَمِي[١٨٩] ٱلْأَصْلِ * حَتَّى أَكُونَ كَمَا كُنْتُ حَيْثُ لَمْ أَكُنْ * وَأَنْتَ كَمَا أَنْتَ حَيْثُ لَمْ تَزَلْ * لَا إِلٰهَ إِلَّا أَنْتَ. إِلٰهِي أَنْتَ ﴿ٱلْفَعَّالُ لِمَا تُرِيدُ﴾ * وَأَنَا عَبْدٌ لَكَ ﴿مِنْ بَعْضِ ٱلْعَبِيدِ﴾ * إِلٰهِي أَرَدْتَنِي وَأَرَدْتَ مِنِّي فَأَنَا ٱلْمُرَادُ وَأَنْتَ ٱلْمُرِيدُ * فَكُنْ أَنْتَ[١٩٠] مُرَادَكَ مِنِّي حَتَّى تَكُونُ أَنْتَ ٱلْمُرَادَ وَأَنَا ٱلْمُرِيدُ * لَا إِلٰهَ إِلَّا أَنْتَ. إِلٰهِي أَنْتَ ٱلْبَاطِنُ فِي كُلِّ غَيْبٍ وَٱلظَّاهِرُ فِي كُلِّ عَيْنٍ * وَٱلْمَسْمُوعُ فِي كُلِّ خَبَرٍ صِدْقٍ وَمَيْنٍ * وَٱلْمَعْلُومُ فِي مَرْتَبَةِ ٱلْوَاحِدِ وَٱلِاثْنَيْنِ * تَسَمَّيْتَ بِأَسْمَاءِ ٱلنُّزُولِ * فَٱحْتَجَبْتَ عَنْ لَوَاحِظِ ٱلْعُيُونِ * وَٱخْتَفَيْتَ عَنْ مَدَارِكِ ٱلْعُقُولِ. إِلٰهِي تَجَلَّيْتَ بِخَصَائِصِ تَجَلِّيَاتِ ٱلصِّفَاتِ * فَتَنَوَّعَتْ مَرَاتِبُ ٱلْمَوْجُودَاتِ * وَتَسَمَّيْتَ فِي كُلِّ مَرْتَبَةٍ بِحَقَائِقِ ٱلْمُسَمَّيَاتِ * وَنَصَبْتَ شَوَاهِدَ ٱلْعُقُولِ عَلَى دَقَائِقِ حَقَائِقِ[١٩١] غُيُوبِ[١٩٢] ٱلْمَعْلُومَاتِ * وَأَطْلَقْتَ سَوَابِقَ ٱلْأَرْوَاحِ فِي مَيَادِينِ ٱلْمَعَارِفِ ٱلْإِلٰهِيَّةِ * فَحَارَتْ ثُمَّ تَاهَتْ فِي إِشَارَاتِ لَطَائِفِهَا ٱلسُّرْيَانِيَّةِ[١٩٣] * فَلَمَّا غَيَّبْتَهَا عَنِ ٱلْكُلِّيَّةِ وَٱلْجُزْئِيَّةِ * وَنَقَلْتَهَا عَنِ ٱلْأَنِيَّةِ وَٱلْأَيْنِيَّةِ * وَسَلَبْتَهَا عَنِ

١٨٨. G, U, V = بِجُودِكَ .

١٨٩. C, R1 + فِي .

١٩٠. U – أَنْتَ .

١٩١. V – حَقَايِقِ ; I, P1, R + وَ ٱلْآيَات ; B2 – غُيُوبِ .

١٩٢. K = عُيُونِ ; B2 – غُيُوبِ .

١٩٣. C, R1 = ٱلرَّبَّانِيَّةِ .

ٱلْكَمِّيَّةِ وَٱلْمَاهِيَّةِ* وَتعَرَّفْتَ لَهَا فِي مَعَارِفِ ٱلتَّنْكِيرِ بِٱلْمَعَارِفِ ٱلذَّاتِيَّةِ* وَحرَّرْتَهَا بِمُطَالَعَاتِ ٱلرُّبُوبِيَّةِ* فِي ٱلْمَوَاقِفِ ٱلْإِلٰهِيَّةِ* وَأَسْقَطْتَ عَنْهَا ٱلْبَيْنَ* عِنْدَ رَفْعِ حِجَابِ ٱلْغَيْنِ* فَٱنْتَظَمَتْ بِٱلنِّظَامِ[194] ٱلْقَدِيمِ* فِي سِلْكِ ﴿بِسْمِ ٱللّٰهِ ٱلرَّحْمٰنِ ٱلرَّحِيمِ﴾. **إِلٰهِي** كَمْ أُنَادِيكَ فِي ٱلنَّادِي* وَأَنْتَ ٱلْمُنَادِي لِلنَّادِي[195]* وَكَمْ أُنَاجِيكَ بِمُنَاجَاةِ ٱلْمُنَاجِي* وَأَنْتَ ٱلْمُنَاجِي لِلنَّاجِي. **إِلٰهِي** إِذَا كَانَ ٱلْوَصْلُ عَيْنَ ٱلْقَطْعِ* وَٱلْقُرْبُ نَفْسَ ٱلْبُعْدِ* وَٱلْعِلْمُ مَوْضِعَ ٱلْجَهْلِ* وَٱلْمَعْرِفَةُ مُسْتَقَرَّ ٱلتَّنْكِيرِ* فَكَيْفَ ٱلْقَصْدُ وَمِنْ أَيْنَ ٱلسَّبِيلُ. **إِلٰهِي** أَنْتَ ٱلْمَطْلُوبُ وَرَاءَ كُلِّ قَاصِدٍ* وَٱلْإِقْرَارُ فِي عَيْنِ ٱلْجَاحِدِ* وَقُرْبُ ٱلْقُرْبِ[196] فِي ٱلْفَرْقِ ٱلْمُتَبَاعِدِ* وَقَدِ ٱسْتَوْلَى ٱلْوَهْمُ* عَلَى ٱلْفَهْمِ* فَمَنِ ٱلْمُبْعَدُ* وَمَنِ ٱلْمُتَبَاعِدُ* وَمَنِ ٱلْمُسْعَدُ* وَمَنِ ٱلْمُسَاعِدُ[197]* ٱلْحُسْنُ يَقُولُ: ﴿إِيَّاكَ﴾ -أَطْلَقَهُ[198]-* وَٱلْقُبْحُ يُنَادِي: ﴿ٱلَّذِي أَحْسَنَ كُلَّ شَيْءٍ خَلَقَهُ﴾* فَٱلْأَوَّلُ غَايَةٌ يَقِفُ عِنْدَهَا ٱلسَّيْرُ* وَٱلثَّانِي حِجَابٌ بِحُكْمِ[199] تَوَهُّمِ ٱلْغَيْرِ. **إِلٰهِي** مَتَى يَتَخَلَّصُ ٱلْعَقْلُ مِنْ عِقَالِ ٱلْعَوَائِقِ* وَتَلْحَظُ[200] لَوَاحِظُ ٱلْفِكْرِ مَحَاسِنَ ٱلْحُسْنَى مِنْ أَعْيُنِ ٱلْحَقَائِقِ* وَيَنْفَكُّ ٱلْفَهْمُ عَنْ أَصْلِ

١٩٤. B = ٱلنِّظَامِ فِي ; K + ٱلْقُدْسِي .

١٩٥. U, V – لِلنَّادِي .

١٩٦. B, I, R1, W = قُرْبُ ٱلْبُعْد ; U, V = وَقُرْبُ ٱلْبُعْدِ لِقُرْبِ ; G = وَقُرْبُ ٱلْبُعْدِ أَقْرَبُ .

١٩٧. G, L, P1 = فَمَنِ ٱلْمُبْعَدُ وَمَنِ ٱلْمُتَبَاعِد ; B2, C, I, K, R, U, V = فَمَنِ ٱلْمُسْعَدُ وَمَنِ ٱلْمُسَاعِدُ .

١٩٨. B, B2, C, G, H, I, K, L, P1, R, U, V – اَطْلَقَهُ .

١٩٩. P1, R, R1 + يَحْكُمُ ; G, L = يُحْكِمُ ; I, V = يحكم .

٢٠٠. R, U, V = وَيَلْحَظُ ; R1 = وَيَلَحّظَ .

ٱلْإِفْكِ * وَيَتَحَلَّلُ ٱلْوَهْمُ مِنْ أَوْحَالِ[٢٠١] حِبَالِ إِشْرَاكِ[٢٠٢] ٱلشِّرْكِ * وَيَنْجُو ٱلتَّصَوُّرُ مِنْ فَرْقِ فِرَقِ ٱلْفَرْقِ[٢٠٣] * وَتَتَجَرَّدُ ٱلنَّفْسُ ٱلنَّفِيسَةُ مِنْ خُلُقِ[٢٠٤] أَخْلَاقِ تَخَلُّقَاتِ ٱلْخَلْقِ. إِلٰهِي أَنْتَ لَا تَنْفَعُكَ ٱلطَّاعَاتُ وَلَا تَضُرُّكَ ٱلْمَعَاصِي * وَبِيَدِ قَهْرِ سُلْطَانِكَ مَلَكُوتُ ٱلْقُلُوبِ وَٱلنَّوَاصِي * ﴿وَإِلَيْكَ يُرْجَعُ[٢٠٥] ٱلْأَمْرُ كُلُّهُ﴾ فَلَا نِسْبَةَ لِلطَّائِعِ وَٱلْعَاصِي. إِلٰهِي أَنْتَ لَا يَشْغَلُكَ شَأْنٌ عَنْ شَأْنٍ * إِلٰهِي أَنْتَ لَا يَحْصُرُكَ ٱلْوُجُوبُ وَلَا يَحُدُّكَ ٱلْإِمْكَانُ * وَلَا يَحْجُبُكَ ٱلْإِبْهَامُ وَلَا يُوضِحُكَ ٱلْبَيَانُ * إِلٰهِي أَنْتَ لَا يُرَجِّحُكَ ٱلدَّلِيلُ وَلَا يُحَقِّقُكَ ٱلْبُرْهَانُ * إِلٰهِي أَنْتَ ٱلْأَبَدُ وَٱلْأَزَلُ فِي حَقِّكَ سِيَّانٌ. إِلٰهِي[٢٠٦] مَا أَنْتَ وَمَا أَنَا وَمَا هُوَ وَمَا هِيَ. إِلٰهِي أَفِي ٱلْكَثْرَةِ أَطْلُبُكَ[٢٠٧] * أَمْ فِي ٱلْوَحْدَةِ * وَبِٱلْأَمَدِ أَنْتَظِرُ فَرَجَكَ * أَمْ بِٱلْمُدَّةِ * وَلَا عُدَّةَ[٢٠٨] لِعَبْدٍ دُونَكَ * وَلَا عُمْدَةَ. إِلٰهِي بَقَائِي بِكَ * فِي فَنَائِي عَنِّي * أَمْ فِيكَ أَمْ بِكَ * وَفَنَائِي كَذٰلِكَ مُحَقَّقٌ بِكَ[٢٠٩] * أَمْ مُتَوَهَّمٌ بِي أَمْ بِٱلْعَكْسِ * أَمْ هُوَ أَمْرٌ مُشْتَرَكٌ * وَكَذٰلِكَ بَقَائِي فِيكَ. إِلٰهِي

٢٠١. B, G, P1, R1, W = أَوْصَالِ .

٢٠٢. B, R, L = أَشْرَاكِ .

٢٠٣. P, P1 = فَرْقِ ٱلْفَرْقِ ; R1 = فَرْقِ فِرَاقِ ٱلْفَرْقِ ; I = غَرْقِ فَرْقِ ٱلْفَرْقِ .

٢٠٤. P1 = خُلُقِ ; B, R, R1 = خَلْقِ ; C - خُلُقِ .

٢٠٥. B, H, P1, R, R1, L = يَرْجِعُ .

٢٠٦. B, R1, U + إِلٰهِي .

٢٠٧. H, L = أَشْهَدُكَ ; B, R, U, V - أَطْلُبُكَ .

٢٠٨. P1, R1 = مُدَّةَ .

٢٠٩. R1 + أَمْ صَحِيح .

سُكُوتِي خَرَسٌ يُوجِبُ ٱلصَّمَمَ٭ وَكَلَامِي صَمَمٌ يُوجِبُ ٱلْبَكَمَ[٢١٠]٭ وَٱلْحَيْرَةُ فِي كُلٍّ وَلَا حَيْرَةَ[٢١١]٭ بِسْمِ ٱللَّهِ[٢١٢] ﴿حَسْبِيَ ٱللَّهُ﴾٭ بِسْمِ ٱللَّهِ ﴿تَوَكَّلْتُ عَلَى ٱللَّهِ﴾٭ بِسْمِ ٱللَّهِ ﴿سَأَلْتُ مِنَ ٱللَّهِ﴾٭ بِسْمِ ٱللَّهِ ﴿وَلَا حَوْلَ وَلَا قُوَّةَ إِلَّا بِٱللَّهِ ٱلْعَلِيِّ ٱلْعَظِيمِ﴾٭ ﴿رَبَّنَا عَلَيْكَ تَوَكَّلْنَا٭ وَإِلَيْكَ أَنَبْنَا٭ وَإِلَيْكَ ٱلْمَصِيرُ﴾. **ٱللَّهُمَّ** إِنِّي أَسْأَلُكَ بِسِرِّ[٢١٣] أَمْرِكَ٭ وَعَظِيمِ قَدْرِكَ[٢١٤]٭ وَإِحَاطَةِ عِلْمِكَ٭ وَخَصَائِصِ إِرَادَتِكَ٭ وَتَأْثِيرِ قُدْرَتِكَ[٢١٥]٭ وَنُفُوذِ سَمْعِكَ وَبَصَرِكَ٭ وَقَيُّومِيَّةِ حَيَاتِكَ٭ وَوُجُوبِ ذَاتِكَ وَصِفَاتِكَ٭ يَا ٱللَّهُ٭ يَا ٱللَّهُ٭ يَا ٱللَّهُ٭ يَا أَوَّلُ يَا آخِرُ٭ يَا ظَاهِرُ يَا بَاطِنُ٭ يَا نُورُ يَا حَقُّ يَا مُبِينُ. **ٱللَّهُمَّ** خَصِّصْ سِرِّي بِأَسْرَارِ وَحْدَانِيَّتِكَ٭ وَقَدِّسْ رُوحِي بِقُدْسِيَّةِ تَجَلِّيَاتِ صِفَاتِكَ٭ وَطَهِّرْ قَلْبِي بِطَهَارَةِ مَعَارِفِ إِلٰهِيَّتِكَ٭ **ٱللَّهُمَّ** وَعَلِّمْ عَقْلِي مِنْ عُلُومِ لَدُنِّيَّتِكَ٭ وَخَلِّقْ نَفْسِي بِأَخْلَاقِ رُبُوبِيَّتِكَ٭ وَأَيِّدْ حِسِّي بِمَدَدِ[٢١٦] أَنْوَارِ حَضَرَاتِ نُورَانِيَّتِكَ٭ وَخَلِّصْ خُلَاصَةَ جَوَاهِرِ جِسْمَانِيَّتِي[٢١٧] مِنْ قُيُودِ ٱلطَّبْعِ وَكَثَافَةِ ٱلْحِسِّ وَحَصْرِ ٱلْمَكَانِ وَٱلْكَوْنِ. **ٱللَّهُمَّ** وَٱنْقُلْنِي مِنْ دَرَكَاتِ خَلْقِي وَخُلُقِي٭

٢١٠. R = سُكُوتِي خَرَسٌ يُوْجِبُ ٱلْبُكْمَ وَكَلَامِي بُكْمٌ يُوْجِبُ ٱلصَّمَمَ.

٢١١. R1 + فِيكَ.

٢١٢. B, L, P1 + وَبِٱللّٰه رَبِّي ٱللّٰه بِسْمِ ٱللّٰه ; R1, W + رَبِّي ٱللّٰه بِسْمِ ٱللّٰه.

٢١٣. L = مِنْ سِرِّ ; B2, K, U, V – سِرِّ ; G, R1, W = بِسِرِّ اسْمِكَ.

٢١٤. B2, G, P1, R, R1, U, V = قُدْرَتِكَ.

٢١٥. G, R = قُوَّتِكَ.

٢١٦. G, I, R, U, V, W = بِمِداد ; R1 = بِمَوَارِدِ.

٢١٧. B, C, I, K, L, P1, U, V, W = جِثْمَانِيَّتِي.

إِلَى دَرَجَاتِ حَقِّكَ وَحَقِيقَتِكَ * أَنْتَ وَلِيِّي وَمَوْلَايَ * وَبِكَ مَمَاتِي وَمَحْيَايَ * ﴿إِيَّاكَ نَعْبُدُ وَإِيَّاكَ نَسْتَعِينَ﴾. اُنْظُرِ ٱللّٰهُمَّ إِلَيَّ نَظْرَةً تَنْظِمُ[٢١٨] بِهَا جَمِيعَ أَطْوَارِي * وَتُطَهِّرُ بِهَا سَرِيرَةَ أَسْرَارِي * وَتَرْفَعُ[٢١٩] بِهَا فِي ٱلْمَلَإِ ٱلْأَعْلَى أَرْوَاحَ أَذْكَارِي * وَتُقَوِّي بِهَا مِدَادَ أَنْوَارِي. اَللّٰهُمَّ غَيِّبْنِي عَنْ جَمِيعِ خَلْقِكَ * وَٱجْمَعْنِي عَلَيْكَ بِحَقِّكَ[٢٢٠] * وَٱحْفَظْنِي بِشُهُودِ تَصَرُّفَاتِ أَمْرِكَ فِي عَوَالِمِ فَرْقِكَ. اَللّٰهُمَّ بِكَ تَوَسَّلْتُ * وَإِلَيْكَ تَوَجَّهْتُ * وَمِنْكَ سَأَلْتُ * وَفِيكَ لَا فِي شَيْءٍ سِوَاكَ رَغِبْتُ * لَا أَسْأَلُ مِنْكَ[٢٢١] سِوَاكَ * وَلَا أَطْلُبُ مِنْكَ إِلَّا إِيَّاكَ. اَللّٰهُمَّ وَأَتَوَسَّلُ إِلَيْكَ فِي قَبُولِ ذٰلِكَ بِٱلْوَسِيلَةِ ٱلْعُظْمَى * وَٱلْفَضِيلَةِ ٱلْكُبْرَى * وَٱلْحَبِيبِ ٱلْأَدْنَى[٢٢٢] * وَٱلْوَلِيِّ ٱلْمَوْلَى * مُحَمَّدٍ ٱلْمُصْطَفَى * وَٱلصَّفِيِّ ٱلْمُرْتَضَى * وَٱلنَّبِيِّ ٱلْمُجْتَبَى. وَبِهِ أَسْأَلُكَ[٢٢٣] أَنْ تُصَلِّيَ عَلَيْهِ صَلَاةً أَبَدِيَّةً[٢٢٤] دَيْمُومِيَّةً قَيُّومِيَّةً إِلٰهِيَّةً رَبَّانِيَّةً * بِحَيْثُ تُشْهِدُنِي فِي ذٰلِكَ[٢٢٥] عَيْنَ كَمَالِهِ[٢٢٦] * وَتَسْتَهْلِكُنِي فِي شُهُودِ[٢٢٧] مَعَارِفِ ذَاتِهِ *

٢١٨. H = تُنْظِمُ ; G, R, R1 = تَنْظُمُ .
٢١٩. L = تَرَفَّعُ .
٢٢٠. L = بِفَضْلِكَ .
٢٢١. B, B2 = لَا أَسْأَلُكَ .
٢٢٢. G, R, W = ٱلْأَوْفَى .
٢٢٣. B, I, U, V + بِكَ .
٢٢٤. B, L, P1, R1 + سَرْمَدِيَّةً أَزَلِيَّةً .
٢٢٥. B, G, R1 = فِي ذٰلِكَ فِي ; B2, H, I, K, P1 = ذٰلِكَ فِي .
٢٢٦. G = كَمَالَ صِفَاتِهِ .
٢٢٧. G, I + عَيْنِ ; B, B2, U, V = عَيْنِ .

وَعَلَى آلِهِ وَصَحْبِهِ كَذٰلِكَ ۞ فَأَنْتَ[٢٢٨] وَلِيُّ ذٰلِكَ ۞ وَ﴿لَا حَوْلَ وَلَا قُوَّةَ إِلَّا بِٱللّٰهِ ٱلْعَلِيِّ ٱلْعَظِيمِ﴾ ۞ وَ﴿ٱلْحَمْدُ لِلّٰهِ رَبِّ ٱلْعَالَمِينَ﴾

وِرْدُ لَيْلَةِ ٱلْجُمُعَةِ

بِسْمِ ٱللّٰهِ ٱلرَّحْمٰنِ ٱلرَّحِيمِ. **إِلٰهِي** كُلُّ ٱلْآبَاءِ ٱلْعُلْوِيَّةِ عَبِيدُكَ ۞ وَأَنْتَ ٱلرَّبُّ عَلَى ٱلْإِطْلَاقِ ۞ جَمَعْتَ بَيْنَ ٱلْمُتَقَابِلَاتِ ۞ فَأَنْتَ ٱلْجَلِيلُ ٱلْجَمِيلُ ۞ لَا غَايَةَ لِابْتِهَاجِكَ بِذَاتِكَ[٢٢٩] ۞ إِذْ لَا غَايَةَ لِشُهُودِكَ مِنْكَ[٢٣٠] ۞ أَنْتَ أَجَلُّ مِنْ شُهُودِنَا وَأَكْمَلُ[٢٣١] ۞ وَأَعْلَى مِمَّا نَصِفُكَ بِهِ وَأَجْمَلُ[٢٣٢] ۞ تَعَالَيْتَ فِي جَلَالِكَ عَنْ سِمَاتِ ٱلْمُحْدَثَاتِ ۞ وَتَقَدَّسَ جَمَالُكَ ٱلْعَلِيُّ عَنْ مُوَاقَعَةِ ٱلْمُيُولِ[٢٣٣] إِلَيْهِ بِٱلشَّهَوَاتِ. أَسْأَلُكَ بِٱلسِّرِّ ٱلَّذِي جَمَعْتَ بِهِ بَيْنَ ٱلْمُتَقَابِلَاتِ أَنْ تَجْمَعَ عَلَيَّ مُتَفَرِّقَ أَمْرِي ۞ جَمْعًا يُشْهِدُنِي وَحْدَةَ وُجُودِي[٢٣٤] ۞ وَٱكْسِنِي حُلَّةَ جَمَالِكَ[٢٣٥] ۞ وَتَوِّجْنِي بِتَاجِ جَلَالِكَ ۞ حَتَّى[٢٣٦] تَخْضَعَ لِيَ ٱلنُّفُوسُ ٱلْبَشَرِيَّةُ ۞ وَتَنْقَادَ إِلَيَّ ٱلْقُلُوبُ

٢٢٨. G = وَأَنْتَ ; C (note), R = فَإِنَّكَ .

٢٢٩. V = لِذَاتِكَ .

٢٣٠. V = لِشُهُودِكَ مِنْهاَ ; R = لِشُهُودِ صِفَاتِكَ مِنْكَ .

٢٣١. V = أَجْمَلُ .

٢٣٢. V = أَكْمَلُ .

٢٣٣. R, R1, W = ٱلْمَيْلِ ; I = ٱلْمَيْلَان .

٢٣٤. G, P, P1 = وُجُودِكَ .

٢٣٥. G, R = جَمَالِ تَوْحِيدِي .

٢٣٦. V - حَتَّى .

ٱلْأَبِيَّةُ[٢٣٧] * وَتَنْبَسِطَ إِلَيَّ ٱلْأَسْرَارُ ٱلْأَقْدَسِيَّةُ * وَأَعْلِ قَدْرِي عِنْدَكَ عُلُوًّا يَنْخَفِضُ لِي بِهِ كُلُّ مُتَعَالٍ * وَيَذِلُّ[٢٣٨] لِي بِهِ كُلُّ عَزِيزٍ * وَخُذْ بِنَاصِيَتِي إِلَيْكَ * وَمَلِّكْنِي نَاصِيَةَ كُلِّ ذِي رُوحٍ نَاصِيَتُهُ بِيَدِكَ * ﴿وَٱجْعَل لِّي لِسَانَ صِدْقٍ﴾ فِي خَلْقِكَ وَأَمْرِكَ * وَٱمْلَأْنِي مِنْكَ * وَٱحْفَظْنِي[٢٣٩] ﴿فِي بَرِّكَ وَبَحْرِكَ﴾ * وَ﴿أَخْرِجْنِي مِنْ قَرْيَةِ﴾ ٱلطَّبْعِ ﴿ٱلظَّالِمِ أَهْلُهَا﴾ * وَأَعْتِقْنِي مِنْ رِقِّ ٱلْأَكْوَانِ[٢٤٠] * وَٱجْعَلْ لِي مِنْكَ بُرْهَانًا يُورِثُ أَمَانًا * وَلَا تَجْعَلْ لِغَيْرِكَ عَلَيَّ سُلْطَانًا * وَٱجْعَلْ غِنَائِي فِي ٱلْفَقْرِ إِلَيْكَ عَنْ كُلِّ مَطْلُوبٍ * وَٱصْحَبْنِي بِعِنَايَتِكَ عَنْ كُلِّ مَرْغُوبٍ[٢٤١] * أَنْتَ وِجْهَتِي وَجَاهِي * وَإِلَيْكَ ٱلْمَرْجِعُ وَٱلتَّنَاهِي * تَجْبُرُ ٱلْكَسِيرَ وَتَكْسِرُ ٱلْجَبَّارِينَ * وَتُجِيرُ ٱلْخَائِفِينَ وَتُخِيفُ ٱلظَّالِمِينَ[٢٤٢] * لَكَ ٱلْمَجْدُ ٱلْأَرْفَعُ * وَٱلتَّجَلِّي ٱلْأَجْمَعُ * وَٱلْحِجَابُ ٱلْأَمْنَعُ * سُبْحَانَكَ لَا إِلٰهَ إِلَّا أَنْتَ * أَنْتَ ﴿حَسْبِي وَنِعْمَ ٱلْوَكِيلُ﴾. ﴿وَكَذٰلِكَ أَخْذُ رَبِّكَ إِذَا أَخَذَ ٱلْقُرَىٰ وَهِيَ ظَالِمَةٌ إِنَّ أَخْذَهُ أَلِيمٌ شَدِيدٌ﴾ * ﴿فَٱنْتَقَمْنَا مِنَ ٱلَّذِينَ أَجْرَمُوا وَكَانَ حَقًّا عَلَيْنَا نَصْرُ ٱلْمُؤْمِنِينَ﴾. **ٱللّٰهُمَّ** يَا خَالِقَ ٱلْمَخْلُوقَاتِ *

٢٣٧. V + تَرْتَاحُ إِلَيْهَا ٱلْأَرْوَاحُ ٱلْأَزْيَجِيَّةُ.
٢٣٨. R = يَدُلُّ ; V = يُدِلُّ.
٢٣٩. V = وَٱمْلَأْنِي مَحْفُوظًا مَلْحُوظًا.
٢٤٠. G = مِن [رِقَةِ] ٱلْأَكْوان.
٢٤١. R = بِعِنَايَتِكَ عَن نَيْلِ مَرْغُوبٍ ; G, R1 = بِعِنَايَتِكَ فِي نَيْلِ كُلِّ مَرْغُوبٍ.
٢٤٢. V = ٱلْجَائِرِين.

وَمُحْيِي ٱلْأَمْوَاتِ * وَجَامِعَ ٱلشَّتَاتِ[٢٤٣] * وَمُفِيضَ ٱلْأَنْوَارِ[٢٤٤] عَلَى ٱلذَّوَاتِ * لَكَ ٱلْمُلْكُ[٢٤٥] ٱلْأَوْسَعُ * وَٱلْجَنَابُ ٱلْأَرْفَعُ[٢٤٦] * ٱلْأَرْبَابُ عَبِيدُكَ وَٱلْمُلُوكُ خَدَمَتُكَ * وَٱلْأَغْنِيَاءُ فُقَرَاؤُكَ * وَأَنْتَ ٱلْغَنِيُّ بِذَاتِكَ عَمَّنْ سِوَاكَ. أَسْأَلُكَ بِٱسْمِكَ ٱلَّذِي ﴿خَلَقْتَ بِهِ كُلَّ شَيْءٍ فَقَدَّرْتَهُ تَقْدِيرًا﴾ * وَمَنَحْتَ بِهِ مَنْ شِئْتَ ﴿جَنَّةً وَحَرِيرًا﴾ * وَخِلَافَةً ﴿وَمُلْكًا كَبِيرًا﴾ * أَنْ تُذْهِبَ حِرْصِي * وَتُكْمِلَ نَقْصِي * وَأَنْ تُفِيضَ عَلَيَّ مِنْ مَلَابِسِ نَعْمَائِكَ[٢٤٧] * وَأَنْ تُعَلِّمَنِي مِنْ أَسْمَائِكَ * مَا يَصْلُحُ لِلْإِذْنِ[٢٤٨] وَٱلْإِلْقَاءِ * وَٱمْلَأْ بَاطِنِي خَشْيَةً وَرَحْمَةً * وَظَاهِرِي هَيْبَةً وَعَظَمَةً * حَتَّى تَخَافَنِي قُلُوبُ ٱلْأَعْدَاءِ * وَتَرْتَاحُ إِلَيَّ أَرْوَاحُ ٱلْأَوْلِيَاءِ * ﴿يَخَافُونَ رَبَّهُمْ مِنْ فَوْقِهِمْ * وَيَفْعَلُونَ مَا يُؤْمَرُونَ﴾. رَبِّ هَبْ لِيَ ٱسْتِعْدَادًا كَامِلًا لِقَبُولِ فَيْضِكَ ٱلْأَقْدَسِ * لِأَخْلُفَكَ[٢٤٩] فِي بِلَادِكَ * وَأَدْفَعَ بِهِ سَخَطَكَ عَنْ عِبَادِكَ * فَإِنَّكَ تَسْتَخْلِفُ مَنْ تَشَاءُ * وَأَنْتَ ﴿عَلَى كُلِّ شَيْءٍ قَدِيرٌ﴾ * وَأَنْتَ ﴿ٱلْخَبِيرُ ٱلْبَصِيرُ﴾. وَصَلَّى ٱللَّهُ عَلَى سَيِّدِنَا مُحَمَّدٍ وَعَلَى آلِهِ وَصَحْبِهِ وَسَلَّمَ * ﴿وَهُوَ حَسْبِي وَنِعْمَ ٱلْوَكِيلُ﴾.

٢٤٣. V - وَجَامِعَ ٱلشَّتَاتِ.
٢٤٤. R, V = ٱلنُّورِ.
٢٤٥. R1 = ٱلْمَجْدُ.
٢٤٦. R1 + وَٱلْحِجَابُ ٱلأَمْنَعُ.
٢٤٧. V = مِن سَوَابِغِ ٱلنَّعْمَاءِ.
٢٤٨. V = يَصْلُحُ مَعَهُ ٱلأَخذ ; G, R1 = ٱلأُذُن.
٢٤٩. R = لِأُخَلِّفُكَ.

وِرْدُ يَوْمِ ٱلْجُمُعَةِ[٢٥٠]

بِسْمِ ٱللّٰهِ ٱلرَّحْمٰنِ ٱلرَّحِيمِ. **رَبِّ** رَقِّنِي فِي مَدَارِجِ ٱلْمَعَارِفِ * وَقَلِّبْنِي فِي أَطْوَارِ أَسْرَارِ ٱلْحَقَائِقِ * وَٱحْجُبْنِي فِي سُرَادِقَاتِ حِفْظِكَ * وَمَكْنُونِ سِرِّ سِتْرِكَ * عَنْ وُرُودِ ٱلْخَوَاطِرِ ٱلَّتِي لَا تَلِيقُ بِسُبُحَاتِ جَلَالِكَ. **رَبِّ** أَقِمْنِي بِكَ فِي كُلِّ شَأْنٍ * وَأَشْهِدْنِي لُطْفَكَ فِي كُلِّ قَاصٍ وَدَانٍ * وَٱفْتَحْ عَيْنَ بَصِيرَتِي فِي قَضَاءِ سَاحَةِ ٱلتَّوْحِيدِ * لِأَشْهَدَ قِيَامَ ٱلْكُلِّ بِكَ شُهُودًا يَقْطَعُ نَظَرِي عَنْ كُلِّ مَوْجُودٍ * يَا ذَا ٱلْفَضْلِ وَٱلْجُودِ. **رَبِّ** أَفِضْ[٢٥١] عَلَيَّ مِنْ بِحَارِ تَجْرِيدِ أَلِفِ ٱلذَّاتِ ٱلْأَقْدَسِ * مَا يَقْطَعُ عَنِّي كُلَّ عَلَاقَةٍ تُعْجِمُ[٢٥٢] إِدْرَاكِي * وَتُغْلِقُ دُونِي[٢٥٣] بَابَ مَطْلَبِي * وَأَسْبِغْ[٢٥٤] عَلَيَّ مِنْ هَيُولَى نُقْطَتِهَا ٱلْكُلِّيَّةِ * ٱلْبَارِزَةِ مِنْ مَلَكُوتِ غَيْبِ ذَاتِكَ مَا أَمُدُّ بِهِ حُرُوفَ ٱلْأَكْوَانِ * مَحْفُوظًا فِي ذٰلِكَ مِنَ ٱلنَّقْصِ وَٱلشَّيْنِ * ﴿يَا مَنْ وَسِعَ كُلَّ شَيْءٍ رَحْمَةً وَعِلْمًا * يَا رَبَّ ٱلْعَالَمِينَ﴾. **رَبِّ** طَهِّرْنِي ظَاهِرًا وَبَاطِنًا مِنْ لَوْثِ ٱلْأَغْيَارِ * وَٱلْوُقُوفِ عَلَى ٱلْأَطْوَارِ * بِفَيْضٍ مِنْ طُهُورِ قُدْسِكَ * وَغَيِّبْنِي عَنْهُمْ بِشُهُودِ بَوَارِقِ أُنْسِكَ * وَٱطَّلِعْنِي

٢٥٠. B + وِرْدُ ٱلْمَعَارِفِ .

٢٥١. B = وَأَفِضْ .

٢٥٢. P1 = تَعْجُمُ ; H, L + عَلَى ; R + عَنْ ; I = تُحْجِبُ .

٢٥٣. V = دُونَ .

٢٥٤. G = اسْبُغْ .

عَلَى حَقَائِقِ ٱلْأَشْيَاءِ * وَدَقَائِقِ ٱلْأَشْكَالِ * وَأَسْمِعْنِي نُطْقَ ٱلْأَكْوَانِ بِصَرِيحِ تَوْحِيدِكَ فِي ٱلْعَوَالِمِ كُلِّهَا * وَقَابِلْ مِرْآتِي بِتَجَلٍّ تَامٍّ مِنْ جَوَاهِرِ أَسْمَاءِ جَلَالِكَ وَقَهْرِكَ * فَلَا يَقَعُ عَلَيَّ بَصَرُ جَبَّارٍ مِنَ ٱلْإِنْسِ وَٱلْجِنِّ * إِلَّا ٱنْعَكَسَ عَلَيْهِ مِنْ شُعَاعِ ذَٰلِكَ ٱلْجَوْهَرِ مَا يُحْرِقُ ﴿نَفْسَهُ ٱلْأَمَّارَةَ بِٱلسُّوءِ﴾ * وَتَرُدُّهُ[٢٥٥] ذَلِيلًا * وَ﴿يَنْقَلِبُ عَنِّي بَصَرُهُ خَاسِئًا﴾[٢٥٦] كَلِيلًا * يَا مَنْ ﴿عَنَتْ لَهُ ٱلْوُجُوهُ﴾ وَخَضَعَتْ لَهُ ٱلرِّقَابُ * يَا رَبَّ ٱلْأَرْبَابِ. **رَبِّ** وَأَبْعِدْنِي عَنِ ٱلْقَوَاطِعِ ٱلَّتِي تَقْطَعُنِي عَنْ حَضَرَاتِ قُرْبِكَ * وَٱسْلُبْنِي مَا لَا يَلِيقُ مِنْ[٢٥٧] صِفَاتِي بِغَلَبَةِ أَنْوَارِ صِفَاتِكَ * وَأَزِحْ ظُلْمَ طَبْعِي وَبَشَرِيَّتِي بِتَجَلِّي بَارِقَةٍ مِنْ بَوَارِقِ نُورِ ذَاتِكَ * وَٱمْدُدْنِي[٢٥٨] بِقُوَّةٍ مَلَكِيَّةٍ * أَقْهَرُ بِهَا مَا ٱسْتَوْلَى عَلَيَّ مِنَ ٱلطَّبَائِعِ ٱلدَّنِيَّةِ * وَٱلْأَخْلَاقِ ٱلرَّدِيَّةِ * وَٱمْحُ مِنْ لَوْحِ فِكْرِي أَشْكَالَ ٱلْأَكْوَانِ * وَأَثْبِتْ فِيهِ بِيَدِ عِنَايَتِكَ سِرَّ حِرْزِ قُرْبِكَ ٱلسَّابِقِ ٱلْمَكْنُونِ * بَيْنَ ٱلْكَافِ وَٱلنُّونِ[٢٥٩] * يَا نُورَ ٱلنُّورِ * يَا مُفِيضَ ٱلْكُلِّ مِنْ فَيْضِهِ ٱلْمِدْرَارِ * يَا قُدُّوسُ * يَا صَمَدُ * يَا حَفِيظُ * يَا لَطِيفُ * يَا رَبَّ ٱلْعَالَمِينَ. وَصَلَّى ٱللّٰهُ عَلَى سَيِّدِنَا مُحَمَّدٍ وَعَلَى آلِهِ وَصَحْبِهِ أَجْمَعِينَ * ﴿وَٱلْحَمْدُ لِلّٰهِ رَبِّ ٱلْعَالَمِينَ﴾.

٢٥٥. H, P1, R1 = يَرُدُّهُ ; P1, R + ضَالًّا .

٢٥٦. I = خَائِبًا ; R1 + حَقِيرًا .

٢٥٧. G = بِصِفَاتِي .

٢٥٨. H, R1 = وَأَمِدَّنِي .

٢٥٩. G, I, P + إِنَّمَا أَمْرُهُ إِذا أَرَادَ شَيْئًا أَنْ يَقُولَ لَهُ كَنْ فَيَكُونُ. فَسُبْحَانَ ٱلَّذِي بِيَدِهِ مَلَكُوتُ كُلِّ شَيْءٍ وَإِلَيْهِ تُرْجَعُونَ .

وِرْدُ لَيْلَةِ ٱلسَّبْتِ

بِسْمِ ٱللّٰهِ ٱلرَّحْمٰنِ ٱلرَّحِيمِ. **سَيِّدِي** دَامَ بَقَاؤُكَ * وَنَفَذَ فِي ٱلْخَلْقِ قَضَاؤُكَ * وَتَقَدَّسْتَ فِي عُلَاكَ[٢٦٠] * وَتَعَالَيْتَ فِي قُدْسِكَ * ﴿لَا يَؤُدُكَ حِفْظُ﴾ كَوْنٍ * وَلَا يَخْفَى عَنْكَ[٢٦١] كَشْفُ عَيْنٍ * تَدْعُو مَنْ تَشَاءُ إِلَيْكَ * وَتَدُلُّ بِكَ عَلَيْكَ * فَلَكَ ٱلْحَمْدُ ٱلدَّائِمُ * وَٱلدَّوَامُ ٱلْأَمْجَدُ. أَسْأَلُكَ وَقْتًا صَافِيًا بِمَا تُرِيدُ * بِمُعَامَلَةٍ لَائِقَةٍ تَكُونُ غَايَتُهَا[٢٦٢] قُرْبَكَ * مِنْ نَتَائِجِ[٢٦٣] ٱلْأَعْمَالِ[٢٦٤] مَوْقُوفَةً عَلَى رِضْوَانِكَ * وَهَبْ لِي[٢٦٥] سِرًّا زَاهِرًا يَكْشِفُ لِي عَنْ حَقَائِقِ ٱلْأَعْمَالِ * وَٱخْصُصْنِي بِحِكْمَةٍ مَعَهَا حُكْمٌ * وَإِشَارَةٌ يَصْحَبُهَا فَهْمٌ * إِنَّكَ وَلِيُّ مَنْ تَوَلَّاكَ * وَمُجِيبُ مَنْ دَعَاكَ. **إِلٰهِي** دَامَ بَقَاءُ نَعْمَائِكَ عَلَيَّ فَأَدِمْ مُشَاهَدَتِكَ[٢٦٦] * وَأَشْهِدْنِي ذَاتِي مِنْ حَيْثُ أَنْتَ لَا مِنْ حَيْثُ أَنَا * حَتَّى أَكُونَ بِكَ وَلَا أَنَا * وَهَبْ لِي مِنْ لَدُنْكَ عِلْمًا تَنْقَادُ[٢٦٧] إِلَيَّ فِيهِ كُلُّ رُوحٍ عَالِمَةٍ * إِنَّكَ أَنْتَ ٱلْعَلِيمُ ٱلْعَلَّامُ * ﴿تَبَارَكَ ٱسْمُ رَبِّكَ ذُو ٱلْجَلَالِ وَٱلْإِكْرَامِ﴾.

٢٦٠. P, P1 = عُلُوِّكَ ; V = عُلَائِكَ .

٢٦١. R = عَلَيْكَ .

٢٦٢. R1 + غِنَاهَا .

٢٦٣. V = يَا مَنْ نَتَائِج ; G = وَأَيِّدْنِي نَتَائِجَ .

٢٦٤. R1 + وَأَيِّدْنِي بِسُلوُكِ مِنْهَاجِ ٱلْأَعْمَالِ فِي ٱلظَّاهِرِ وَٱلْبَاطِنِ حَتَّى تَصِيرُ نَتَائِجِ ٱلْأَعْمَالِ .

٢٦٥. R1 = وَهَبْنِي .

٢٦٦. P, P1 = وَمُشَاهَدَتِك لَدَيَّ ; V = أَدِمْ عَلَيَّ نِعَمَكَ حَتَّى اتْنَعَم بِدَوامِ مُشَاهَدَتِكَ .

٢٦٧. R = يَنْقَادُ .

﴿وَعِنْدَهُ مَفَاتِحُ ٱلْغَيْبِ لَا يَعْلَمُهَا إِلَّا﴾ أَنْتَ.[٢٦٨] رَبِّ أَفِضْ عَلَيَّ شُعَاعًا مِنْ نُورِكَ يَكْشِفُ لِي عَنْ كُلِّ مَسْتُورٍ فِيَّ ۞ حَتَّى أُشَاهِدَ وُجُودِي[٢٦٩] كَامِلاً مِنْ حَيْثُ أَنْتَ لَا مِنْ حَيْثُ أَنَا ۞ فَأَتَقَرَّبُ إِلَيْكَ بِمَحْوِ صِفَتِي مِنِّي ۞ كَمَا تَقَرَّبْتَ إِلَيَّ ۞ بِإِفَاضَةِ نُورِكَ عَلَيَّ[٢٧٠]. رَبِّ ٱلْإِمْكَانُ صِفَتِي وَٱلْعَدَمُ مَادَّتِي ۞ وَٱلْفَقْرُ مُقَوِّمِي وَوُجُودُكَ عِلَّتِي ۞ وَقُدْرَتُكَ فَاعِلِي وَأَنْتَ غَايَتِي ۞ حَسْبِي مِنْكَ عِلْمُكَ بِجَهْلِي ۞ أَنْتَ كَمَا أَعْلَمُ ۞ وَفَوْقَ مَا أَعْلَمُ ۞ وَأَنْتَ مَعَ كُلِّ شَيْءٍ ۞ وَلَيْسَ مَعَكَ شَيْءٍ ۞ قَدَّرْتَ ٱلْمَنَازِلَ لِلسَّيْرِ ۞ وَرَتَّبْتَ ٱلْمَرَاتِبَ لِلنَّفْعِ وَٱلضَّيْرِ ۞ وَأَثْبَتَّ مِنْهَاجَ ٱلْخَيْرِ ۞ فَنَحْنُ فِي ذٰلِكَ كُلِّهِ بِكَ ۞ وَأَنْتَ بِلَا نَحْنُ ۞ فَأَنْتَ ٱلْخَيْرُ ٱلْمَحْضُ ۞ وَٱلْجُودُ ٱلصِّرْفُ ۞ وَٱلْكَمَالُ ٱلْمُطْلَقُ. أَسْأَلُكَ بِٱسْمِكَ ٱلَّذِي أَفَضْتَ بِهِ ٱلنُّورَ عَلَى ٱلْقَوَابِلِ ۞ وَمَحَوْتَ بِهِ مِنْ ظُلْمَةِ ٱلْغَوَاسِقِ ۞ أَنْ تَمْلَأَ وُجُودِي نُورًا مِنْ نُورِكَ ۞ ٱلَّذِي هُوَ مَادَّةُ كُلِّ نُورٍ[٢٧١] ۞ وَغَايَةُ كُلِّ مَطْلُوبٍ ۞ حَتَّى لَا يَخْفَى عَلَيَّ شَيْءٌ مِمَّا أَوْدَعْتَهُ فِي ذَاتِ[٢٧٢] وُجُودِي ۞ وَهَبْ لِي ﴿لِسَانَ صِدْقٍ﴾ ۞ مُعَبِّرًا عَنْ شُهُودِ حَقٍّ ۞ وَٱخْصُصْنِي مِنْ ﴿جَوَامِعِ ٱلْكَلِمِ﴾ بِمَا تَحْصُلُ بِهِ ٱلْإِبَانَةُ وَٱلْبَلَاغُ[٢٧٣] ۞ وَٱعْصِمْنِي فِي كُلِّ كَلِمَةٍ

٢٦٨. P, P1 = هُوَ وَيَعْلَمُ مَا فِي ٱلْبَرِّ وَٱلْبَحْرِ... .
٢٦٩. V = وُجُودِكَ .
٢٧٠. R – عَلَيَّ .
٢٧١. G, I, R + وَكَمَالٍ ; V = كُلِّ كَمَالٍ .
٢٧٢. P, P1 = ذَرَّاتِ ; R, R1 = ذَاتِي وَ .
٢٧٣. P, P1 = ٱلْبَلَاغَةِ .

مِنْ دَعْوَى مَا لَيْسَ لِي بِحَقٍّ * ﴿وَٱجْعَلْنِي عَلَى بَصِيرَةٍ﴾ مِنْكَ ﴿أَنَا وَمَنِ اتَّبَعَنِي﴾. اَللّٰهُمَّ إِنِّي أَعُوذُ بِكَ مِنْ قَوْلٍ يُوجِبُ حَيْرَةً * أَوْ يُعْقِبُ فِتْنَةً * أَوْ يُوهِمُ شُبْهَةً[٢٧٤] * مِنْكَ تُتَلَقَّى ٱلْكَلِمُ * وَعَنْكَ تُؤْخَذُ[٢٧٥] ٱلْحِكَمُ * أَنْتَ مُمْسِكُ[٢٧٦] ٱلسَّمَاءِ * وَمُعَلِّمُ ٱلْأَسْمَاءِ * لَا إِلٰهَ إِلَّا أَنْتَ * اَلْوَاحِدُ ﴿ٱلْأَحَدُ﴾ * اَلْفَرْدُ ﴿ٱلصَّمَدُ﴾ * اَلَّذِي ﴿لَمْ يَلِدْ وَلَمْ يُولَدْ * وَلَمْ يَكُن لَّهُ كُفُوًا أَحَدُ﴾[٢٧٧]. وَصَلَّى ٱللّٰهُ عَلَى سَيِّدِنَا مُحَمَّدٍ وَعَلَى آلِهِ وَصَحْبِهِ أَجْمَعِينَ * ﴿وَٱلْحَمْدُ لِلّٰهِ رَبِّ ٱلْعَالَمِينَ﴾.

وِرْدُ يَوْمِ ٱلسَّبْتِ[٢٧٨]

بِسْمِ ٱللّٰهِ ٱلرَّحْمٰنِ ٱلرَّحِيمِ. ﴿وَمَنْ يَعْتَصِمْ بِٱللّٰهِ فَقَدْ هُدِيَ إِلَى صِرَاطٍ مُسْتَقِيمٍ﴾ * اَلْحَمْدُ لِلّٰهِ ٱلَّذِي أَحَلَّنِي حِمَا لُطْفِ ٱللّٰهِ * اَلْحَمْدُ لِلّٰهِ ٱلَّذِي أَنْزَلَنِي[٢٧٩] جَنَّةَ رَحْمَةِ ٱللّٰهِ * اَلْحَمْدُ لِلّٰهِ ٱلَّذِي أَجْلَسَنِي فِي مَقَامِ مَحَبَّةِ ٱللّٰهِ * اَلْحَمْدُ لِلّٰهِ ٱلَّذِي أَذَاقَنِي مِنْ مَوَائِدِ مَدَدِ ٱللّٰهِ * اَلْحَمْدُ لِلّٰهِ ٱلَّذِي وَهَبَ لِي بِطَاقَةَ[٢٨٠] ٱلْإِضَافَةِ لِاصْطِفَاءِ ٱللّٰهِ * اَلْحَمْدُ لِلّٰهِ ٱلَّذِي سَقَانِي مِنْ

٢٧٤. R = يُوْجِبُ حَيْرَةً اَوْ يُعْقِبُ شُبْهَةً .

٢٧٥. G = تُجِدُ .

٢٧٦. R, V = مُسَكِّنُ .

٢٧٧. R – ٱلْفَرْدُ . . . أَحَدُ .

٢٧٨. B + وِرْد ٱلْاِعْتِصَام .

٢٧٩. G (note), R1 = اَدْخَلْنِي .

٢٨٠. B2, K, P, P1, R = لَطَافَةَ ; H, L = لَطَّائِفَ .

مَوَارِدِ وَارِدِ وَفَاءِ ٱللّٰهِ[٢٨١] * ٱلْحَمْدُ لِلّٰهِ ٱلَّذِي كَسَانِي حُلَلَ صِدْقِ ٱلْعُبُودِيَّةِ لِلّٰهِ * كُلُّ ذٰلِكَ عَلَى ﴿مَا فَرَّطْتُ فِي جَنْبِ ٱللّٰهِ﴾ * وَضَيَّعْتُ مِنْ حُقُوقِ ٱللّٰهِ * ﴿فَذٰلِكَ ٱلْفَضْلُ مِنَ ٱللّٰهِ﴾ * ﴿وَمَنْ يَغْفِرُ ٱلذُّنُوبَ إِلَّا ٱللّٰهُ﴾. **إِلٰهِي** إِنْعَامُكَ عَلَيَّ بِٱلْإِيجَادِ * مِنْ غَيْرِ جِهَادٍ وَلَا اجْتِهَادٍ * وَجَرَّأْتَ[٢٨٢] مَطَامِعِي مِنْ كَرَمِكَ عَلَى بُلُوغِ ٱلْمُرَادِ[٢٨٣] * مِنْ غَيْرِ اسْتِحْقَاقٍ لِي وَلَا اسْتِعْدَادٍ * فَأَسْأَلُكَ بِوَاحِدِ ٱلْآحَادِ * وَمَشْهُودِ ٱلْأَشْهَادِ * سَلَامَةَ مِنْحَةِ ٱلْوِدَادِ * مِنْ مِحْنَةِ ٱلْبِعَادِ * وَمَحْوَ ظُلْمَةِ ٱلْعِنَادِ * بِنُورِ شَمْسِ ٱلرَّشَادِ * وَفَتْحَ أَبْوَابِ[٢٨٤] ٱلسَّدَادِ * بِأَيْدِي مَدَدِ ﴿إِنَّ ٱللّٰهَ لَطِيفٌ[٢٨٥] بِٱلْعِبَادِ﴾. **رَبِّ** أَسْأَلُكَ فَنَاءَ أَنِيَّةِ[٢٨٦] وُجُودِي * وَبَقَاءَ أَمْنِيَّةِ[٢٨٧] شُهُودِي * وَفِرَاقَ بَيْنِيَّةِ شَاهِدِي وَمَشْهُودِي * بِجَمْعِ عَيْنِيَّةِ[٢٨٨] مَوْجُودِي لِوُجُودِي[٢٨٩]. **سَيِّدِي** سَلِّمْ عُبُودِيَّتِي بِحَقِّكَ مِنْ عَمَاءِ وَهْمِ رُؤْيَةِ ٱلْأَغْيَارِ * وَأَلْحِقْ بِي كَلِمَتَكَ ٱلسَّابِقَةَ ﴿لِلْمُصْطَفَيْنَ ٱلْأَخْيَارِ﴾ * وَٱغْلِبْ عَلَى أَمْرِي بِٱخْتِيَارِكَ فِي ٱلْأَوْطَارِ وَٱلْأَطْوَارِ * وَٱنْصُرْنِي بِٱلتَّوْحِيدِ وَٱلِاسْتِوَاءِ فِي ٱلْحَرَكَةِ وَٱلِاسْتِقْرَارِ. **حَبِيبِي** أَسْأَلُكَ سَرِيعَ ٱلْوِصَالِ *

٢٨١. G, R1 = سَقَانِي مِنْ شُرَابِ صَفَاءِ ٱللّٰهِ .
٢٨٢. G, P = وجرت ; B, K, P1, R1 = وَجَرَّأْتُ .
٢٨٣. G, H = عَلَيَّ لِبُلُوغَ ٱلْمُرَاد ; R1, W = عَلَيَّ بِبُلُوغِ ٱلْمُرَاد .
٢٨٤. G = بَابِ .
٢٨٥. V = روف .
٢٨٦. G, H = أَيْنِيِّةِ ; L = إِنِّيَّةِ .
٢٨٧. L, R = أُمْنِيَّةِ .
٢٨٨. R = بِجَمْيعِ غَيْبِيَّةِ ; B2 = بِجَمِيعِ غَيْبَةِ ; G = بِجَمْعِ غَيْبَةِ .
٢٨٩. B = وُجُودِي لِمَوْجُودي ; L, P1, R = مَوْجُودِي لِمُوْجِدي ; B2 = شُهُودِي لِمُوْجِدي ; G, U, V = مَوْجُودِي لِمَوْجُودي ; I, R1 = مَوْجُودِي بِمَوْجُودي .

وَبَدِيعَ ٱلْجَمَالِ * وَمَنِيعَ ٱلْجَلَالِ * وَرَفِيعَ ٱلْكَمَالِ * فِي كُلِّ حَالٍ وَمَآلٍ. يَا مَنْ هُوَ هُوَ هُوَ[٢٩٠] * يَا هُوَ * وَيَا مَنْ لَيْسَ إِلَّا هُوَ. أَسْأَلُكَ ٱلْغَيْبَ ٱلْأَطْلَسَ * بِٱلْعَيْنِ ٱلْأَقْدَسِ * وَٱلرُّوحِ ٱلْأَنْفَسِ[٢٩١] * ﴿فِي ٱللَّيْلِ إِذَا عَسْعَسَ * وَٱلصُّبْحِ إِذَا تَنَفَّسَ﴾ * ﴿إِنَّهُ لَقَوْلُ رَسُولٍ كَرِيمٍ * ذِي قُوَّةٍ عِنْدَ ذِي ٱلْعَرْشِ مَكِينٍ * مُطَاعٍ ثَمَّ أَمِينٍ﴾ * ﴿بِلِسَانٍ عَرَبِيٍّ مُبِينٍ﴾ * ﴿وَإِنَّهُ لَتَنْزِيلُ رَبِّ ٱلْعَالَمِينَ﴾[٢٩٢] * حُكْمُ مُحْكَمُ[٢٩٣] ٱلْأَمْرِ بِرُوحِهِ ٱلْمُتَلَوِّنِ[٢٩٤] فِي صِيَغِ[٢٩٥] ٱلتَّبْيِينِ * بِصِبْغِ[٢٩٦] ٱلتَّمْكِينِ. وَأَسْأَلُكَ ٱللّٰهُمَّ حَمْلَ[٢٩٧] ذٰلِكَ لِذَاتِي * عَلَى يَدِ نَسِيمِ حَيَاتِي * بِأَرْوَاحِ تَحِيَّاتِي * فِي صَلَوَاتِكَ ٱلطَّيِّبَاتِ * وَتَسْلِيمَاتِكَ ٱلدَّائِمَاتِ *[٢٩٨] عَلَى وَسِيلَةِ حُصُولِ ٱلْمَطَالِبِ * وَوُصْلَةِ وُصُولِ ٱلْحَبَائِبِ * وَعَلَى كُلِّ مَنْسُوبٍ إِلَيْهِ فِي كُلِّ ٱلْمَرَاتِبِ * إِنَّهُ ﴿عَلَى[٢٩٩] ٱلْحَقِّ ٱلْمُبِينِ﴾ * وَٱجْعَلْنَا مِنْ خَوَاصِّهِمْ آمِينَ[٣٠٠]. وَصَلَّى ٱللّٰهُ عَلَى سَيِّدِنَا مُحَمَّدٍ وَآلِهِ وَصَحْبِهِ أَجْمَعِينَ * ﴿سُبْحَانَ رَبِّكَ رَبِّ ٱلْعِزَّةِ عَمَّا يَصِفُونَ * وَسَلَامٌ عَلَى ٱلْمُرْسَلِينَ * وَٱلْحَمْدُ لِلّٰهِ رَبِّ ٱلْعَالَمِينَ﴾.

٢٩٠. B1, H, K, L, N, P = يَا مَنْ هُوَ هُو .

٢٩١. B, B2, I, K, R, U, V – وَٱلرُّوحَ ٱلْأَنْفَسَ .

٢٩٢. G + نَزَلَ بِهِ ٱلرُّوحُ ٱلْأَمِينُ عَلَى قَلْبِكَ لِتَكُونَ مِنَ ٱلْمُنْذِرِينَ .

٢٩٣. H = حَكَمَ مُحْكِمٍ ; R = حَكَمَ مُحْكَمُ .

٢٩٤. G (note), H, I, R = ٱلْمُتَكَوِّنِ .

٢٩٥. G, I, K, V, W = صِبْغِ .

٢٩٦. H, L, V = بِصِيَغِ ; G, K = بِصُنْعِ ; B2 = بِصُنِيعِ .

٢٩٧. R = حَلَّ .

٢٩٨. R + عَلَى وَسِيلَةِ ٱلْعُظْمى وَٱلْفَضِيلَةِ ٱلْكُبْرى وَ .

٢٩٩. P1 = إِنَّهُ ; G, I, W = إِنَّكَ أَنْتَ ٱللّٰه ; B1, B2, H, L = أَلَا هُوَ ; K, P, R1 = إِلٰهِ .

٣٠٠. G = أَجْمَعِين .

Manuscripts used for *Awrād al-usbūʿ* (RG 64)

B = Berlin 3774 lbg 737, fols. 1a–24b, n.d., morning prayers only
B1 = Berlin spr 784, fols. 1b–24a, n.d., morning prayers only
B2 = Bodleian Pococke 78, fols. 183a–191b, 1012h, morning prayers only
C = Carullah 1094, fols. 70b–72a, 939H, Tues, Wed and Thurs morning only
G = Genel 43, fols. 1a–28a, Damascus 1179H, all prayers (with alternative readings in margin)
H = Haci Mahmud Efendi 4179, pp. 2–45, n.d., facsimile, morning prayers only
I = India Office, Arabic Loth 339, fols. 1a–36a, n.d., all prayers
K = Köprülü Ahmed Paşa 338, fols. 33b–51a, morning prayers only
L = Laleli 1520, fols. 1a–30b, *ca.* 1164H, morning prayers only
N = Nafiz Paşa 702, fols. 3b–159b, n.d., all prayers
P = facsimile edition of original private ms., n.d., all prayers, published as *Wird Ibn ʿArabi* (Oxford, 1979, repr. 1988)
P1 = Ahmed Gümüshhanevi, *Majmūʿat al-aḥzāb* (Istanbul, 1880), vol. 1, pp. 40–76, all prayers
R = Reşid Efendi 509, fols. 9b–88a, *ca.* 1020H, all prayers
R1 = Reşid Efendi 501, fols. 23a–41a, 12th century H, all prayers
S = Shehit Ali 2796, fols. 56a–56b, n.d., Thursday morning only
U = University A3184, fols. 245b–247a, 406a–409a, *ca.* 972H, morning prayers only
V = Veliyuddin 1833, fols. 99b–104b (eve), 189b–197a (morning), *ca.* 977H
W = Waṭaniyya 1049, fols. 1a–34a, n.d., all prayers